Gender and Literacy

Gender and Literacy

A Handbook for Educators and Parents

Karen A. Krasny

Forewords by Tom Bean and Didi Khayatt

HANDBOOKS FOR EDUCATORS AND PARENTS
James T. Sears, Series Editor

 PRAEGER

AN IMPRINT OF ABC-CLIO, LLC
Santa Barbara, California • Denver, Colorado • Oxford, England

Library of Congress Cataloging-in-Publication Data

Krasny, Karen, 1958–
    Gender and literacy : a handbook for educators and parents / Karen A. Krasny.
        p. cm. — (Handbooks for educators and parents)
    Includes bibliographical references and index.
    ISBN 978–0–313–33675–1 (hard copy : alk. paper) — ISBN 978–0–313–06342–8
(ebook)
1. Sex discrimination in education. 2. Literacy. I. Title.
LC212.K73   2013
302.2′244—dc23   2012040631

ISBN: 978–0–313–33675–1
EISBN: 978–0–313–06342–8

17 16 15 14 13   1 2 3 4 5

This book is also available on the World Wide Web as an eBook.
Visit www.abc-clio.com for details.

Praeger
An Imprint of ABC-CLIO, LLC

ABC-CLIO, LLC
130 Cremona Drive, P.O. Box 1911
Santa Barbara, California 93116-1911

This book is printed on acid-free paper ∞

Manufactured in the United States of America

To Peter, and our sons, Jon and Rob.

This book is also dedicated to the many parents and educators I have been privileged to listen to for over a quarter of a century and in whose hopes and dreams for our children I found inspiration.

Contents

Series Foreword

How can I advocate for my child? What are the best school practices in teaching diverse learners? What programs are most effective in enhancing learning? These simple but profoundly important questions are the heart of this book series.

This handbook is a practical guide for parents/families and a standard reference resource for educators and libraries. The entire series provides an overview of contemporary research, theories, practices, policy issues, and instructional approaches on a variety of timely and important educational topics. It also gives straightforward recommendations for evaluating curriculum and advocating for strategies for supporting their (and others') children through involvement in schools and civic life.

Schooling is one of the most essential institutions within a democratic society and education the single most important family investment. For citizens and parents, though, there are few "owner's manuals" to determine the quality of their investment. Too often we rely on others' judgments and standardized tests to infer value. But, just as quantity does not equal quality, the judgment of others is no substitute for our own. Handbooks for Educators and Parents provide manuals for a new millennium of learning and teaching.

This volume, *Gender and Literacy*, reflects our goal of communicating within the public square. Dr. Krasny articulates the paramount role that gender continues to play in our schools. Degendering schools requires the efforts of all. But the most important partners in this effort are students, parents, and teachers. It is for this reason that *Gender and Literacy* exists. Although those in academia too often choose to *theorize* "essentialization" of this or that, in this case, gender really matters in everyday school life; it is this site of contestation. And, thus, knowing the research, who to contact, and what to do when your child (or sibling, or grandchild, or foster child) suffers the impact of gender stereotyping is critical—and is the raison d'être of this series.

Foreword by Tom Bean

As I set out to compose this Foreword, I consulted with a second-grade informant, Camille. Camille is an active second grader interested in a variety of sports including basketball, football, boogie boarding, ping pong, golf, badminton, and other physically active sports. In the spirit of qualitative interviewing, I asked Camille to comment on her views about gender stereotyping in her world. She said, "If a girl walks up to a bunch of boys playing tag and asks if she can play they will snap at her and tell her no, because you are a girl."

This and many other examples affirm the words of gender scholar Karen Krasny when she notes:

> One idea that resounds throughout this book it is that there is nothing neutral about gender. Feminine and masculine codes of behavior that can look very different across cultures and times are nevertheless so pervasive that they cannot help but shape who we are and how we act. In writing this book, I hope to promote the idea we cannot even begin to deal effectively with gender stereotyping and bias until we recognize the extent to which we ourselves consciously or unconsciously abide by these codes. (Krasny, p. 14)

Gender and Literacy: A Handbook for Educators and Parents is a compelling and comprehensive effort to synthesize a complex array of information for educators and parents interested in the intersection of gender and literacy practices. It is inspiring and filled with a rich array of ideas designed to transform gendered social practices in ways that challenge simplistic solutions to complex social issues.

Students view themselves through the socially constructed prism of other peoples' words and actions on the playground, in classrooms, at home, and in their communities. These "voices in the head" can reify gender stereotypes that signal who has power and who is silenced. For example, in my doctoral seminar on critical literacy, we deconstruct various texts and songs that locate power within certain groups (e.g., football, hockey, or rugby players in high school), leaving out gay, disabled, transgender, studious, shy, bullied, or other possible ways of being in the world. In addition to deconstructing these texts, we seek to transform who gets voice and agency in these contested sites.

Karen Krasny's comprehensive book explores gender as a performative social practice that often involves hegemonic power and the need for relational critique about what it means to be a girl, guy, queer, or different in the context of educational spaces that claim to offer equal opportunity and increased social capital. This work goes to the heart of social justice through critical, transformative pedagogy. As the author notes, "Gender bias is embedded in the very language that shapes our thinking and creates our worldview" (p. 2).

Schools should be sites of inquiry into forms of social difference with a focus on expanding human freedom and potential in a democratic society (Bean & Harper, 2007). This book delivers on this vision with specifics that go well beyond arguing for and theorizing a transformative pedagogy. The author troubles simplistic, essentialized notions of the perceived crisis in boys' reading through a lens that illuminates issues of self-selected reading and guided instruction. Book talk matters, but simply channeling boys (or girls for that matter) into reading narratives that reify patriarchal systems of dominance may do little to alter the status quo. Thus, book talk should involve shared conversations that create spaces to deconstruct stereotypes and ways of being in the world that limit both boys' and girls' life trajectories. This is by no means an easily accomplished vision in our classrooms.

Professor Krasny reviews studies of girls' silencing in science classrooms and other settings that speak to a long-established history of inequitable promotion of boys' voices in these formal settings. It is not hard to find studies that validate male voices in science, technology, engineering, and mathematics while illustrating the lateral climb in these spaces for girls to find their agency and voice.

Importantly, this book goes beyond a critique of gender and literacy practices to include a wealth of teaching resources including children's and young adult literature to support critical conversations. If we are going to change current gendered practices in literacy instruction, resources such as Karen Krasny's book offer both a hopeful sense of what is possible and exemplars of how to move forward. I hope you enjoy this work as much as I did, and it will be an important resource for my students in literacy and cultural studies seeking to alter experiences that limit students' potential and futures.

Tom Bean
University of Nevada, Las Vegas

REFERENCE

Bean, T., & Harper, H. (2007). Reading men differently: Alternative portrayals of masculinity in contemporary young adult fiction. *Reading Psychology* 28, 11–30.

Foreword by Didi Khayatt

December saw me engrossed in grading papers, writing a syllabus for each of the courses I was to teach in the winter term, and writing letters supporting various applications for a number of my graduate students. So when Professor Krasny approached me to write a foreword for her forthcoming book, I groaned with the weight of one more item to add to my "to do" list. What I did not realize at the time was the pleasure that awaited me.

I have worked for close to 40 years in the area of gender and education and have written on the topic from a feminist perspective for at least 30 of those years. I came to this book with the confidence of someone who has read and thought about the topic for longer than most of my graduate students have been alive. Krasny's book made me pause, made me think, made me ask new questions, and even better, inspired me to read further because she brings such a fresh outlook to gender and education. Much of what she writes about was not new to me, but how she writes it and to whom it is addressed is what makes this book inimitable: she combines an intellectual rigor and a profound knowledge of the subject area with a clear language to produce an invaluable asset to any teacher or parent who is curious about the topic of how gender is relevant to literacy, how it shapes it and is shaped by it. Krasny's book is filled with small gems: statistics that are not easily dismissed, class activities that are both interesting and appropriate for classroom use, and sections she names "Explore" that forces the reader to think and to try out some ideas that might be challenging and that may push the reader to think about aspects of literacy that she or he might have resisted previously.

In my long career of writing and publishing in the area of gender and sexuality, I have come across many ways of teaching these subjects. Years of teaching about social issues at the university level have shown me how difficult it is to present these topics without putting the readers or listeners on the defensive, be they men or women. Young men in my classes often deal with documented instances of sexism by either laughing it off or by saying that these were from a different era and that sexism does not exist to the same extent or in the same way as it did in the past. Young women in these same classes often feel they have to speak up to defend the men against the unjust allegations of this rabid feminist professor. Years of covering the topics of gender and sexuality have taught me the pitfalls of just presenting facts to the students, of imparting my scholarship only to be accused of bias and prejudice against men. Indeed, I have found it easier to teach about the effects of racism on our society than it is to teach about gender and sexuality.

Krasny's book tackles issues of gender as these pertain to literacy. She takes nothing for granted, always exploring and explicating each term, presenting the literature and the debates, writing tactfully yet tenaciously about the pervasive effects of gender discrimination and how these are glaring for some people, subtle for others, and totally nonexistent for many. Krasny presents the debates about how gender affects and is affected by literacy in a consistent, considerate, and compelling prose, a voice of reason, and a reasoned text. There is not a chapter in the book that does not have a practical use in the classroom, from intelligent exercises to statistical validations to scholarly references. I read the manuscript with great pleasure, highlighting some sections for later use in my own classroom. Krasny's text is well written, intelligent, and convincing. Her measured prose pulls the reader and yet challenges the intellect. Her arguments are both compelling and convincing, and she presents each of her chapters in such a way that these can be used individually or read in their entirety. Finally, there is much that I could write about this text, but the one element that stands out for me is that the reader is in for a thoughtful, challenging, and excellent read.

Didi Khayatt
York University, Toronto, Canada

Acknowledgments

I wish to express my gratitude to a number of people who assisted in the production of this book. Thanks go to my research assistants, Maria Bojagora, Alecia Wagner, and Sonia Malfitano, in York University's Graduate Program in Education, who tirelessly hunted down articles and carefully tended to a growing list of bibliographic references. Throughout this project, I have been inspired by the many conversations held with colleagues old and new, in and outside of the academy, that focused on the complex relationship between gender and literacy. Their dissatisfaction with hasty solutions proffered by politicians and policy makers further convinced me of the worthiness of writing this book. In particular, Pat Adamson, who some years ago now stepped into my position as English Language Arts Coordinator for the St. James-Assiniboia School Division (Winnipeg), generously read and commented on the first chapters. I am grateful to Thomas Bean from the University of Nevada, Las Vegas, and to Didi Khayatt from York University for their thorough reading of the manuscript and their enthusiastic forewords written from their perspectives as eminent scholars in their respective fields. My sister Deborah Peabody, M.D., graciously agreed to read and review the manuscript from her perspective as a pediatrician with more than 20 years in practice. Less directly, but no less important, as a young woman admitted to medical school at the age of 19, her life and work have always provided this older sister with an unwavering model of women's intellectual autonomy. I would be remiss if I did not acknowledge the teachers, students, and families at École Laura Secord School in Winnipeg with whom I once worked, who taught me a great deal about the curricular limitations imposed by heteronormative discourse practices and about the very real possibility of working together to make schools and communities sites of equity and social justice. And finally, my deepest gratitude to my husband Peter and our sons Rob and Jon for their constant support and their willingness to once again give over large areas of our home to stacks and stacks of books, journals, drafts, and articles.

CHAPTER 1

Why a Handbook on Gender and Literacy?

Are schools delivering gender-equitable education? How accurate are claims that girls and boys continue to achieve significantly different levels of success with literacy? Assuming that such differences occur, what school initiatives are effective in eliminating the gender gap? How does popular culture and media—television, the Internet, and magazines—play an influential role in determining how children create their identities as girls and boys? What types of literacy activities do girls and boys engage in? The continuing debate surrounding the provision of equitable education for all signals the need for a practical guide to assist educators and parents in recognizing how gender is constructed through literacy practices at home, at school, and throughout the community.

AIM AND SCOPE

The aims of this handbook are to offer educators and parents a practical guide to understanding the ways literacy practices expand and limit our views of male and female identities and to provide recommendations for addressing gender inequities in schools and in the community. It focuses on issues related to the gendered experience of students from prekindergarten to grade 12 and the social, cultural, and political conditions that structure those experiences. The content of this book promotes an understanding that issues surrounding gender cannot be reduced to broad generalizations. It seeks to make clear the complex notion of gender construction located within the intersections of race/ethnicity and socioeconomic status and how we are redefining what constitutes legitimate literacy practices in schools and society. The handbook includes annotated bibliographies and serves as a helpful resource in the selection and evaluation of print and media resources. *Gender and Literacy* is part of a reference series designed to provide an overview of contemporary research theories, practices, policy issues, and instructional approaches on a variety of timely and important educational topics. It is written in a style accessible to both parents or families and educators. In addition, college educators and prospective professionals will find it a valuable classroom resource. School administrators, too, will find information useful in developing and setting policy related to the creation of gender-equitable learning environments.

How Is This Book Organized?

Gender and Literacy: A Handbook for Educators and Parents is organized into nine chapters. The handbook provides readers with an overview of research, theory, practices, policy issues, and instructional approaches related to gender and literacy in education. In this first chapter, I begin by responding to the question, "Why a handbook on gender and literacy?" and by conveying some sense of the complex and ever-expanding definitions of both *gender* and *literacy*. This introduction is intended to make those of us who work and interact with our youth aware of how gender bias is embedded in the very language that shapes our thinking and creates our worldview. I hope that it will provoke interest among parents and educators to look for and discover the underlying assumptions in teaching practices, school curricula, and policies that limit the possibilities for both girls and boys. Beyond providing a much needed guide to what research can tell us about the construction of gender identities and their impact on literacy achievement, the chapters that follow should assist readers in identifying and working through their personal assumptions and gendered practices.

In Chapter 2, readers are introduced to the need for a critical approach to reading the literature and research on gender and literacy. It features some guidelines for critically assessing the contribution of popular rhetorical and practice-oriented literature to our understanding of gender differences in attitudes and achievement relating to K–12 literacy practices and for considering some of the social, economic, and political conditions that direct current trends in research. It describes types of classroom interventions aimed at closing the achievement gap between girls and boys and examines the effectiveness of several of these in closer detail.

Chapters 3 through 5 provide readers with a review of historical and contemporary research on gendered literacy practices and a discussion of the findings. Chapter 3 begins by briefly describing how the global economy has shaped educational discourse into a corporate rhetoric where competition between nation-states ascribes major importance to national and international tests measuring students' skills and knowledge within the aim of evaluating school systems worldwide. The chapter presents a summary of the findings from national and international assessments and continues with a critical discussion to qualify and, in some cases, dispel some of the myths surrounding the reported gender gap in academic achievement levels. At a time when there appears to be a national uproar about boys' underperformance on state- or province-wide, national, and international literacy assessments, I feel compelled to make clear that any attempt to account for the discrepancies in achievement levels between girls and boys needs to begin by understanding gender and how socially constructed codes of masculinity and femininity determine the manner in which boys and girls approach literacy and learning. The claim that girls appear to outperform boys on literacy measures and, correlatively, the claim that boys have *traditionally* outperformed girls in secondary mathematics and science is not in question, although it must be pointed out that girls have made significant gains in the later. I do, however, wish to problematize such claims by demonstrating that gendered achievement patterns are not so clear once we begin to take into consideration the intersections of socioeconomic status, culture, class, and race. I also wish to show that efforts to characterize boys as "marginalized" in response to girls' apparent gains (Sommers, 2000) are potentially dangerous in a global society that clearly remains under patriarchal domination. This chapter provides a careful analysis of reported results from the Programme for International Assessment (PISA) (Organization for Economic Cooperation and Development, 2003) and the National Assessment of Educational Progress (NAEP) that includes measures of reading literacy. Nevertheless, I believe that readers need to arrive at some understanding of the role international standards tests such as PISA play in the creation of knowledge-based societies and their potentially marginalizing effects on specific populations.

In Chapter 4, particular emphasis is placed on research investigating classroom discourse practices. A review of qualitative studies on gender and talk in classrooms documents a number of emerging patterns including the tendency among female adolescents to silence themselves in classroom discussions and for males to occupy the conversational floor. Research also indicates a tendency among girls to use talk to cultivate friendships and foster cooperation in small group settings. Nevertheless, these patterns are influenced greatly by the instructional method within which students are given the opportunity to interact. In Chapter 5, readers can familiarize themselves with a wide range of studies related to gender and reading. In the first part of the chapter, I discuss the findings from a number of studies that investigate gendered responses to literature. Later in the chapter, attention shifts to a review of the research investigating gendered reading preferences. A historical overview demonstrates that the reading preferences of both boys and girls change over time. Moreover, both girls' and boys' expressed book preferences and choices are often made in response to opportunities for reading structured by the schools and mass marketing.

How gender is constructed in children's and adolescent literature is the subject of Chapter 6. It deals specifically with identifying gender bias and stereotypes in children's and young adult fiction and nonfiction. Through the presentation of specific examples, parents and educators are able to develop general criteria for evaluating books. A number of works are highlighted for their potential to expand possibilities for both girls and boys. To this end, considerable attention is paid to young adult literature with gay and lesbian characters and to queering reading practices. There is also educative value in engaging students in the deconstruction of popular favorites, well-known classics, and virtually any text that reinforces traditional gendered expectations. Of particular interest to readers is likely to be the critique of gender-role construction in J. K. Rowling's *Harry Potter* series. A key feature of this chapter is the references to works that may assist teachers and librarians in addressing the documented gender bias in the literary canon used to teach reading in the language arts and English classroom. For those intent on providing more than mere equal representation of female and male protagonists, the chapter references novels with strong heroines, books that portray girls and boys performing a range of masculinities, picture books about children's family and social worlds, and a critique of gender representation in multicultural literature and folktales and their variants. Nevertheless, it cannot be emphasized enough that *how* literary works are taken up in a classroom is as important as *which* works are selected for study, and therefore I would advise parents and educators to resist the didacticism associated with treating any list of works as a prescription for "teaching" gender equity but rather to use them as ways of "thinking through" gender.

In Chapter 7, I present an overview of the policy, practice, and research on gender in education. While most of the early research relevant to gender and literacy generated by female scholars working from feminist perspectives clearly focused on issues related to girls and schooling (American Association of University Women, 1992; Orenstein, 1994; Pipher, 1994; Sadker & Sadker, 1994; Walkerdine, 1990), a number of scholars both female and male (AAUW, 2001; Brozo, 2010; Faludi, 1999; Martino & Kehler, 2007; Moss, 2007; Smith & Wilhelm, 2002; Sommers; 2000; Weaver-Hightower, 2003) have attempted to account for the underlying causes for the recent "boy turn" (Weaver-Hightower, 2003) in gender research in education that continues to claim headlines. The purpose of this chapter is to grant parents and educators a much needed opportunity to sift through various arguments and major critiques. The hope is that readers come to some understanding that efforts to account and correct for some boys' failure to achieve need to happen in ways that do not work to the detriment of girls (Moss, 2007). The overview provided will enable parents and educators to actively engage in the debate over literacy, gender, and educational reform so that they might be better positioned to interpret the role of schools and community in creating gender-equitable environments and to identify new ways of research and thinking about being gender literate.

For example, Chapter 7 provides teachers, administrators, school board members, and policy makers with information about the historical contribution of feminist researchers and teachers' organizations in lobbying for legislation. Readers, too, are introduced to Didi Khayatt's (2006) cross-cultural analysis of hegemonic masculinities and the idea that attitudes toward sexual orientation in schools are not likely to change until we are willing to take up gender *in conjunction* with sexuality. Title IX of the U.S. Educational Amendments of 1972 states that schools cannot deny any student participation in an educational program or activity on the basis of sex. Yet the construction of femininities and masculinities enacted in school discourse in the United States and in schools elsewhere can actively work to deny children of both sexes access to educational opportunities and can contribute to sustained forms of sexual harassment. I draw readers' attention to the effectiveness of a number of current programs and approaches in support of gender diversity and in making schools safe and welcoming. Emphasis is placed on adopting more proactive means by making gender literacy an integral part of both policy making and curriculum development in an effort to create a more inclusive school organization.

In Chapter 8, I invite readers to examine how educators and students can take action in the classroom. Through the presentation of concrete examples of theoretically informed practice, I hope to validate the work of students and educators in demonstrating that the promotion of gender literacy is possible within regular classroom instruction. Building upon the discussion on developing school policy in Chapter 7, I draw readers' attention to the critical literacy practices employed by a group of grade 8 students at Avondale Middle School in working through the problem of sexual harassment. The chapter continues with a discussion of how students and teachers can unlock the potential of literature to actively work through notions of gender and identity. I relate how my former class of grade 4 students and I assumed a critical stance in exploring gender issues in E. L. Konigsburg's (1993) young adult novel, *T-Backs, T-Shirts, COATS, and Suit.* I also describe for readers the social and instructional context within which rich discussion took place. Critical literacy practices are also central to Laraine Wallowitz's (2004) unit exploring gendered messages in literature and media in her women's studies class for high school seniors. Her work is reminiscent of Deborah Appleman's (2000) earlier research in which she instructs students in critical perspectives and then directs them to assume a particular stance in rereading various works from familiar folktales to Shakespeare. Wallowitz (2004) wants her students "to understand that reading a text from a feminist perspective changes their understanding of its meaning, that literature and media both reflect and create images of femininity and masculinity, and that readers project their own assumptions about gender onto a text" (p. 26). I conclude with my recent research with co-investigator Farra Yasin that examined how adolescents in a multicultural suburban middle school in the Greater Toronto area represented their identities through the production of comic strips. The research yielded considerable insight into students' gendered patterns of behavior as they relate to their ideas about friendship, the body, and their imaginative choices. The entire chapter is a rather passionate discussion about why reading and writing matter beyond the neoliberal rhetoric of accountability and test scores. I argue that in thinking about the complex relation between gender and literacy and the function of literacy, we would do well by our children if we took up Hannah Arendt's (1961) question: "What do we educate children for?" To this end, this section provides readers with insights into how reading practices in and out of school can lead to psychic fulfillment, psychological affirmation, moral deliberation, and a chance to mull over our own intentions and assumptions (Krasny, 2011). Moreover, in Chapter 7, I wish to convey to readers that overcoming the limitations imposed through socially sanctioned practices related to gender requires nothing less than a deliberate attentiveness to the political role of education in making children critically responsible for creating the world anew.

Throughout my years of teaching, I have gained an appreciation for the need to stop and reflect often in the course of coming to new understandings. In classrooms, we employ strategies such as "Think, Pair, Share," "Think Alouds," and simply a quick "Turn and Talk" to give time for students and teacher to verbally work through their thoughts and beliefs in response to a particular topic for study or text for interpretation. In order to engage educators and parents in an ongoing dialogue with the ideas and arguments presented in this handbook, each chapter features suggestions for exploration. The idea to engage readers through exploration is grounded in a desire to encourage readers to actively apply knowledge acquired while helping them recognize that knowledge is always open-ended and subject to experience. The explorations borrow from well-known interactive strategies for inquiry and reading comprehension. The decision to include these points of inquiry drew considerable inspiration from my undergraduate and graduate students' success with suggestions for further investigation contained in a number of textbooks for teaching English and language arts. I hope that educators and parents will find the suggestions for further exploration in *Gender and Literacy* equally inciting in ways that allow for personal reflection and collaborative change. In this handbook, "Exploring with Children" offers parents a chance to contemplate particular ideas presented in the section and think about how such ideas might be applied to inform, shape, and in some cases alter gender and literacy practices at home. Similarly, "Exploring with Students" aims at assisting educators in using the theories and ideas presented to think through issues of gender and literacy with students and examine how gender and literacy are enacted in classrooms and schools. The highlighted boxes designated simply "Explore" describe a task that all readers may find useful in taking stock of and possibly revising their assumptions about literacy and gender. Some invitations to explore are simply guiding questions designed to focus readers' attention and activate prior knowledge before reading on. In academic and professional settings, some may serve as the impetus for action-based research or spawn study groups around a particular question of interest.

In Chapter 9, the final chapter of the book, readers will find an annotated bibliography of suggested further reading for those interested in following up on particular ideas, debates, or concepts introduced in each chapter. The list is by no means comprehensive, and readers will note that I have included works that may contain content that seems contrary to the arguments presented herein. I do so in the hope that parents and educators explore the range of perspectives and theories surrounding issues related to gender and literacy and that this book and the works referenced will spur readers on to consciously take action in the quest to create gender-equitable learning environments.

Explore

This initial exploration borrows from an idea in Nodelman and Reimer's (2003) text on children's literature. I invite readers to open the handbook to any page and begin reading until you come to an idea that you find strange or intriguing. The idea may lend confirmation to something you have thought about before, or you may find that the idea does not fit entirely with your thoughts and beliefs. Think about the experiences in your life that would cause you to accept or reject this new idea about gender and/or literacy. Readers are encouraged to mark the intriguing passage with a sticky note and return to it later. Teacher candidates can record the identified passage, write a brief response, and then share their responses in small groups or pairs.

Why a Handbook on Gender and Literacy?

It can be argued that there has always been a need to uncover the ways in which human potential is determined by our habits and presumptions regarding gender. Beginning at birth, children are assigned to either female or male roles and immediately receive different behavioral messages from their parents (Smith & Lloyd, 1978). From the moment a child is born, parents and members of society tend to adjust their behavior and response according to the child's perceived sex (Paechter, 1998). Moreover, much of children's play is directed at learning how to be "grown up" men and women. Toys such as kitchen centers, tool benches, auto garages, action figures, and fashion dolls teach children a great deal about gender expectations and contribute to children's first ideas about career goals and aspirations. Thorne (1993) found that boys and girls experience overwhelming pressure from both peers and adults to fill gender roles in the classroom and on the playground. She also notes that the process of separating girls and boys into "opposite sides" is often reinforced by teachers through the creation of separate teams, separate seating arrangements, and separate competitions. In kindergarten and nursery classes, it is not unusual to still find that children separate according to gender when it is center time. In my experience as a language arts coordinator in public schools, I repeatedly observed teachers and librarians identify "boys' books" and "girls' books" in making their selection for classroom and school libraries. It is not surprising, therefore, that boys and girls inevitably demonstrate different discourse patterns emerging from their interaction with different activities and materials. Recent developments in cognitive science (Damasio, 2003; Edelman, 1992; Paechter, 1998) provide evidence to suggest that repeated experiences emerging from interactions with peers and adults and with objects build different neural connections. In other words, much of what we might think comes naturally to girls or to boys is instantiated in the brain as children grow into their expanding social environment. As a result, their attraction and aversion to certain activities, people, and objects are learned behaviors.

Exploring with Children

Take a quick survey of your child's toys. How do they reflect gendered expectations (e.g., tool bench, cars, and action figures for boys; kitchens, dolls, and glitter pens for girls)? What messages do these objects convey about gendered roles and professions? How is this reinforced by the toys' color, form, and marketing? What gendered expectations do you hold for these toys as they relate to your child? Think about introducing an activity to your child that falls outside of gendered expectations? How might you do this without relying on mass-marketed toys?

Whenever we use biological determinism to explain human behavior and account for observed differences between females and males, we are making an *essentialist* argument. We are saying that certain behaviors are attributed to a person's assigned sex. Over the years, essentialist arguments have been used to justify gender and racial inequities. But in fact biology tells us that there is very little that comes "naturally" to either boys or girls. For example, essentialists would argue that boys are genetically predisposed to have higher levels of aggression due to higher levels of testosterone, but in fact, girls have similar levels of testosterone up until the age of 10 (Constantino,

Grosz, Saenger, Chandler, Nandi, & Earls, 1993). While male adolescence is marked by a surge in testosterone, we know that not all boys are aggressive (Archer, 1997). Also, there is evidence to suggest we might have the causal relationship between testosterone and aggression backwards. Kindlon and Thompson (1999) report that elevated levels of testosterone might be a direct effect of committing aggressive acts and not the precipitating cause.

Biological essentialists provide much of the evidence that fuels the hot debate over single-sex schooling, and for that reason we need to examine such claims carefully. No doubt biology plays a role in the development of girls and boys, but there is overwhelming evidence to support the idea that gender is shaped by sociocultural conditions within our environment. It is only when we begin to examine gender as a social construction that we can gain the necessary insight to transform what appears as gendered realities into new possibilities.

DEFINING GENDER AND LITERACY

Before we can begin to arrive at a clear understanding of the complex relationship between gender and literacy, we need to define these terms. While this might seem fairly straightforward, defining *gender* and *literacy* in such a way as to reflect contemporary research from diverse disciplines including language and literacy, linguistics, feminist scholarship, queer theory, masculine theory, biological sciences, cognitive psychology, and cultural studies might prove complicated, confusing, and for some even disconcerting. But such an exercise might also prove mind expanding in ways that help us develop a critical understanding of the issues related to the gendered experience of students from prekindergarten to grade 12. In this section, we examine how an enhanced understanding of gender and literacy might lay the ground for challenging traditional boundaries.

Gender

According to Judith Butler (1990), gender appears to us as a particular form—girl/boy, woman/man—and any description of gender relies on making a normative judgment "about those appearances and the basis for what appears" (p. xxi). Butler asks us to ponder what conditions determine the appearance of gender itself. While we may be tempted to seek a descriptive account of gender that would include the conditions that make gender intelligible (e.g., a boy has a penis/a girl has a vagina; girls wear dresses and pants/boys wear pants but no dresses; girls are passive/boys are active), such descriptions invariably lead to a normative account. Accordingly, the conditions that color our conception of gender contribute to our view of how the gendered world ought to be to create a normative operation of power. Language and social discourse, as will we see, are primary means of maintaining that order. The underlying premise of this book is that gender is, by and large, socially constructed and performative.

It might be helpful to define *gender* in relation to the term *sex*. It is generally accepted that one's biological sex refers to one's chromosomal makeup as either genetically male (XY) or female (XX). Most often it is assigned according to one's genitalia; however, many children are born with ambiguous genitalia, and still others are *intersexed*, that is to say, born with genitalia or secondary sex characteristics that are neither exclusively female nor male or that combine features of both the male and female sexes. It is estimated that as many as 1 percent of all live births exhibit some degree of sexual ambiguity (Fausto-Sterling, 2000). Others (Sax, 2002) adopt a narrower definition of the conditions that determine intersexuality and therefore claim that the incidence of those born with intersexed conditions is far below 1 percent. We will learn that even scientific arguments about sex and nature are grounded in interpretation and influenced by social and political forces. One thing seems to be apparent: We are gaining an increasing awareness of the difficulties associated with assigning sex based solely on physical characteristics.

In her book *Sexing the Body: Gender Politics and the Construction of Sexuality*, Fausto-Sterling (2000) opens with the example of Spain's top female hurdler, Maria Patiño, who in 1988 entered the Olympic field of competition completely unaware that her career as an athlete was about to take a downward turn. Patiño was headed for her first race when officials informed her that she had failed the sex test. Despite the fact that Patiño grew up as a female and developed a female form, examinations revealed that her cells supported a Y chromosome and she had hidden testes. The doctors confirmed that she had a condition known as *androgen insensitivity*. Fausto-Sterling explains that while Patiño's testes produced a lot of testosterone, her body was not capable of detecting this masculinizing hormone. As a result, at puberty, Patiño's body read instead the *estrogen* produced by the testes—her breasts grew, her waist narrowed, and her hips widened. In short, until this revelation, neither Patiño nor anyone else had any reason to suspect that she was anything but female.

After a lengthy and trying legal battle, Patiño was eventually reinstated by the International Amateur Athletic Federation, and in 1992 she returned to the Spanish Olympic Squad as an athlete eligible to compete. Her case is a highly publicized one, and it advances the argument of Fausto-Sterling and others (Butler, 1990; Sears, 1997) that a person's sex is more complex than many of us are prepared to believe and that there are "shades of difference" (Fausto-Sterling, 2000, p. 3). Patiño's story is not unique. Santhi Soundarajan, an Indian track-and-field athlete, was stripped of her silver medal for the 800-meter race in the 2006 Asian Games held in Doha, Qatar, for failing a gender verification test. And in 2009, officials of the International Association of Athletics Federations stripped 18-year-old

South African Castor Semenya of her gold medal for the 800-meter race at the world track-and-field championships in Berlin after undergoing sex-determination testing. In an interview with *New York Times* reporter Christopher Clarey in the wake of the Semenya controversy, Alice Dreger, a professor of medical humanities and bioethics at Northwestern University, explained the difficulty facing these athletes thus: "It turns out genes, hormones and genitals are pretty complicated.... There isn't really one simple way to sort out males and females. Sports require that we do, but biology doesn't care. Biology does not fit neatly into simple categories...." (Clarey, *New York Times*, Aug. 19, 2009).

Money and Ernhardt (1972) popularized the idea that whereas *sex* is anatomically and physiologically determined, *gender* is a social expression of an inner psychological conviction that one is either male or female. Accordingly, having a vagina as opposed to a penis is a *sex difference*. Girls outperforming boys on standardized reading tests is considered a *gender difference*. Fausto-Sterling (2000), however, argues that while we may use scientific knowledge to label a person as female or male, our beliefs about gender shape what kind of knowledge scientists produce about sex in the first place, advancing the idea that sexuality, too, can be socially constructed. In this regard, the terms *gender* and *sex* are said to be mutually complicit, a view shared by feminists Judith Butler and Monique Wittig. The extent to which gender affects our definition of sex is still a subject of debate, but one thing seems to be clear: The social forces and belief systems that define what it means to be male or female and what it means to act in a masculine and feminine fashion are constantly evolving. In other words, gender roles and behaviors change in response to cultural and ideological influences and are closely related to issues of power.

Valerie Walkerdine (1990) has long employed a Marxist perspective and a critical psychology to demonstrate how social and economic organization shapes the culture of girlhood. Walkerdine explains how the feminized culture of early education—for example, the inclusion of math problems relying on shopping and cooking scenarios—works to link the domestic space between home and school and discourage boys, who are socialized to resist such content. The flipside of this, of course, is that historically adolescent girls have been less successful at advanced mathematics and physics because these subjects are presented in a more abstract and socially irrelevant manner. The feminization of elementary education and its traditional link to domesticity is further enhanced by the fact that most early educators are female. But as I hope to make clear in later chapters, replacing female teachers with male teachers inadequately addresses the problem of deconstructing the complex set of social structures that would cause us to form an association between domesticity and femininity in the first place. Arguably, girls have always been better at "doing school." Moreover, Burman (2005) claims that the fact that girls appear to be overtaking boys in all but the traditionally "masculine" areas of the school curriculum is consistent with the body of educational literature indicating that girls perform best on the kind of continuous assessment and cumulative study that characterizes the structure, form, and standards of assessment currently adopted by many Western countries. In other words, boys feel they are supposed to achieve success effortlessly, and therefore they are less likely to benefit from the cumulative effect of ongoing preparation and study (Stipek, 1984). In contrast to girls, boys tend to opt for last-minute cramming to make up for what they didn't get done throughout the term.

For more than two decades, Walkerdine's research (1981, 1988, 1990; Walkerdine, Lucey, & Melody, 2001) has demonstrated that girls' overperformance is not a new phenomenon; it simply hasn't been recognized as such nor have girls necessarily been rewarded for it. As a matter of fact, there is considerable evidence to suggest that adolescent girls' high academic achievement may result in their low self-esteem and loss of potential. In a study investigating cross-gender teasing in literature-discussion groups, Evans, Alvermann, and Anders (1998) reported that the boys eventually thwarted any efforts of the girls in the group to take a leadership role, to keep the group on task, or to initiate new topics. Overwhelmingly, in situations like this, girls "chose silence as a means of self-protection" (Guzzetti, Young, Gritsavage, Fyfe, & Hardenbrook, 2002, p. 21). Despite documentation that girls outperform boys in the comprehension of reading narrative text, the research (Cherland, 1992; Evans, Alvermann, & Anders, 1998; Marks, 1995) indicates that generally girls play a submissive role in literature-discussion groups. *Female silencing* is but one of the devastating consequences for girls' psychological development resulting from the negative sociocultural influences that contribute to the vast discrepancies between girls' high academic abilities and their low self-esteem. Incidences of eating disorders, self-mutilation, and depression; increased aggression in peer and intimate relationships; criminal arrests; and conventional career choices can be directly attributed to girls' loss of self-esteem (Brown & Gilligan, 1992; Kerr, 1997; Kilbourne, 1999; Orenstein, 1994).

Masculinity studies is an interdisciplinary field that began in response to feminist political action but in more recent years has taken up the question of boys' underachievement and problems of violence and aggression by adopting perspectives that are sympathetic to feminist scholarship. Martino's extensive research (1995a, 1995b, 1998, 2001) inquiring into the construction of masculinities among Australian youth builds upon Walkerdine's (1990) work. Walkerdine found that the conscious reinforcement of the traits identified with a dominant male hierarchy is a dangerous practice and may contribute to the alarming rate of sexual harassment perpetrated by boys in British schools. This concern is echoed in a report by the American Association of University Women (AAUW; 1995) documenting the educational consequences of gender construction in American schools throughout childhood and adolescent development. The AAUW maintains that patriarchal power structures and pressure on girls and boys to conform to idealized conceptions of femininity and masculinity can have destructive consequences for both sexes. Much of the recent research into the culture of boys emerges from a concern for boys' psychological health and what has been termed their emotional illiteracy. The seemingly impossible task of living up to masculine-defined attitudes and behavior takes a serious toll on male youth and, in far too many cases, their victims. Those arguing from a biological orientation (Faludi, 1999; Gurian, 1996) that "boys will be boys" and we needn't interfere with their natural development surely cannot be blind to the manifestations of culturally embedded codes of masculinity that have been linked to violence, desperation, depression, isolation, addiction, and attitudes that are not conducive to learning and achievement in school (Garbarino, 2000; Gilbert & Gilbert, 1998; Gilligan, 1997; Salisbury & Jackson, 1996; Walkerdine, 1990). In Chapter 5, we will examine more closely Martino's study of Australian boys' stated reading preferences that makes clear that, for many boys, literacy simply does not fit with traditional conceptualizations of performing masculinity. In response to the current furor surrounding boys and literacy, Smith and Wilhelm (2002) argue that if indeed boys are "in trouble in the area of literacy because of gender, then our systems of belief both about literacy and about gender can be changed in ways to help them" (p. 18).

James Sears (1997) explores teaching for critical sexual literacy. He contends that a universal, unidimensional, and stable conception of sexuality grounded in biblical or biological arguments fails to consider "the pervasive influence of culture on understandings of our sexual selves and . . . behaviours" (p. 273). He describes how individuals within a society may construct gendered and sexual relationships differently. Social class, race, religion, and region "intersect to form the cultural bounds within which individuals make meaning of their sexual and gendered selves" (p. 276). Sears conducted a number of case studies of young people from various cultural, regional, and ethnic backgrounds within the United States to determine their constructions and valuations of gender and sexuality. He found that American youth living in a Cherokee village, an urban housing tenement, a rural Southern community, and an affluent Midwestern suburb all hold very different views about what it means "to be heterosexual or homosexual; to be a woman or man, or to act in a masculine or feminine manner" (p. 276).

Critical theories deriving from feminist scholarship, queer theory, masculine theory, and cultural studies can provide us with lenses to examine and think through our assumptions about sexuality and gender and help us interpret and challenge the evidence presented through research findings. As I hope to point out to readers, literature can be a valuable medium for testing those critical lenses and exercising our moral imagination. Critical theories can help us examine the extent to which our social world and the ways we act within it are not natural but rather are shaped by culture, ideology, and power. Such perspectives allow us to see how we are positioned socially and historically and the consequences of our positioning. Most importantly, by rendering the familiar unfamiliar, such perspectives can provoke alternate visions of how we might redefine our role as parents and educators and transform teaching and learning. Gaining an awareness of how our identities are constructed through participation in our social world should incite us toward integrating a developing understanding of sexuality and gender in curriculum development.

One idea that resounds throughout this book is that there is nothing neutral about gender. Feminine and masculine codes of behavior that can look very different across cultures and times are nevertheless so pervasive that they cannot help but shape who we are and how we act. In writing this book, I hope to promote the idea we cannot even begin to deal effectively with gender stereotyping and bias until we recognize the extent to which we ourselves consciously or unconsciously abide by these codes.

Explore

Take a few minutes to list the ways that you routinely perform gender according to cultural expectations—anything from playing linebacker to wearing pantyhose. Can you imagine a cultural milieu in which such behaviors would be gender neutral? Are some behaviors considered more gendered than others? For example, is it culturally more acceptable for girls and women to play linebacker than for boys and men to wear pantyhose? Why or why not?

Literacy

The UN Educational, Scientific and Cultural Organization (UNESCO)'s traditional definition of literacy as the ability to "read and write a short simple statement about his/her life" was thought to have provided a straightforward, measurable definition of literacy. This definition, once accepted by the international literacy assessments discussed in Chapter 3, comes under increasing criticism as it fails to account for the complex set of skills and abilities required to understand and communicate using the dominant symbol systems of a culture including alphabets, characters, numbers, and visual icons. In a technologically advanced society, the definition of literacy clearly encompasses more than the basic skills of listening, speaking, reading, and writing. The term *multiliteracy* attempts to account for the complex social, cultural, and linguistic skills needed to communicate in an ever-changing world marked by new technologies. The New London Group (1996) advances the idea "that the multiplicity of communications channels and increasing cultural and linguistic diversity in the world today call for a much broader view of literacy than portrayed by traditional language-based approaches" (p. 60).

An integrated language arts curriculum emphasizes the interconnectedness of listening, speaking, reading, and writing and extends it to include viewing and representing. Such an extension is necessary if we are to understand how we make meaning from visual and media texts. Moreover, today's multiliteracies relate to our capacity to apply acquired skills and knowledge about language, symbols, and images to making critical judgments about the oral, visual, and written information and texts we interact with each day. A more expansive view of literacy puts the results of many of the literacy assessments used to compare girls' and boys' literacy achievement into question. In addition to usurping traditional notions about what it means to be literate, multiliteracies paint a very different picture about how girls and boys engage in literate activities. Information and communication technologies that make possible the Internet, electronic mail, instant messaging, videoconferencing, hypermedia, social networking, and digital media effectively change the ways students acquire and apply literacy (Leu, 2000; Leu & Kinzer, 1999, Reinking, Labbo, & McKenna, 2000). Recent studies are beginning to shed some light on the gender differences associated with how girls and boys use these new literacies in the process of identity formation and social communication.

It is important to note that, like gender, literacy too is influenced by culture, ideology, and power. The value placed on the various strands—listening, speaking, reading, writing, viewing, and representing—and how literacy is enacted vary from context to context. For example, Willinsky (1990) describes how attaining new levels of literacy was seen by the working classes in the mid-nineteenth-century England as a means to achieving better working conditions and making political gains. Before the provision of public schooling, the working classes organized "Sunday Schools" so that workers and their children could learn to read and write on their day off. The ruling classes soon felt threatened by the possibility of the working class gaining political power through their new-found literacy practices, and as a result, compulsory public schooling was soon introduced. At first glance, one might view this as a genuine advance for the working classes, but in reality the elite saw it as a way of undermining the social agency associated with literacy gains. Willinsky continues to describe how the socially transformative project of literacy gave way to an emphasis on literature. Throughout the history of public schooling, literature education in British and American schools largely served to maintain the status quo and advance the project of colonization and nativism in which the interests of the native-born or established inhabitants are protected. In Chapter 6, "Reading Gender in Children's and Adolescent Literature," we look more closely at how literature education has actively reinforced stereotypic gendered roles and existing power structures and, conversely, how it has worked to challenge these same roles and structures through reading's potential for transformative change.

Regardless of how literacy is defined by a particular culture at a particular time in history, it pervades every aspect of individual and social life. In Western society, we recognize literacy as fundamental to learning and purport to value it as a basic human right. A century after the introduction of public schooling in Anglo-America, Freire (1970) saw the ability of Brazilian peasants to read and write as a nonviolent means toward achieving human freedom. His model for critical pedagogy has been adapted in developing nations throughout the world, and the idea that literacy is a form of *praxis*, that is to say, a way of acting on the world, has been adopted by those working toward implementing an antioppressive and antiracist pedagogy in North American schools. It has been often noted that literacy is a double-edged sword insofar as it can work to both subvert and maintain dominant (or *hegemonic*) power structures.

Exploring with Students

Ask students to share their understanding of what it means to be literate. Present the idea of multiple literacies as the knowledge and skills about language, symbols, and images we use to make sense of oral, visual, and written information and texts. Prompt students by asking them to think about the messages conveyed in a picture-book illustration, an advertisement, a painting, or the lyrics to a popular song. Ask them to consider whether music and dance can be considered forms of literacy. Why or why not? Ask primary aged-students to brainstorm the different ways people share or communicate their thoughts and feelings.

GENDER AND LITERACY

Throughout this handbook, we examine the ways language often acts as the means through which we organize and shape our world. Gender differences imply a corresponding social order within a culture, and these differences are inscribed in the culture's language (Millard, 1997). For example, authority is generally believed to be located within the male culture. Feminist scholar Deborah Cameron (1998) shows how the simple act of naming—the fact that family names pass down through the male line—is a means of reinscribing male authority. The frequent use of the words *woman* and *female* as qualifiers for "doctor" (as in *woman doctor*) or "athlete" (as in *female athlete*) and the addition of the suffix *–ess* to form the feminine form of *poet* (*poetess*) and *actor* (*actress*) effectively relegate women to the status of other. Showalter (1977), Gilbert and Gubar (1979), and Schweickart (1989) have illustrated how

Western literature has been largely written according to a male script. At the same time, these scholars have detailed how writers like Emily Dickinson, Jane Austen, Mary Shelley, and Virginia Wolff managed to write themselves out of the male-inscribed literary text in ways to reject woman as angelic ideal (Snow White) or monster (Wicked Stepmother). Such work highlights the potential of a feminist perspective on reading and writing to bring gender and politics to prominence. For example, investigations into writing women's lives (Krasny, 2006; Wagner-Martin, 1994) reveal that until recently, biographies about women were primarily stories about the "woman behind the man." *Critical literacy* practices derive from Freire and Macedo's (1987) conviction that reading the world and the word expands our social imagination in ways that make possible the kind of actions needed to change oppressive social relations. Harste (2002) explains that critical literacy needs to keep moving so as not to be captured and packaged in some particular way. To my mind, the active creation of gender-equitable classrooms requires that we recognize alternate perspectives to revise and reimagine new ways of being in the world.

Children begin to construct gendered realities based on what they see, hear, and read (Fox, 1993; Turner-Bowker, 1996). Whether we like it or not, we live in a society in which our individual and group identity is defined, to a startling degree, by our gender. Advertisers are skilled at exploiting gendered identities to sell us the clothes we wear, the cars we drive, the shampoo giving our hair bounce and shine, the deodorant to keep us dry, and even the food we eat.

Over the years, in an attempt to promote an understanding of the pervasive construction of gender in media discourse, I have regularly asked school-aged and university students to watch two consecutive hours of prime time network television at their leisure and to try to find a single commercial that does *not* include gender stereotyping of any kind. Needless to say, most students have a difficult time. Even when they come to class armed with an example, more often than not, another student challenges the example and it is soon discounted with exclamations of "Oh, yeah! I never saw it that way before." I am always amazed at how even elementary school–aged children come away from this simple exercise more critically aware of how the media directs their thinking about who they are and what is expected of them as boys and girls. They have also caught on to how subtle some of the messages can be and the degree to which humor in television often depends upon a shared view of gendered identities.

For example, in one grade 4 class, students commented on a trailer for what was then a new television series called *Due South*. The series featured a "handsome" Royal Canadian Mounted Police (RCMP) officer working south of the border in Chicago. The short clip depicted a group of women huddled around an office window making lewd and suggestive remarks as they gazed out at the street below where the "Mountie" stood outfitted in his red uniform, wide-brimmed hat, and knee-high riding boots. After some discussion, the students arrived at the conclusion that the joke depended on everyone knowing the all-too-often-portrayed scenario of male construction workers whistling and harassing young women as they passed by. Even 9- and 10-year-olds were not prepared to accept the possibility of reversing stereotypes as a means of amending the limitations of gendered identities. Both boys and girls decided that the trailer was degrading to both sexes, but they also recognized that even though they found aspects of the trailer sexist, many of the students and their families would probably continue to watch the show and enjoy it. This brings us to the question of whether it is even possible to eliminate all forms of gender bias and stereotyping. Clearly, sexist stereotyping persists because it continues to validate conscious and unconscious assumptions about ourselves and others. Critical literacy should help us uncover some unforeseen part of ourselves, what it is that we identify with, and help us recognize how our daily habits and actions might be contributing to harmful practices.

Exploring with Students

Play a network trailer or opening scene from a current popular sitcom and one from an older series rerun. Then ask students to watch each again and make a list of gendered stereotypes (e.g., "the nagging wife," "the sexy but dumb blond," "the hunky but dumb jock," "the conniving husband," "the nosey gossip," "the interfering or overbearing mother-in-law," "the science-fiction nerds," etc.). Compare how humor in each of the sitcoms relies on gendered stereotyping. Challenge older students to rewrite a scene in either of the sitcom trailers without relying on gendered stereotypes. Is it possible? If so, is the scene still funny?

One way to come face to face with personal and shared assumptions is to pay attention to mental images formed about persons and events. For example, I have often shared the example of the grade 4 students' response to the trailer for *Due South* in university classrooms and professional development sessions for educators in the United States and Canada. I ask students and teachers unfamiliar with the show's actor to imagine the Mountie featured in the trailer. Most descriptions comply with contemporary Western masculine codes about the perfect male and include a combination of the following features: tall, physically fit, broad shoulders, white teeth, clear skin—and despite the fact that there are significant numbers of aboriginal, Asian, South Asian, and black male and female RCMP officers, no one yet has pictured the actor as anything but white. The Royal Canadian Mounted Police are a symbol of power and justice. In Canada, as in the United States, white men have historically controlled both.

On the problem of eliminating sexist stereotypes from books, children's literature critic Michelle Landsburg (1986) points out:

> Sexist and racist stereotypes are an immensely difficult question. . . . It's no use simply dismissing [any book] that smacks of bias because, provokingly enough, some of the best-written books carry traces of thoughtless stereotyping—and some of the worst-written stuff available is conscientiously liberated and free from every trace of prejudice against women, blacks, homosexuals, the aged, the disabled . . . the list goes on. . . . Some of this determinedly progressive fiction for youth has an eerily Victorian ring to it; didacticism clangs on every page like an iron bell—heavy, clumsy, reverberant with good intentions. (p. 186)

Ridding our libraries of books containing sexist stereotypes is problematic and not recommended. Apart from leaving us with very little to read, doing so would erase an important historical record. Characters in the best of young adult and children's fiction speak and act according to the societal parameters established for them within a particular time and place. Fantasy can sometimes liberate characters from traditional gender roles as, for example, in Ursula LeGuin's (1969) *The Left Hand of Darkness* and Cynthia Voigt's (1990) *On Fortune's Wheel*. But even in fantasy, the author must create in the mind of her readers a fictional world with a well-established system of social order. Literature remains a valuable record of our *historical consciousness*, and while this does not excuse insensitivity on the part of writers and publishers, censorship as a means of correcting gendered stereotypes is likely to contribute to *cultural amnesia*, or the tendency to forget about anything that does not paint society in a positive light as judged by contemporary standards. This handbook is intended to provide readers with critical frameworks for analyzing young adult and children's texts. From a critical perspective, *how* literature is taught is as important as *what* literature is taught.

MOVING ON

Hopefully, this introduction to gender and literacy has piqued considerable interest in taking up the challenge to provide gender-equitable learning environments for our children and students. In the chapters that follow, we begin to take a critical look at what research can tell us about the impact of gender constructions on literacy practices and levels of achievement. Chapter 2 begins by providing some guidelines for developing a critical understanding of the body of research on gender and literacy and discusses concerns about some of the initiatives spawned by a growing fixation on the gender gap in literacy performance.

Taking a Critical Approach to Interpreting the Research and Literature on Gender and Literacy

Parents and educators can access a wide array of resources on issues related to gender and literacy. These include research studies, reports issued from government and nongovernmental organizations and institutions, newspapers, journal articles, trade books, magazines, podcasts, and webpages. Weaver-Hightower (2003) warns that popular rhetorical literature that includes newspapers, magazines, and trade books is often construed as *the* source of information, receiving its considerable attention through the deployment of the loudest voices and media-grabbing headlines. Bestsellers such as Michael Gurian's *Wonder of Boys* (1996), recently reissued as a 10th anniversary edition (2006), provides testimony to the resiliency of the "boy turn" in research and education in much the same way as popular books about the educational disadvantages of girls occupied the media headlines during the 1990s. The aim of this chapter is to encourage educators and parents to read beyond the headlines and assist them in the critical assessment of independent research investigating the relation between gender and literacy conducted in schools and other educational environments.

RESEARCH AS DISCOURSE

Research contributes to a form of discourse that both appropriates and generates language to convey the purpose, method, and results of an investigation. For any discourse to be effective, it must fashion conventions and routines to implicate its audience and facilitate understanding within the community it oversees. Traditionally, research has been regarded as an academic or scientific domain in which scholars ply their trade as both producers and consumers, sometimes, but not always, making their results available to the wider public. Knowledge mobilization, or the widespread dissemination of research data, is viewed by many as putting to work

available knowledge generated through public funding and other sources so
that it might be of maximum benefit to others in making informed decisions
about everything from family and community affairs to national and global
social and economic policy. Nevertheless, wider dissemination of research
findings does not necessarily guarantee that studies will be accessed by a
wider audience. As a particular form of discourse, research relies on specific
language to support a certain set of relations, activities, and identities (Gee,
2005), suggesting that it privileges certain communities of readers and
excludes others. Handbooks, trade books, and practice-oriented literature
are often employed to summarize and make practical the findings and implications of research to interested audiences.

Explore

What types of literature inform your thoughts and beliefs about gender and literacy? How much of your understanding comes from
popular media sources (e.g., newspapers, magazines, television interviews, trade books)? What issues related to gender and literacy currently claim your attention?

Educational Research as Economic Discourse

Open-access online journals and data repositories play an active role in
the promotion of knowledge mobilization, as do national nonprofit organizations such as the National Research Council (NRC) in the United States
and the Canadian Council on Learning (CCL). But where open-access publishing advocates the democratization of knowledge and mutually supportive rights to know and be known (Willinsky, 2005), organizations such
as the CCL, the federally funded NRC, and the international Organisation
for Economic Co-operation and Development (OECD) responsible for
the Programme for International Student Assessment (PISA) discussed in
Chapter 3 are clearly invested in linking education to nation-building agendas that focus on the creation of human capital as lifelong learners in a
highly competitive global economy.

To this end, such organizations tend to act as knowledge brokers, decid-
ing what is worthy of investigation and dissemination and, oft times, who
is commissioned to undertake such investigations and under what conditions. With regards to the present discussion, the extent to which transnational, national, and state-run organizations have linked standards and
testing to educational reform policy has had considerable impact in fueling
the furor over boys and reading. I am not contending that we cannot glean
something from the reports generated by these agencies, but in the interest

of being judicious and critically aware, it pays to be familiar with the mission of the organization or institution brokering the knowledge. This information can usually be found on the organization's website. For example, the OECD professes to "promote policies that will improve the economic and social well-being of people around the world" by creating "a forum in which [participating] governments can work together to share experiences and seek solutions to common problems" through the measurement of "productivity and global flows of trade and investment" and the analysis and comparison of data to "predict future trends" and "set international standards on a wide range of things, from agriculture and tax to the safety of chemicals" (OECD, http://www.oecd.org/about/). To date, however, the OECD has yet to conclusively attribute causation to the correlation between economic growth rates and trends in educational performance documented through PISA, that is to say, whether improved schooling leads to economic growth or economic growth leads to improved schooling (Bils & Klenow, 2000; OECD, 2010). One also has to consider how minor economic gains may have come at a cost of local autonomy and control over the aims of public schooling. For example, how have free-trade agreements and corporate intervention shaped the educational system and the economic and social well-being of people in countries striving to participate economically on a global scale? Do internationalizing efforts directed at the comparative assessment of nations contribute to a new form of cultural imperialism? If so, what are the gendered consequences? Is it reasonable to apply the same economic systems of analysis to project growth in educational performance as we would with hog futures? While there is insufficient space within the pages of this book to fully unpack the complexities implicating education in the creation of global economic citizenship, readers not familiar with the repressive effects of globalization on public schooling might find Jill Freidberg's (2005) documentary film *Granito de Arena/Grain of Sand* insightful.

Neoliberal Educational Reform and the "Boy Turn" in Educational Research

The question that looms large in the present discussion is to what extent the "boy turn" in educational research (Weaver-Hightower, 2003) has been grounded in the neoliberal reforms that prompted standards testing results to be made public. In the 1990s, education took on greater "exchange value" as free-market economists like Milton Friedman "entered the American educational arena arguing in favor of school vouchers and schools of choice as a response to perceived failings of schools" (Krasny, 2006). Similarly, in the United Kingdom, the widespread publication of league tables of standardized test scores in newspapers and on the Internet linked student performance to job security and keeping school doors open (Gillborn & Youdell, 2000; Weaver-Hightower, 2003). As a direct result, school administrators felt compelled to direct teachers' attention and limited funding resources toward improving the performance of boys, who outnumber girls in the lowest test score ranks, to improve overall school standings. In effect, the structure of educational reform as it relates to accountability and school choice has given rise to overt and less obvious forms of political backlash that draw life from repeated claims that girls have made gains and, in some respects, have surpassed boys (Kenway & Willis, 1998; Lingard & Douglas, 1999; Weaver-Hightower, 2003).

As Weaver-Hightower (2003) points out, "backlashes feed on anxieties, threatened beliefs, and self-interest" (p. 477) and are not new to gender politics. The "increasingly unstable set of circumstances in the work sphere threatening the conventional basis both of masculinity and its associated ideal of the male as breadwinner" (Arnot, David, & Weiner, 1999, pp. 125–26), the dislocation of males in more feminized work environments (Gee, Hull, & Lankshear, 1996), and the fear voiced among white middle-class parents that their sons are faced with the possibility of not doing as well as previous generations (Comaroff & Comaroff, 2000; Yates, 2000) converge in ways that place high-status forms of masculinity in competition with femininities and other masculinities. I, therefore, invite educators and parents to consider carefully arguments advancing the crisis in masculinity in response to girls' gains.

Scholarly Peer-Reviewed Journals

Scholarly peer-reviewed journals arguably offer the most reliable source of research investigating gender and literacy. Peer-reviewed journals generally provide readers with a mission statement that summarizes the aim of the journal and the type of articles featured within. These may include summaries of important studies, reviews of existing literature on a particular topic or issue, book essays and reviews, theoretically and empirically informed opinion pieces, and nonreviewed invited editorials. The journal mission statement usually indicates the intended audience (researchers and/or practitioners) and its disciplinary (language acquisition, mathematics, engineering, etc.), interdisciplinary, or multidisciplinary appeal. For example, gender studies and literacy journals have an interdisciplinary and multidisciplinary appeal insofar as they potentially raise issues particular to any number of disciplines or foster an understanding of the connections among and across disciplines. As a general rule, the peer-review process whereby authors submit their manuscripts for blind review by noted scholars in a particular field is intended to ensure that any research carried out reflects standards in the field and that the article addresses critical issues of importance in a style and format accessible to its intended readers. For many readers, however, research articles may prove daunting. Quantitative studies require specific knowledge about statistical procedures, and both qualitative and quantitative studies often employ a particular jargon, making comprehension difficult for those outside the field of study. Handbooks like this one often function to summarize and highlight research with a specified focus for a wider audience. The studies featured in this handbook can all be found in print-based or online peer-reviewed publications or were presented at high-profile peer-reviewed academic conferences. The International Reading Association (IRA) and the National Council of Teachers of English (NCTE) publish journals that are aimed at both a scholarly and practitioner audience. For example, *The Reading Teacher* (IRA), the *Journal of Adolescent and Adult Literacy* (IRA), and the *English Journal* (NCTE) feature peer-reviewed articles with a definite emphasis on the practical implications of research for classroom instruction. Nevertheless, social, economic, and political forces shape educational research, especially in determining what receives funding for large-scale investigations, and therefore informed readers need to assess both the merits and the limitations of any study, that is to say, what specific questions does it address about which populations, and what questions still remain?

RESEARCH DOCUMENTING GIRLS' EDUCATIONAL DISADVANTAGES

Not surprisingly, the majority of early research on gender and education has come from female scholars who focused on the achievement, social outcomes, and schooling experiences of girls (Arnot, David, & Weiner, 1999; Weiner, 1994). Initial findings pointed squarely at the need for policy and practice that would address and correct for the educationally disadvantaged experience of girls. Early research in this area culminated in the American Association of University Women (AAUW) report *How Schools Shortchange Girls* in 1992, which aimed at dispelling any myth that "girls and boys have identical educational experiences in school" (p. 1). The authors argued that the math and science curriculum, bias in standardized tests, and learning environments favored boys in ways that left girls out in the cold and worked to render girls' achievement invisible. It charged education policy makers to address the relationship between education and the conditions that underscore the cycle of poverty among women and children. At the time of its publication, girls had fallen behind their male counterparts in key areas of higher-level mathematics and measures of self-esteem. The report lays out in detail why even girls who excel in math and science are much less likely to pursue careers in science, technology, engineering, or mathematics (STEM).

Nearly a decade later, Hill, Corbett, and St. Rose (2010) authored the AAUW report *Why So Few? Women in Science, Technology, Engineering and Mathematics* to highlight eight research findings that point to social and environmental factors relating to the continued underrepresentation of women in science and engineering, especially at the upper levels of these professions. They point out that the "rapid increase in the numbers of girls achieving very high scores on mathematics tests once thought to measure innate ability suggests that cultural factors are at work" (p. 15). In other words, girls' recent gains in science and math achievement scores tell us that changes to the learning environment can make a difference in the cultivation of interests and abilities. The authors point out that roughly as many girls as boys leave U.S. high schools prepared for science or engineering majors, yet by graduation, men outnumber women in virtually every science and engineering field, with the most dramatic differences occurring in physics, engineering, and computer science, in which women earn a scant 20 percent of the bachelor degrees. The disparity between female and male representation in the STEM fields widens further at the graduate level and yet again as graduates transition to the workplace.

The reality of the situation gives us pause to think that while learning environments appear to have been altered in ways that have made a difference in girls' achievement levels in elementary, middle, and high school, the fact that girls remain systematically limited in their progress in scientific and engineering fields strongly suggests that cultural bias is still at work and can seriously affect the way girls self-assess or view their own abilities in math and science. Furthermore, Hill, Corbett, & St. Rose (2010) describe how the classic formulation "that men 'naturally' excel in mathematically demanding disciplines, whereas women 'naturally' excel in using language skills" (p. xvi) continues to work to the detriment of women. If the truth be known, despite the documented global pattern of boys' underachievement in literacy, boys ultimately outperform girls on literacy measures that count when it comes to college entrance exams in the United States such as the Scholastic Assessment Test (SAT) and American College Test (ACT) and hold considerable sway in advanced philosophy classes demanding high levels of language competence. It is here, too, that girls and women have traditionally been made to feel that their ideas do not have relevance to the wider world, reflecting the widespread notion that contributions to Western thought are largely a product of dead white males.

Why does all this research matter in a discussion of gender and literacy? Because as I strive to maintain throughout, our aims for literacy need to project a wider scope than the achievement of narrowly defined success on reading test scores. Literacy practices have a way of circumscribing life's narrative and material possibilities. Language is so closely associated with thought that it becomes a primary means through which we frame our world. In social environments, where discourse has a way of shaping our relations with others, we need to be aware of the bias that exists in order to be in a better position to work to interrupt it. It is not, as some may assume, that I object to changing learning environments in ways that foster ~~~' enhanced engagement with literacy. What I am looking to advance is ~nderstanding of how many of the interventions suggested may ~ of girls and some boys and of how the research to date has indicated that quick-fix solutions are inadequate in producing any sustainable effects.

While the work of the AAUW is directed at bringing to the fore the conditions that shortchange girls, the AAUW (1992) maintains throughout that "public education is plagued by numerous failings that affect boys as negatively as girls" (p. 1). The association is insistent, however, that hundreds of studies support the claim that "in many respects girls are put at a disadvantage simply because they are girls" (p. 1). Orenstein's (1994) *School Girls,* Pipher's (1994) *Reviving Ophelia,* and Sadker and Sadker's (1994) *Failing at Fairness* closely followed the initial AAUW report. Each of these oft-cited works seemed to echo Gilligan's concern for girls' eventual loss of voice and self-confidence as they succumb to the social pressures of being female and relating in a patriarchal society. The authors argue that the resulting psychological damage can contribute to a radical drop in self-esteem, depression, withdrawal, and in more serious cases eating disorders and self-mutilation. Research in this area has made a notable difference. For example, studies documenting the achievement gap and enrollment numbers in science and mathematics and the number and quality of responses to girls' comments and questions in these classes led to a better understanding of the obstacles girls face in attaining entry and success in the fields of math, science, and technology (Correll, 2001; Eisenhart & Finkel, 1998; Fennema, Carpenter, Jacobs, Franke, & Levi, 1998). Such focused attention to research on the effects of gender has given rise to policies and programs that have resulted in narrowing the gender gap in math and science and also has seen girls' enrollment numbers climb in university classrooms. Yet our job is far from done. Educational researchers must recognize the importance of being vigilant about gender equity and assume some responsibility for monitoring the conditions that promote or restrict access to opportunities. For example, Guzzetti's (1998) study, described in Chapter 4, documents the discourse practices in a high school physics class to help illustrate that the processes at work that have traditionally put girls at a disadvantage continue to operate in the twenty-first century.

THE "BOY TURN" IN RESEARCH ON GENDER AND EDUCATION

The mid-1990s began to see a shift in research on gender and education from documenting the disadvantaged educational experience of girls toward an examination of the state of boys in schools (Weaver-Hightower, 2003). Many of these more recent works signaling the boy turn in research on gender and education provide considerable evidence of the psychologically damaging effects on boys, among them increasing depression, drug use, academic failure, and violence. Some, like William Pollack (1998), see the active reinforcement of boys' emotional connections with parents and significant adults as a corrective. Boys are more likely than girls to drop out of school, to be suspended from school, to be placed in special education classes, and to be diagnosed with attention deficit disorder. And, as we will examine in considerable detail, boys have consistently fallen behind girls on literacy measures. As Weaver-Hightower (2003) points out, these are fairly robust findings but made problematic in the hands of those like Christina Hoff Sommers (2000) who rely on popular rhetoric—newspapers, magazines, and trade books—to argue that boys' difficulties are a direct result of advocacy for girls and feminist attempts to "pathologize" boys' manly nature. Essentialist arguments abound, and some contend that neurological differences predetermine boys' different educational needs and that schools have proven inadequate in meeting such needs (Gurian, Henley, & Trueman, 2001; Sax, 2005). Biological determinism is also behind arguments justifying boys' behaviors on the basis of testosterone levels and the contention that boys have a specific gendered role to perform (Biddulph, 1998).

In the chapters that follow, we first look at what research has to say about gender and literacy and consider carefully possible implications for policy and practice and further questions for investigation. I begin with three concerns about evaluating existing research, offered by literacy researchers Michael Smith and Jeffrey Wilhelm (2002), and add two important concerns of my own. The first is that there is a tendency (albeit sometimes unintentional) in many of the works that focus on boys and literacy to portray good teaching practice as having exclusive benefits for boys. This tendency, I believe, grows directly out of what I have identified as a second concern, one I share with British researcher Gemma Moss (2007), that many of these works are misguided in predicating girls' success on their "inclusion" in the literacy curriculum. As a result, popular interventions aimed at closing the gender gap in literacy achievement are often aimed at "(re)masculinizing" the curriculum. As many of the highlighted studies attest, the literacy curriculum and inherent practices can both benefit and disadvantage boys and girls in rather complex ways. In this chapter, I take a critical approach to taking up some of the popular trade books and teacher resource materials published in the midst of the current furor on boys and literacy. I conclude with a discussion of Laura Sokal's (2010) recent summary of research investigating the long-term effects of literacy interventions designed to raise boys' performance scores on reading tests.

Explore

What beliefs do you hold about girls' and boys' reading practices? How did you arrive at these beliefs?

THREE CONCERNS ABOUT EXISTING RESEARCH

Smith and Wilhelm (2002) in their book *Reading Don't Fix No Chevys: Literacy in the Lives of Young Men*, voice three concerns about the existing research on boys and literacy that I feel can be relevant to evaluating all studies related to gender. First, the authors caution against *essentializing or oversimplifying children*. Smith and Wilhelm point out that much of the current research is motivated by the belief that gender impacts literacy achievement. We need to recognize that any individual's so-called gendered behavior may look different when performing certain tasks or interacting with specific groups. In other words, how an individual enacts his or her gendered identity varies from situation to situation. Citing McCarthy (1998), Smith and Wilhelm suggest that researchers investigating gender pay attention to the following:

1. The influence of context in which children are observed (e.g., at home, at school, at the sports arena, in a restaurant)

2. The specific task being performed (e.g., discussing literature, watching television, shopping, doing homework)

3. The specific group of others with whom they are interacting (e.g., peers, parents, siblings, teachers, teammates, same-sex and mixed-sex groupings)

Second, Smith and Wilhelm (2002) remind us that *it is easy to lose sight of individuals* when we rely on categorizing or grouping individuals in order to make comparisons. Aggregating boys and girls into two separate but single categories assumes that all boys and all girls behave according to the general tendencies identified for their group. The constant pressure in education to find that "magic bullet" or "one-size-fits-all" solution often leads to hasty and superficial interpretations of research results. As Smith and Wilhelm explain, teachers are tempted to reinforce general tendencies rather than attend to individual differences that might provide greater insight into the range of instructional possibilities.

Third, Smith and Wilhelm caution against maintaining a *narrow vision of success* when assessing literacy achievement. Citing the work of a number of literacy scholars (Heath & McLaughlin, 1993; Mahiri, 1998; Moje ^ Telford, 1999), they argue that young people employ n~~ tices outside of school that are seldom valid~~ my son is an avid hockey card collector story but spent as much or more time ~ I recall that any fears I might have had at as phonetically irregular words in English, there is not a clear one-to-one sound-syn versus *cat*) were completely allayed when he recognized and read aloud the names of hockey stars Jaomir Jagr, Keith Tkachuk, and Dominik Hasek. He also demonstrated an ability to *read multisyllabic words, read statistical information* to compare players, *select information* to *write short biographies* on his favorite players, *scan* catalogues to identify the potential value of cards, and *create* a variety of *criteria for organizing* his collection. These are all literacy skills that we wish to promote within a balanced language arts program. Many of today's youth, both girls and boys, readily and skillfully engage in literacy practices related to a growing array of texts including magazines, websites, electronic games, comic books, and graphic novels. They create their own homepages, navigate intertextual hyperlinks, participate in online social networks like Facebook and Twitter, read and write rap, produce zines, and critique film. Smith and Wilhelm (2002) noted that the boys in their study engaged in an extensive range of literate activities at home including reading gaming manuals and hobby-related magazines but were unable to see themselves as readers or validate these as literate behaviors because they were not recognized as such at school. I want to caution, however, that in a quest to provide a corrective to the perceived problem of boys and literacy, parents and educators do not unintentionally contribute to establishing technology as an exclusively male domain or perpetuate the assumption that narrative reading is intrinsically a feminized activity.

The disconnect between home and school literacies extends to the way schools tend to overlook how immigrant and migrant families are often involved in literacy practices related to running family businesses, translation and interpretation, shared reading of religious texts, and scanning community newspapers and fliers for advertisements and coupons to economize (Lynch, 2009). Educators working with pre-K to grade 12 students and beyond need to pay attention to how both girls and boys are engaged in a range of complex social, cultural, and linguistic skills outside of school (Orellana & Gutiérrez, 2006). Once we begin to recognize and validate the literate lives of our students, we are in a much better position to leverage multiliteracies in ways that can support learning and development. In other words, by gaining an awareness of students' interests, hobbies, and family responsibilities, teachers may be more able to help students recognize how they use literacy in their day-to-day life to enhance their confidence and enable them to apply their acquired skills to perform a wider range of activities.

CRITICAL PERSPECTIVES ON RECENT INITIATIVES ON BOYS AND LITERACY

[...]ren's hobbies and interests can also provide us with an insight into [...]ered identities. This brings me to adding yet another caution of [...] I stated earlier, the issues surrounding gender are complex, [...] not hasten to adopt the latest panacea in response to boys' underachievement on reported literacy measures. While it is important that we validate children and adolescents' literacy practices that derive from their interests, we must also be mindful that to incorporate them into our instructional programming uncritically is irresponsible. I have observed throughout this current furor over boys and literacy a trend in catering to traditional masculine values in a quest to hook boys into reading. This has resulted in an overemphasis on books with gratuitous "burping" and "farting," a burgeoning proliferation of books with male protagonists, sports stories, and the widespread implementation of boys-only book clubs, which, as one of my graduate students teaching middle school observed, amounted to "Pick up a donut and read!" Apart from negatively impacting the national health agenda, it would be hard not to see the problem of trying to promote boys' literary engagement through the very attitudes that contribute to the societal belief that reading, especially fictional reading, is not an acceptable pastime for boys (Hall & Coles, 1999). I hasten to add, no one need worry that there are not enough books with male protagonists. Overly determining boys' interest is a recurring theme in popular rhetoric that can actively work to disadvantage girls and many boys.

The Ontario Ministry of Education (2004) in Canada, in its zeal to correct the achievement gap between girls and boys on test scores obtained by the province's Education Quality and Accountability Office, published a document addressing the problem of boys and literacy titled *Me Read?, No Way!: A Practical Guide to Improving Boy's Literacy Skills.* Let me go on record that as the mother of twin boys, a former K–12 teacher, curriculum coordinator in language arts, and now professor in preservice teaching, I support the publication and distribution of materials intended to help teachers meet the formidable challenge of engaging all students in reading and writing well. What is off-putting is the boldness of a title that clearly essentializes boys and reading as being incompatible and positions reading as an obstacle for boys to overcome. Voiced in the negative in this way, what attitudes does the title reinforce about boys who already like to read? If we are to believe the data collected by Smith and Wilhelm (2002), many boys do enjoy reading and can express their preferences for a wide range of texts. What many of the books on boys and reading have failed to do is address the disparate degrees to which boys and girls have been socialized to seek the immediacy and guarantee of success (Stipek, 1984) and how that might have affected their sustained engagement with text. A number of studies documenting boys' negative attitudes and resistance toward reading cite boys' belief that reading is work (Bardsley, 1999; Blair & Sanford, 1999; Millard, 1994, 1997) but also assert that boys' perceptions are strongly influenced and reinforced by both gendered expectations of family, peers, and teachers and instructional constraints (Bardsley, 1999; Valentine, 1999). In the United States, Michael Sullivan's (2009) *Serving Boys through Reader's Advisory*, published by the American Library Association, also focuses on "highlighting fun over challenge" to cater to boys' "sense of accomplishment" and their "need to finish a book" (p. 8). Further emphasizing that race to get boys to the bottom of the page, Sullivan argues reading shorter books can fulfill boys' competitive need to boast about the number of books read. Let's face it: reading and writing well can be hard work for anyone, and both benefit from cumulative practice and a tacit acceptance that comprehension and composition are highly recursive activities that demand a lot of rereading and revision. The tendency in popular rhetoric to project reading as "fun" for girls and "work" for boys is far too superficial an assessment of a complex process and ignores the bigger questions of how social forces and the pressures of performing gender are at work actively making it so and what we can do to effect meaningful change.

Explore

Locate the Ontario Ministry of Education's (2004) *Me Read? No Way* online at http://www.edu.gov.on.ca/eng/document/brochure/ meread/index.html. Read and review the ministry document with the following questions in mind:

1. In what ways does the cover's photo collage reinforce traditional masculinities or normative ideas about what it means to be a boy?

2. What statements and suggestions essentialize the relationship between boys and reading?

3. What suggestions made about best practices for improving boys' literacy skills do you think might be equally applicable to girls?

CLOSING THE ACHIEVEMENT GAP: WHO'S LEFT OUT IN THE COLD?

Feminists have taken issue with two aspects of the current political attention to gender inequalities in the performance data on literacy (Moss, 2007). First, feminists feel it necessary to respond to the manner in which the neoliberal managerial conditions responsible for bringing test scores and achievement data to such prominence adopt a politics of erasure in treating the differences in achievement as something that can be quickly fixed without regard to wider social inequalities (Gilbert & Gilbert, 1998; Rowan, Knobel, Bigum, & Lankshear, 2002). Arguably, *Me Read? No Way!* appears to fall into this category as it fails to take into consideration factors related to immigration, migration, socioeconomic status, presence of cultural artifacts, and race/ethnicity that have been shown to contribute to educational performance of both boys and girls. Second, a number of feminists have focused on the curriculum interventions intended to redress the achievement gap in girls' and boys' performance (Barrs & Pidgeon, 1998; Millard, 1997). These scholars draw from existing literature on girls and education and then work to apply this knowledge to boys and education where appropriate. Feminist scholars working from this perspective are intent in ensuring that any recommendations for closing the gendered achievement gap in literacy be applied in ways that do not come at girls' expense or reinforce stereotypic aspects of masculinity (Moss, 2007).

While Smith and Wilhelm (2002) lay out a number of theoretical perspectives on gender and literacy in *Reading Don't Fix No Chevys*, their study of the literate lives of 49 male middle and high school students has alerted me to the extent to which a singular focus on boys and literacy may unintentionally work to leave readers with the impression that somehow boys' learning needs are consistently and distinctly different from those of girls. For example, Smith and Wilhelm emphasize that certain factors such as feeling competent and in control assisted the boys in their study in accomplishing literacy activities but that many seldom felt this way in school. On the flip side, there is nothing about how young women are still expected to achieve when we know full well that feelings of being in control elude them, too, even in areas where they prove competent (AAUW, 1991, 1992; Brown & Gilligan, 1992; Davis, 1994; Gilligan, 1993; Hey, 1997). There is an unstated assumption underlying the suggestions proffered by Wilhelm and Smith and the ministry document *Me Read? No Way!* that girls' relative success is somehow due to their inclusion in the literacy curriculum and therefore the curriculum needs to be amended in ways to match boys' interests.

As the title makes clear, *Reading Don't Fix No Chevys* is a book about boys and literacy, and the data yielded through in-depth interviews and observations are insightful in terms of demonstrating that boys *do* live literate lives. Nevertheless, given the racial and ethnic diversity of the participants and the prominence with which the authors have noted it on the inside cover and in participant profiles, I would have appreciated a stronger analysis on how the dynamics of gender, race, cultural identity, and social class have interacted in shaping boys' literacy practices inside and outside of school. Such an analysis may have proven helpful in accounting for why Smith and Wilhelm's findings differed from Martino's (1998) study of Australian boys' codes of masculinity and from Ogbu and Fordham's (1986) study of African Americans' resistance to the white culture of schools.

Smith and Wilhelm drew on Martino's (1998) research in which Martino asked Australian boys to respond to a set of fictional profiles representative of the different ways boys engage with school. Their responses led Martino to conclude that boys see literacy and reading as feminized activities inconsistent with hegemonic codes of masculinity and therefore reject these activities. Smith and Wilhelm developed their own set of eight profiles and conducted a series of profile interviews to get participants' responses to the fictive lives of the students portrayed. The profiles of "James" and "Chris" were intended to elicit participants' attitudes toward "the interaction between gender, on the one hand, and race and social class, on the other" (p. 78). In creating the fictional profile of "James," the researchers drew on Ogbu and Fordham's (1986) research at Capital High in Washington, DC, that found some black students resisted attitudes and behaviors they perceived as "acting White" in the belief that these ways of acting could compromise their collective racial identity. In response to what he saw as widespread misinterpretation of his research with Fordham, Ogbu (2003) later clarified findings, stating,

> Black students in Shaker Heights and probably elsewhere [Washington] did not reject making good grades *per se* because it entailed acting White.... These students seemed to reject certain attitudes and behaviors that they perceived or interpreted as White, but that were conducive to making good grades. (p. 198)

Smith and Wilhelm paint "James" as an African American high school student who grows more disinterested in the English curriculum because of his belief, "The stuff we read makes me feel White!" (p. 61). Smith and Wilhelm report that attitude toward reading among the African American students in their study was not influenced by a rejection of acting white and that one participant was even offended at the thought of linking school success with being white (this, by the way, is not Ogbu's contention). Nevertheless, in the same response, the student revealed that the profile provoked the need to probe "James" further, something that Smith and Wilhelm did not do in response to their participants' initial responses. Consider the following exchange highlighted in Smith and Wilhelm's study.

> Chris (student): ... So, there is no stereotype when it comes to writing in my opinion, and that would really make me get thinking about what's going through James' head, and then I would end up reevaluating his whole attitude.
>
> Michael (researcher): You'd press him on that.
>
> Chris: Right, I'd keep pushing him until he really said the whole reason of why he said that. Stereotypes or race-related stereotypes really annoy me. I don't know. They just do. (pp. 78–79)

Chris's response here seems to beg the question, "What stereotypes or race-related stereotypes really annoy you?" There is a lost opportunity to investigate further Chris's knowledge of racial stereotyping and how it relates to gender and literacy. Johnny, another African American participant, claimed to be "color-blind" when it came to such things. Rather than question the participant further in an attempt to critically challenge the notion of "color-blindness," the researchers appear to have been prepared to accept students' initial responses at face value to draw the rather contradictory conclusion that *"[n]one* of the participants reported feeling the tension that *James* felt. *Or if they did*, it was overcome by their profound belief in school as the engine that drives future success" (p. 78, emphasis added). Smith and Wilhelm appear unaware of the inherent tension in their observation that any rejection of whiteness was "overcome" by a "profound belief" (p. 78). I am left to wonder whether the erasure associated with "color-blindness" and an unquestioned faith "in school as the engine that drives future success" may be indicative of the extent to which these students' responses reflect both the need to "act White" and values and attitudes consistent with being raised in middle- to upper-middle-class homes. The authors admit that they made assumptions regarding the middle- to upper-middle-class status of participants based on their responses, and it would appear that information about parents' highest level of education was not obtained. These factors have been shown to account for critical differences in students' attitude toward school and literacy and would make for more detailed profiles of individual participants. Despite the stated emphasis on gender construction and the sociocultural positioning of participants, Smith and Wilhelm more frequently relied on disparate theories of language and cognition (e.g., Vygotsky, Bakhtin, Dewey, Thorndike, Csikszentmihalyi) and Rosenblatt's theory of reader response to account for their observations and participants' comments. As a result, many of the conclusions drawn with regard to boys' needs as learners are ones that are easily applied to learners of both sexes, and therefore their specific relevance to the impact of gender on literacy is not always clear.

INTERVENTIONS TO ADDRESS THE ACHIEVEMENT GAP

We need to recognize when suggested interventions to address the gender achievement gap focus on changing the content of the literacy curriculum rather than pupil attributes (Moss, 2007). For example, literature circles have been seen as a means of engaging boys in a wider range of texts than they would normally have selected for themselves. Many educators see literature circles as extending the space in which boys can begin to express a wider range of emotions (Fokias, 1998). The ultimate aim here is to adopt a particular curricular approach that will foster changes in boys' expressed attributes. By contrast, as I alluded to earlier, other gender-based reforms are designed to alter the curriculum in response to the belief that the curriculum has actively worked to include girls and exclude boys. The absurdity of statements such as "language teachers 'reward particular kinds of literacy practices which girls take to like ducks to water' " (Simpson, in Brozo, 2010, p. 78) used to preface the need for "remasculinizing" the curriculum panders to political backlash in ways that uncritically deter teachers from the real job of helping all students understand how gender stereotypes have guided their behaviors and limited their imagination. Moreover, the general inference that language teachers are to bear the sole burden of responsibility for shutting out boys is unfair and unjustified. Remasculinizing interventions are devised to compensate for what many see as the absence of male role models, a feminized curriculum that favors narrative reading over nonfiction, or a lack of technologies to capture boys' fascination. Readers need to be aware of the challenges to the viewpoint that the literacy curriculum has somehow shortchanged boys.

"BOY-FRIENDLY PRACTICES": A DISCUSSION OF THE FINDINGS

Canadian researcher Laura Sokal (2010) investigated the long-term effects of interventions that rely on quick fixes aimed at addressing deficits in some boys' reading performance and by and large found them to be inadequate in tackling this complex issue. Consistent with the views expressed in this handbook, Sokal's review of existing research confirms that many of the variables underpinning burgeoning "boy-friendly" practices seldom lead to any sustainable effects. Critics of the essentialist "boys will be boys" approach contend that these interventions are overly simplistic, can constitute a gross misdirection of funds, detract from more strategic interventions, direct unnecessary attention to boys who are not at risk, and can unintentionally marginalize some boys and girls in the process (Alloway, 2007; Luke, Freebody, & Land, 2000: Martino & Kehler, 2007; White, 2007). I performed my own reading of a number of highlighted studies appearing in Sokal's review of the literature. The following summary cites research from the United States, Canada, the United Kingdom, and Australia on three types of interventions generated in response to a perceived need to remasculinize the curriculum.

Male Teachers as Literacy Models

Sokal (2010) points to numerous large-scale and international studies that demonstrate that having a male teacher does not produce any significant differences in boys' performance scores over when they have a female teacher (see Allan, 1993; Butler & Christianson, 2003, Carrington & Skelton, 2003; Carrington, Tymms, & Merrell, 2005; Coulter & McNay, 1993; Ehrenberg, Goldhaber, & Brewer, 1995; Froude, 2002; Martin, 2003; Sokal, Katz, Adkins, et al., 2005). Dee's (2007) post hoc analysis of data from the National Education Longitudinal Study of 1988 constitutes one exception. I hasten to caution, however, that the study uses old data to provide new evidence. From my reading of the study, Dee, an economics professor, relied on previous data obtained from a U.S. national sample of

24,000 eighth-grade boys and girls through the National Education Longitudinal Study of 1988 to examine "whether assignment to a same-gender teacher influences student achievement, teacher perceptions of student performance, and student engagement" (p. 528). Findings from Dee's study indicated that both sexes performed better for same-gender teachers. His results led him to conclude that spending one year with a male language arts teacher would eliminate one-third of a 1.5-year gap in reading achievement between female and male students. Nonetheless, my further reading of Dee's post hoc analysis reveals that he too harbors serious concerns about making any hasty conclusions. He adds that according to his calculations, the implementation of such a plan to improve the performance of boys would simultaneously harm the performance of girls. Dee is left to conclude that "this study's results for policy efforts to promote gender equity are not clear and would turn critically on understanding more about the structure of interactions within classrooms" (p. 551). Furthermore, he is clear that his findings *do not* speak to the probable effects of proposals for single-sex schooling, changes to the gender distribution of students, or training in gender-specific teaching methods as advocated by Leonard Sax (2005) that, in his opinion, would invariably "raise a variety of other moral and practical concerns" (Dee, 2007, p. 551).

Engaging Boys through the Use of Technology

Those advocating for upping "boy-friendly practices" in schools see the incorporation of technology as a means to engage boys in reading (Booth, 2002). Sokal's (2010) limited review reveals that the use of computers has been shown to help increase boys' achievement in school, with the greatest gains being among boys with low achievement (Bangert-Drowns, Kulik, & Kulik, 1985; Niemiec & Walberg, 1985). My first reaction is to caution readers that the cited research is considerably dated and may not begin to account for how more than two decades of technological change and increased market penetration might have impacted those findings. Whitley's (1997) meta-analysis of 82 studies led him to conclude that boys have more positive attitudes toward computers than do girls. Again, the increasingly pervasive use of information technology across genders especially as it relates to social networking may make some of the conclusions drawn from studies in Whitley's 1997 meta-analysis obsolete or the findings less significant. Following up further on cited studies in Sokal's article, Mathews (1996) and Pearman (2003) compared second- and third-grade students' reading comprehension of CD-ROM storybooks to reading comprehension of traditional texts and reported that students gave richer story retellings after reading CD-ROM books. Another study, by Doty, Popplewell, and Byers (2001), found that second graders scored better on comprehension questions after reading CD-ROM storybooks. Lefever-Davis and Pearman (2005) also found that CD-ROM storybooks could enhance comprehension but that the group of 11 participants differed in their use and reaction to the electronic features. Implications for further research might analyze students' approach to the use of electronic storybooks by gender, that is to say, how girls and boys differ in their deployment of hyperlinks, digital pronunciations, and animated features to support reading or to enhance entertainment value, or whether they choose to access them at all in their reading of electronic text.

A number of researchers and educators have taken issue with the use of computers to support boys' reading. The findings from Clark's (1985) study suggest a novelty effect and that the positive gains obtained through the use of computers decline over time. Again, although Clark's findings support Sokal's overall contention that the use of technology has no sustainable effects on boys' reading engagement, we are also left to question whether what was novel in 1985 is, by now, relatively mainstream. Lewin's (1996) study confirmed that interactive computerized books create greater interest among boys but that they may lead to an overdependence on features that decode words rather than promote strategies for comprehension. Lefever-Davis and Pearman (2005) noted that "hot links" and animation features in CD-ROM books were sometimes a distraction, increased reading time, and could lead to reader fatigue. Again, we must consider all of these findings in light of the fact that technology seems to be a moving target and our relationship with it ever evolving. There is little research to show how negotiating meaning from multimedia texts may have changed the cognitive processes and strategies associated with reading and writing. For example, web browsing requires us to skim and scan for information, taking in both visual, print, and oft times auditory text. We scroll up and down a screen to read and reread. Our eyes move between multiple windows containing related or very different content. How do girls and boys engage with multilayered texts and hypertexts differently from traditional printed texts? Beyond spelling and grammar, do students take advantage of word processing features to actively delete, cut, copy and paste, move, and insert to thoughtfully revise while writing to improve the overall quality? How might students be disadvantaged when asked for handwritten responses to essay questions on high-stakes exams once, or possibly twice, a year when over much of their academic career they have consistently used word processing for projects and term papers and are likely to continue to do so in work-related environments? Many questions remain largely unanswered, and as I have suggested before, more research is needed if we are to correct for any gendered disadvantages.

Where Millard (1997) sees that boys are "staking a claim to technology," which makes them "differently literate," Rowan, Knobel, Bigum and Lankshear (2002) object to the "techno-push" to engage boys in reading on the basis that it caters to the "thrill and kill" of video play and societal expectations regarding masculinity and stereotypic gender roles. At the time of writing, electronic readers and tablets are gaining currency, and in both my personal and professional life, I am experiencing the portable advantages of being able to scan texts more quickly, move between screens at the touch of a finger, access multimodal representations of knowledge, highlight and recall passages, bookmark pages, link to related sites, share and use files across several devices, access reference materials at will, archive, and travel with a library. Computer-based reading incorporates a wide range of activities, and technology has enhanced our capacity for reading the word and the world—and this capacity brings with it a host of ethical concerns. I loathe to think, however, that as educators we are still at the point where we see technology as a mere motivator—a carrot on a stick— rather than an evolutionary tool for negotiating life and learning. You can put me on record as having nothing to do with any classroom practice that singles out boys as the exclusive purveyors of information technology.

Explore

I invite educators and school and district administration to consider whether there are populations of students within the community who are actually disadvantaged by the integration of technology. What are the technological expectations related to homework and assignments? Do all students have access at home to computers, laptops, the Internet, and printers?

Explore with Children

Think about the various ways your family benefits from information technology. In mixed-gender families, are there differences in the way females and males engage in technology? You can help your children be selective in using technology by taking an active interest in the websites they visit for learning and entertainment and in their video game choices. Grab a controller and have your child guide you through a favorite game.

Providing Choice in Reading

A review of the research on the effects of providing students choice in their reading materials on reading engagement and performance is more complicated that one might think. The pervasive belief among teachers and many researchers that providing choice to students will lead to an increase in students' efforts and motivation and, ultimately, to greater gains in learning goes largely unchallenged (Baumann, Hoffman, Moon, & Duffy-Hexter, 1998; Flowerday & Schraw, 2000). Teachers tend to maintain even greater faith in the power of choice to effect changes when it comes to at-risk learners (Schraw, Flowerday, & Lehman, 2001). Indeed, the assumption that choice relates to ultimate gains in reading achievement characterizes much of the teacher resource literature on boys and reading. It is the underlying premise of many of the recommendations made in the Ontario Ministry's *Me Read? No Way*, and it is a recurring theme reinforced by references to students' responses in Smith and Wilhelm's *Reading Don't Fix No Chevys* and William Brozo's (2010) *To Be a Boy, To Be a Reader: Engaging Teen and Pre-Teen Boys in Active Literacy* (2nd edition). For example, "Joe" in Smith and Wilhelm's (2002) study remarked, "I don't like it if I have to read it, but if I read it on my own then it would probably seem a little better" (p. 33). To my mind, Smith and Wilhelm's contention that Joe's response supports the notion that choice equates with control over reading may be slightly overstated. Clearly, the tentativeness of the student's reply—"would probably seem a little better"—indicates that there is far more operating in this young man's aversion to reading that a lack of choice.

As William Brozo (2010) sees it, interest, which is much broader and different from choice, that is to say, from the actual selection of something, is central to actively engaging reluctant boy readers. In *To Be a Boy, to Be a Reader*, Brozo describes at length one student's bonding with *Lockie Leonard, Human Torpedo* (Winton, 1993). The student, Delfino, an avid surfer but a far less enthusiastic reader, ultimately comes to the conclusion "if when I was a kid teachers let me read books about surfing and stuff I think I would be a better reader now" (p. 82). But from Brozo's description, we see that Brozo is a masterful teacher who deftly guides Delfino through his reading of the text, helping him build comprehension skills and questioning him to elicit critical responses and personal connections to the character Lockie Leonard and the events depicted in the book. Brozo exemplifies that gradual-release-of-responsibility model in Pearson and Gallagher's (1983) *Model of Explicit Instruction* that derives from Vygotsky's social constructivist approach in which the teacher gradually relinquishes the role of the expert other as the student increasingly assumes greater responsibility for learning through guided practice until she or he reaches some level of independence and is ready to move on to related or more demanding challenges. The success of this reading event may have benefitted as much or more from sound guided practice and extended one-to-one student-teacher interaction as it did from the student's stated interest.

As I indicated in the introduction, I am in total agreement that students' existing interests can be a way into reading. Like Brozo, I can easily recall how interest in a particular subject catapulted a reluctant reader into literature, but I can also think of countless situations where teachers have tapped into students' prior knowledge in ways to get them engaged in works for which, upon first glance, they held no immediate interest. The chance to expand one's worldview seems an equally compelling reason to read on. To this end, strategies such as anticipation guides and a directed reading thinking activity (DRTA) (Appendices A and B) help all students activate prior knowledge and set purposes for reading to provide the necessary "hook" to generate interest in opening the book and turning the page. Potential for engaging readers is further enhanced by the capacity of these strategies to exploit cooperative learning and promote cooperation in mixed-gender groupings. Readers' interests, however, should not be confused with interest in reading, which, as we will see in Chapter 3, appears to correlate positively with gains in achievement (OECD, 2000). The results regarding the provision of choice of reading materials are not so robust (Parker & Lepper, 1992; Schraw, Flowerday, & Reisetter, 1998), and as Weaver-Hightower (2003) concludes, studies examining the literacy practices of boys have to reach beyond preferences and habits and focus instead on gaining a better understanding of the effects of masculinities on learning.

BOOK TALK

What I find most encouraging, however, in both Smith and Wilhelm's study and Brozo's book of proposed strategies is that their stories of students' literate lives demonstrate the power of talking about books, which to my mind goes a long way to building a literacy culture at home and in schools and classrooms. Beginning in the preschool years, one-to-one book sharing is an important way parents can support young children in their ability to comprehend a book by describing pictures, labeling objects, explaining events, asking questions, and relating the story to the child's life experiences (Price, van Kleeck, & Huberty, 2009). From a social constructivist perspective (Vygotsky, 1978), parents' extratextual utterances create a supportive context that assist children in achieving higher levels of comprehension and more sophisticated linguistic expression that they would have been capable of achieving otherwise. Moreover, the effects of early book sharing are sustained over time. As much as 8 percent of the variance in later language and literacy outcomes measures can be accounted for by the variation in frequency of book sharing in the toddler and preschool years, and this holds true regardless of socioeconomic status (Bus, van Ijzendoom, & Pellegrini, 1995). As children advance in age, book talk is no less important.

Comprehending and composing are complex strategic and social processes that benefit from instruction that makes visible to students these processes before, during, and after working with text (Mariage, 1995).

Explore with Children

Talking about books with children and adolescents before, during, and after reading helps build and extend their understanding. Sharing books with your child can present an enjoyable opportunity that can enrich your child's vocabulary and help her or him recognize that reading matters. When reading a picture book with young children, encourage your child to ask questions and comment on the story and illustrations in a book. Begin by examining the cover illustration and asking your child what she or he thinks the book is about. Then read the title aloud. Read the book, stopping now and then to ask your child what is happening in the illustrations or what she or he thinks will happen next. Encourage children to participate through drama and by chiming in when reading books with repeating phrases or choruses.

Continue reading aloud to your child after she or he has learned to read. I encourage educators to do the same. Choose books that may be slightly beyond your child's independent reading level with more complex plots. Ask questions to explore characters' motivation for certain actions and help your child make connections to her or his experience and knowledge. Be attentive to the construction of gender and raise questions about assumptions in the text.

Book talks are an enjoyable and arguably a more meaningful alternative to traditional book reports insofar as they have an immediate and genuine audience and purpose beyond writing for a grade. In addition, they encourage students of all ages to interpret and respond to a wider range of literature, entice students to read peer-recommended selections, and help teachers and librarians monitor students' interest in books. Book talks may also foster cross-gender discussions in the literacy classroom through which girls and boys might find common literary ground. A book talk is a short presentation generally, anywhere from 30 seconds to 3 minutes, that aims to convince others that a particular book is worth reading. Many readers will recall that the former PBS show *Reading Rainbow* concluded each episode with book talks by elementary school–aged children. The presenter begins with a statement or question that establishes the context of the book. For example, a book talk introducing Natalie Babbitt's *Tuck Everlasting* might begin with "Have you ever thought about what it might mean to live forever?" The presenter then provides a preview of the characters, the setting, and the central conflict in the book without revealing the resolution. Students can read aloud a short passage or show an illustration during their book talk.

Throughout 1999 and 2000, while working as Manitoba's provincial language arts specialist, I conducted a number of Book Talk workshops across the province with teachers and students and subsequently provided further mentorship through feedback in response to classroom observations. During that time, language arts instruction favored cooperative learning environments with an emphasis on peer interaction informed by social constructivist theory, and early childhood classrooms professed a child-centered curriculum. In addition, the arts flourished in the many schools I attended, and with the increase in the use of technology and the popularity of home videotaping, for the first time, visiting artists working with students in the schools included documentary film makers. In several classes, children as young as six and seven years old applied their developing media-literacy skills to videotape the book talks, which they then played for parents in the waiting area during parent-teacher interviews. Copies of the highlighted books were on hand for parents to peruse. In all of my observations, however, it is important to note that not a single child recommended a particular book as being a good choice for either gender despite the fact that many bookstores and school book markets have taken up the practice of merchandising titles as "boy books" and "girl books." While the content of some of the children's choices may have reflected gendered stereotypes, at the time, the idea of designating books as gender specific simply was not on their radar, or mine either. From my observations and discussions with teachers, the books most likely to be taken up by other students in response to the book talks were those that featured the best "sales pitches." As an academic looking back, I can't help but think that students' responses to book talk recommendations merit further study. A number of articles, many of which are contributed by librarians (Frank, 2002; Riesterer, 2002), document how book talks increase interest and library circulation. From my experience, students appeared more open to a wider range of choices in classes where they were already comfortable working cooperatively and discussing in mixed-gender groupings and where it was clear that *both* students and teachers were actively participating in making reading and writing relevant.

Explore with Students

The following suggestions may help teachers and librarians with launching successful book talks with students:

1. The teacher or librarian demonstrates book talks several times before asking students to prepare and present their own.

2. When initiating book talks with students, ask for volunteers.

3. Give students adequate time to prepare their book talk for presentation, usually two to three days.

4. The audience is encouraged to ask questions.

5. Schedule regular (even daily) short sessions with two to three book talks at a time.

6. Book talks may be linked to nominations for literature circle selections.

7. Display the featured books prominently in the class or library. Students may also create a book jacket or poster advertising their book to be posted in the class or school library.

A number of cooperative instructional frameworks such as reciprocal teaching, book clubs, and literature circles are designed to create communicative contexts that allow students to collaboratively construct meaning from texts before, during, and after reading. These contexts are often structured to assist students in activating prior knowledge; in helping students make text-to-self, text-to-text, and text-to-world connections; and in increasing overall engagement. Nevertheless, in establishing peer-group discussions, we need to be aware of the problems associated with well-established gendered discourse patterns and practices emerging from classroom power relations that honor the voice of some and exclude the voice of others. In Chapter 4, I review a number of studies in which the researchers document and analyze the discourse in mixed- and same-gender group literature discussions. Later, in the introduction to Chapter 5, I describe how traditional patterns of male discourse contributing to men's perceived inability to adapt to more feminized work environments and to build work relationships in a globalized economy has been cited as a catalyst for the moral panic surrounding boys' literacy achievement. If this is indeed the case, how likely is it that literacy initiatives spawned in response to the threat to male dominance will challenge male-female dualisms? Readers are asked to consider, on the one hand, whether advocating for boys-only book clubs and policies mandating the hiring of male teachers aims at having boys learn to relate better to other boys in a quest to ensure a future for patriarchal order or, on the other hand, whether working with boys in these various ways can fulfill more progressive ends such as helping boys develop an emotional repertoire and an understanding, recognition, and appreciation of multiple masculinities and respecting the intellectual, creative, and productive contribution of girls in mixed-gender collaborations. Educators and parents need to be attentive to the ways of operating to determine the degree to which particular communicative contexts can be both liberatory and oppressive.

LITERARY ARCHETYPES

In this regard, I find Brozo's (2010) argument for using literary male archetypes in young adult books (no shortage here) as a means to assist boys in finding their reading comfort zone disconcerting, despite the obvious afterthought to use these works in "deconstructing aspects of teenage masculinity" (p. 80). In literature, an archetype has come to represent a universal symbol or prototype for a character or situation—an ideal upon which all others are based. Common character archetypes include "the hero," who like a knight in shining armor arrives just in time to save the day (e.g., the handsome prince in fairytales; D'artagnan in Alexandre Dumas's *The Three Musketeers*); "the outcast" (e.g., Piggy in William Golding's *Lord of the Flies*); "the shrew" (e.g., the nagging and abusive wife; Zeena from Edith Wharton's *Ethan Frome*); "the star-crossed lovers" (e.g., Shakespeare's Romeo and Juliet); and "the scapegoat" or "Christ figure," who is on the receiving end of negative punishment or blame and often given to self-sacrifice (e.g., Tessie in Shirley Jackson's short story "The Lottery"). Archetypes, which structure much of mythology and folklore (see Campbell, 1998, 2008) and are prominent in various forms of artistic expression and popular media, contribute to many of our conscious and unconscious beliefs about gender. For example, Deborah Tannen (1984) has meticulously researched the history of the Genesis stories of ancient Israel and subsequent Biblical adaptations to demonstrate how reiterations of the Eve story in postbiblical and Western canonical works serve a universal view of women as helpmates and lower-order companions often cast in the light of a temptress responsible for all sinfulness and cursed by the pain of childbirth.

In his use of archetypes to capture boys' interest in reading, Brozo fails to see how he cannot, on the one hand, validate the essentialism associated with having boys identify with archetypal ideals of masculinity while, on the other, engage in deconstruction's rigorous pursuit of exposing inherent contradictions. Brozo's brand of selective deconstructionism would have us conveniently ignore the archetypal aspects or traits that he has determined to be desirable in hooking boys into reading or use them to get what we want and then hold them up to critique. Whether intentional or not, references to Jean Jacques Rousseau and Samuel Johnson appear to ground Brozo's argument for "boy work" in centuries of patriarchal entitlement whereby boys are painted as victims of an uncaring curriculum with reading as "torture," and girls simply don't figure into the equation:

> I would let [a boy] at first read any book which happens to engage his attention; because you have done a great deal when you have brought a boy to have

entertainment from a book. He'll get better books afterwards. (Johnson, cited in Brozo, 2010, p. 78)

Explore with Students

Hero archetypes come in many forms. Post a list of archetypes and an example of each (Appendix C) and have students brainstorm other examples from literature, film, and television that fit the descriptors. Similarly, you can do the same with the list of villain archetypes. Leave the posting up in the classroom or on a class-based open-source management platform such as Moodle or WebCT and invite students to add to the list as they think of others. Debrief a week or so later and examine how these archetypes function in stories. What kinds of actions in the story compel characters to either maintain or relinquish their archetypal roles in particular works of literature or film? For example, what happens to make the kind and responsible "boyfriend" take a walk on the wild side? How often is the "go-getting, take charge female" brought down, and by whom? How have certain actors been typecast? What are the physical characteristics that are attributed to particular archetypes? How do archetypes create female/male binaries? In what ways do some writers and film makers successfully break through archetypal structures? Extend students' critical media-literacy skills by asking them to identify how advertisers employ archetypes to sell products.

MOVING ON

No doubt, Chapter 2 has left readers with the impression that researchers have their work cut out for them. Girls' gains in the areas of math and science and their growing enrollment numbers in university classrooms are an indication that *research does matter* in ways that can inform educational policy and practice to correct for gender inequities. Parents and educators have a job to do, too, in adopting a critical stance toward popular rhetoric to determine whether claims made in newspapers, magazines, textbooks, and teacher resource materials are well supported through research or are based on long-held assumptions or opinions. They need to think seriously about claims grounded in biological determinism for if, indeed, girls and boys are universally and biologically predisposed to learn differently, then educational efforts aimed at ameliorating girls' and boys' achievement in specific areas are likely to yield limited effects.

In the following chapter, I look at national and international studies comparing the literacy achievement of elementary and secondary students, including the Progress of International Reading Literacy Study (PIRLS) (Mullis, Martin, Kennedy, & Flaherty, 2002), which reported that grade 4 girls performed better than boys in all 34 countries where the assessment was administered[1] and the PISA (OECD, 2003), which indicated that girls outperformed boys on the reading test in all 41 participating countries. But as many researchers have pointed out, numbers don't begin to tell the whole story. In Chapter 3, I have attempted to provide readers with the critical information needed to understand reported findings and assess the limitations of such studies. There is a growing recognition that we need to see beyond what may be immediately perceived as a global pattern of female superiority in literacy achievement and focus our attention on *which boys* and *which girls* are not achieving well and why. From this vantage point, what becomes increasingly clear is that we need to examine how systemic factors such as family, school and community, peer culture, student-teacher interactions, and classroom practices interrelate and work together to affect performance and outcomes of girls and boys. Furthermore, it soon becomes clear that a more systematic review of applied research in schools and non-school-based learning environments is warranted if we are to identify with greater confidence instructional approaches and strategies that effectively engage girls and boys in more equitable literacy practices.

---

[1]Girls' outperformance in reading literacy measures has also been found for subsequent 2006 and 2011 PIRLS studies and recorded for reading measures in 2006 and 2009 PISA results.

CHAPTER 3

International and National Literacy Assessments

International and national assessments are by and large regulatory devices used to impose order on national educational systems through normative notions of effective schools and student performance (Abi-Mershed, 2010; Taubman, 2009). The OECD is a transnational organization whose PISA advances a standards discourse that links education to the economic progress of knowledge-based societies. Increasingly, globalization is seen as the path toward modernization and economic success. Defined by the global economy, global societies construct people as "the capital of a knowledge driven economy" (Singh, 2007, p. 534), ready and willing to adapt to meet the changing demands of a competitive and dynamic labor market. The intent is to transform citizens into highly skilled lifelong learners. In Chapter 2, readers were introduced to how the alignment of public education policy with economic aims accounts in some part for the crisis in masculinity as it relates to literacy achievement. This chapter is intended to acquaint parents and educators with the findings from international and national assessments that compare performance on tests of literacy, with the hope that readers will consider these findings within the broader social, economic, and political context. I cannot stress enough that policy makers eager to use the data from these assessments to confirm a pattern of female superiority in literacy and then make the leap to funding quick-fix "compensatory" strategies may be missing the proverbial boat, and hasty action may lead to the gross misdirection of funds and human resources. Parents and educators should seek detailed and critical analyses that disaggregate the data according to gender, race, socioeconomic status, and geographical region and then make a concerted effort to identify and address the underlying reasons why specific groups of students are or are not achieving well. Gender differences appearing in one group can be significantly different from those appearing in another. Furthermore, the ultimate consequences and long-term outcomes of those documented differences may be critically different. For example, there is much documented on how low literacy levels among African American males have been linked to grade retention, drop-out rates (Darling-Hammond, 2004), unemployment, violence, incarceration (Baer, Kutner, Sabatini, & White, 2009), and poor health outcomes and lack of access to proper health care (Birru & Steinman, 2004; Shea, Beers, McDonald, Quistberg, Ravenell, & Asch, 2004). It would be hard to imagine a white European male who achieves a lower NAEP reading score than his female counterpart but still manages to graduate high school with a higher SAT as suffering disadvantages in any way remotely resembling those faced by growing numbers of poor black and Hispanic students in the urban United States (regardless of gender) whose educational experience is marked by overcrowded and poorly maintained schools, lack of qualified teachers, and inadequate instructional resources resulting in impoverished curricula emphasizing "basic skills" in contrast to more challenging curricula enacted in more affluent school districts (Kozol, 2005; Dudley-Marling, 2007).

Bernadette Baker (2011) interrogates "the presumption of the nation as a unified, personified actor in PISA reports" and the widespread "belief that comparing two entities tells us something rather than nothing." For example, on the surface of things, knowing that Canada as a nation ranked fifth in reading proficiency and scored well above the OECD average according to 2009 PISA results does little to address the more pressing issue of high drop-out rates among Aboriginal students, who have historically performed two to four years behind in measured reading levels (Heit & Blair, 1993). We need to carefully examine the degree to which the actual mechanics of measurement are actively relegating groups of students to the margins with little hope of ever receiving the strategic funding and attention needed to make a critical difference in the lives of the disenfranchised. To date, I know of no sustained research that examines the influence gender may have on achievement among Canadian Aboriginal students, where lack of educational attainment has been linked to a host of social ills including violence and property crime and to negative effects on health and welfare (Mendelson, 2009). The American Association of University Women (2008) notes that data disaggregated by gender, race/ethnicity, and family income are not widely available, although NAEP results are disaggregated by race/ethnicity (white, black, Hispanic, Asian/Pacific Islander, American Indian/Alaska Native), gender (male, female) and type of school (public, private). But digging even deeper, Baker challenges us to question the distributive logic of assessments that preselect, predetermine, isolate, and stabilize what counts as worthy of comparison and then link these measures to status and funding. There is a fervent push to use data from international and national assessments as support for the creation of "boy-friendly" curriculum while, to my mind, it is clear we continue to remain, as Ted Sizer observed (2004), historically silent on the "most sensible, indeed stunningly obvious remedy" which is "to create a seamless support and ministering system" one that would "administer to *all aspects* of each child's situation, *in deliberate, sustained combination*" (emphasis added, p. 5).

Explore

Before reading the summary of results from recent PISA and NAEP assessments, think about the following:

1. What information do you expect to gain from the results of these assessments?

2. As an educator, how do the results of these assessments inform your instructional practice in meeting the diverse needs of your students?

3. As a parent, what information can educators provide that will allow you to best support your child's literacy development? Is it more helpful to know where your daughter or son ranks in the class or what books she or he likes to read?

PROGRAMME FOR INTERNATIONAL STUDENT ASSESSMENT (PISA)

PISA is a triennial survey conducted by the OECD that measures and compares learning skills among 15-year-olds. Around 470,000 students representing approximately 26 million 15-year-olds in 65 participating countries and economies took part in PISA 2009, with its main focus on reading, up from the 250,000 participants representing 41 countries surveyed in 2003. The number of participants and participating countries continues to increase since the original PISA survey in 2000, giving some indication of mounting status accorded to the survey results by policy makers worldwide. The assessment entails a two-hour paper-and-pencil test in the students' schools and measures student performance in mathematics, problem solving, science, and reading. It also includes a survey of students' approaches and attitudes toward school, providing information related to a range of individual, home, and school factors. Principals of participating schools are also asked to complete a survey. The survey data is helpful in terms of identifying and explaining cross-national patterns of reading literacy test performance.

PISA (OECD, 2003) defines reading literacy as "understanding, using and reflecting on written texts, in order to achieve one's goal's, to develop one's knowledge and potential and to participate in society" (p. 108). PISA's broader definition of literacy attempts to tap into multiple literacies insofar as it encompasses the ability of students to read and make meaning from a wide range of written materials. In constructing its reading literacy assessment, PISA recognizes three important dimensions: the format of the reading material, the type of reading task, and the situation or the use for which the text was constructed.

At first glance, the 2003 PISA results continue to indicate a global pattern of female superiority in reading. For the most part, there was little change in the average performance among the 25 participating countries from the 2000 PISA and the 2003 PISA assessments. The inclusion of new countries in 2003 accounts for the slight decline in the overall OECD mean literacy score.

The 2003 PISA findings indicated several trends. Students of parents with better-paying jobs and more education, and of homes with more "cultural" possessions, performed on average significantly better in all countries than those students without such advantages. Nevertheless, the overall socioeconomic status (SES) of the school population had an impact greater than that of the SES of individual students. In other words, careful attention to the socioeconomic ethos and culture of a school may potentially alleviate the impact of the SES of individual students. Girls continue to outperform boys on the combined reading literacy scale in all countries. And in most countries, results showed the majority of the least capable students were males of low SES.

One of the most powerful findings of the original 2000 PISA survey that focused on reading was that the effect of high levels of engagement can also reduce the effect of SES. This finding continues to resonate in the most recent 2009 report. PISA (OECD, 2000) results indicated that the motivation to read and the amount of time spent on reading might account considerably for the gap between good and poor readers. Nevertheless, it must be noted that while females outperformed males on the combined reading literacy scale in all participating countries and while the performance difference may be attributed in part to engagement in reading, males in some countries are more engaged in reading than females in other countries. For example, male participants in Denmark, Finland, Iceland, Japan, and Korea reported being either as engaged or more engaged in reading than females in Belgium, France, and Spain. This would seem to dispel any essentialist myths about girls being universally any more predisposed to reading than boys and compels us to look at the sociocultural factors that would account for overlapping results between males and females across nations.

Engagement in reading, that is to say, the amount of time spent reading and the extent to which students exercise control over the reading process, should not be conflated with interest in reading. In fact, while interest in reading did show a positive correlation with achievement, high interest does not necessarily lead to high engagement. Overall, males tended to show a higher interest in using computers for learning activities than females, and this interest too was correlated with higher reading performance. Generally, females were shown to be more reflective and evaluative in their approach to reading and reported spending much more time reading for enjoyment than did males. Females reported reading more fiction than males, who by contrast read more newspapers, comics, e-mails, and webpages.

Report of the International Reading Association PISA Task Force

A task force established by the International Reading Association (IRA; Topping, Valtin, Roller, Brozo, & Dionisio, 2003) issued a report in response to the first PISA assessment results (OECD, 2000) summarizing key findings and the implications for policy and practice. With regard to the provision of equitable education, IRA determined that comparative international analyses such as PISA can be helpful for the following three reasons:

1. Assessing the relative standing of each country in terms of the overall level of performance

2. Identifying groups of at-risk students

3. Identifying the characteristics of students who perform poorly

In summarizing their recommendations for policy and practice in response to the 2000 PISA results, IRA emphasizes the need to foster gains in boys' reading performance. The members of the task force are careful to note that schools need to consider the methods of reading instruction to ensure that implicit culture or gender bias is not present. Rather, schools should seek to broaden the definitions, models, and expectations of literacy embedded in school and teacher culture. The task force offers three possible explanations for the persistent gender gap in literacy achievement.

First, the task force points to the cultural penetration of television and popular electronic media promoting iconographic and stereotypic models of gendered behavior in which boys and men are portrayed as "action figures" while girls and women are cast in more passive, nurturing, and domestic roles. Stereotypic models of masculinity do not include contemplative time for traditional book reading. Gendered codes of behavior may be even more restrictive for children of color and for those in lower socioeconomic communities. IRA suggests that boys of lower SES would benefit from preventive measures in the early years aimed specifically at raising engagement in reading. In response to PISA results (OECD, 2000), the association also supports opportunities for enhancing student interest in a wide range of reading activities but notes that sustaining high engagement with reading is more important. Accordingly, IRA advocates schools provide numerous and rich opportunities for reading multimedia and Internet texts as an approach for boys of low SES who also demonstrate low levels of reading engagement. Nevertheless, the potential consequences of this approach have been discussed in Chapter 2, and more research is needed to confirm the sustainable effects of technology on the level of reading engagement among boys of low SES.

Second, the task force suggests that the "feminization" of school environments may affect boys' literacy development and perceptions. Approximately 75 percent of classroom teachers in the United States are women, and at the elementary level this jumps to 90 percent. IRA notes that the teaching forces in Canada, Australia, and the United Kingdom reflect a similar gender makeup. The IRA task force speculates that female teachers may sanction certain texts that may be in conflict with masculine culture but do not cite any evidence. While I agree that, traditionally, reading and teaching reading has been seen as women's work, there simply isn't enough research to indicate whether or not female teachers actually assume attitudes and select texts that are actively contributing to why some male youth are rejecting reading as a "girl thing." From my experience as both teacher and curriculum coordinator and in my present role supervising teacher candidates in schools, I have witnessed increasing efforts on the part of both female and male teachers to widen the range of forms and genres of texts offered to students despite many standardized curricula that adhere to a classic canon. IRA's speculation on female teacher attitudes, no matter how indirect, is an unfortunate example of how easy it is to incorporate assumptions about women's sense of decorum and literary tastes and, conversely, assumptions about what boys like to read. There is an implicit suggestion here that somehow, by their presence, women are to blame. Such a suggestion completely ignores the very real problem of male attitudes toward professional women in authority (Leathwood, 2005; Walkerdine, 1998). The gender imbalance between female and male teachers in the work force has much to do with the extent to which, historically, women's career choices and salaries have been limited and how their professional identities continue to be subject to derision. Misplacing the blame for boys' lower literacy achievement on the disproportion of women who have been relegated to nurturing professions and lower salaries is unjustifiable. Furthermore, the review of the research on the effects of same-sex teachers on reading achievement highlighted in Chapter 2 indicates that there simply isn't sufficient evidence to support IRA's suggestion that changes to the gender makeup of the teaching force would have any sustainable positive effects on raising boys' performance scores in reading. Dee's (2007) post hoc analysis of the National Educational Longitudinal Study of 1988 points out that such changes are likely to have negative consequences for girls and the employment status of women. Efforts might be more effectively and ethically directed toward changing the attitudes of boys toward women in authority and enhancing the professional profile of teachers at all levels.

Finally, IRA attempts to account for the gender gap in reading achievement reported in the PISA (2000) results to the type of texts sanctioned in secondary school language arts curricula. They suggest that if boys are repeatedly asked to read books unrelated to their needs and interests, they may become disengaged. Common to this argument is the assumption that the protagonist's gender determines girl-appropriate and boy-appropriate titles. IRA's analysis fails to note that many of the books selected in secondary school classrooms may hold little interest for girls either. Arguably, canonical texts read in secondary school—Shakespeare's plays, William Golding's *Lord of the Flies*, J. D. Salinger's *Catcher in the Rye*, and even books written by female authors such as Harper Lee's *To Kill a Mockingbird*—overwhelmingly reflect a world dominated by males, as do many books written about women by women. In fairness, this is the world within which all authors exercise their craft. To compensate, girls and woman often read and write in "resistant" ways outside of the male canon. If anything, Huck (2001) notes that schools tend to make girls read books with male protagonists because there is a pervasive belief that boys won't read (or listen to) stories about girls but girls will read anything. Again, such actions on the part of educators advance the perception of girls as compliant and boys as resistant. The suggestion that we need to masculinize the curriculum further detracts from the real issue of how girls and boys construct their identities as readers according to gendered codes of behavior and the extent to which schools consciously or unconsciously reinforce these codes. A gender-equitable approach to literacy would entail addressing the issues surrounding girls' apparent compliance as well as the factors contributing to boys' documented low engagement in reading.

NATIONAL ASSESSMENT OF EDUCATIONAL PROGRESS (NAEP)

The NAEP is a nationally representative and continual assessment that attempts to capture what U.S. students know and can do in a number of subject areas including reading, mathematics, science, writing, history, and geography. The assessment seeks to provide policy makers at the national, state, and local levels with objective information on student performance. In developing its framework for assessment, NAEP also recognizes that different contexts for reading may lead to differences in what readers can do. The NAEP reading framework assesses grade 4 students in two different contexts. Assessing reading for literary experience entails having students read literary materials such as short stories, legends, and myths. Assessing reading for information requires students to read from informational pieces such as magazine articles and biographies. The grade 8 reading framework includes a third context. At this level, students are assessed on reading to perform a task. Eighth-grade students are required to read and respond to a variety of practical texts such as bus schedules, directions, forms, and charts. Reading achievement results for grades 4 and 8 are reported as a 0–500 scale score and at three achievement levels:

1. *Basic*: indicates partial mastery of the knowledge and skills deemed fundamental for proficient work at a given grade

2. *Proficient*: indicates solid academic performance. NAEP states that students at this level have demonstrated competency over challenging subject matter.

3. *Advanced*: indicates superior performance

The average scale scores and achievement-level results in reading reported by gender for both grades 4 and 8 reveal that girls have consistently outperformed boys between the years 1992 and 2005. In 2005, the average scale score in reading for grade 4 females was 222 compared to 216 for grade 4 males. Findings indicate that the average scale score for grade 4 boys has increased by 1 point from 2003 to 2005 while the average scale score for grade 4 girls has remained the same since 2002. In 2005, 61 percent of grade 4 males achieved a level of "Basic" or higher. This represents a significant increase of 1 percentage point over 2003. Sixty-seven percent of grade 4 females achieved a level of "Basic" or higher on the 2005 assessment. Again, this is consistent with results dating to 2002.

NAEP 2005 results for grade 8 also indicate that girls outperformed boys on measures of reading achievement for the years between 1992 and 2005. In 2005, 68 percent of grade 8 males achieved a level of "Basic" or higher. This represents a decrease of 1 percentage point from 2003. From 2003 to 2005, the percentage of grade 8 females achieving a level of "Basic" or higher also dropped 1 percentage point from 69 percent to 68 percent. The NAEP scale scores and achievement-level percentages are helpful insofar as they provide a picture of national and regional trends over time. NAEP publishes the results in *The Nation's Report Card*. The recent 2005 report card in reading, however, offers very little in actually accounting for the gender gap. Only when we consider the results reported by gender in relation to the findings associated with other variables such as race/ethnicity and SES indicators do we begin to form some ideas about which girls and which boys are not attaining the "Basic" achievement level in reading.

When we examine NAEP findings in relation to other national standardized tests in the United States such as the SAT and ACT, we see that children from the lowest-income families consistently have the lowest average test scores and that an incremental rise in income is associated with a rise in test scores. So, too, can we see that African American and Hispanic girls and boys score lower than white and Asian American children. With reference to NAEP reading scores, gender differences in achievement also vary by race/ethnicity and family income. Girls generally outperform boys within each racial/ethnic group on the NAEP reading assessment, but this gender gap in achievement is most consistent among white students, less so among African American students, and least among Hispanic students (AAUW, 2008). Overall, boys have outperformed girls on both the math and verbal portions of the SAT, but when we disaggregate the data by family income level, the gender gap in achievement favoring males is consistent only among students from low-income families. In other words, overall patterns of achievement do not necessarily reflect patterns found in subgroups, nor are gender differences appearing in one group necessarily replicated in another.

MOVING ON

In reviewing the literature on gender and literacy, I wish to note that I have done my best in the following chapters to make clear what are actual findings from research studies and what are personal observations used to assist the reader in making connections to a wider range of contexts. This is an important distinction because a significant number of teacher resource materials and professional development sessions on gender and literacy are not so much based on research findings as they are a response to the popular rhetoric on boys and reading and the taken-for-granted assumptions about the differences between girls and boys. Actual research examining gendered literacy practices involves empirical or observational data that does not lead to "proving" anything but rather provides us with quantitative and qualitative data to create a picture of what is going on within or across particular contexts. The findings from many studies investigating the same phenomenon across a variety of settings begin to offer us insight into patterns of behavior, and we begin to get some idea of what conditions contribute to shaping those behaviors. I caution readers, however, to understand what may be lost in broad sweeping strokes. For example, PISA (OECD 2009) results over time have indicated that there is no significant relationship between a country or economy's mean performance and the proportion of students with an immigrant background. Here again, we may lose sight of linguistic and socioeconomic factors that determine the extent to which particular groups of immigrants experience inferior or superior schooling conditions in host countries relative to their native peers (p. 71). For example, considerable research documents the benefits of implementing bilingual school and family literacy programs to enhance immigrant children's literacy development by valuing and maintaining children's home or first language (Cummins & Schecter, 2003).

I have also attempted to point out where the current body of research has inadequately addressed some of our questions. Every day, I am made aware of new investigations that will continue to contribute to our understanding of the complex relationship between gender and literacy. It is impossible to reference everything written on the subject of gender and literacy, but I have worked to provide readers with a broad range of studies that will inevitably provoke as many new questions as it answers. I am also aware that any selection is constructed in such a way as to convey a particular argument, and no doubt readers will have noted a concern that the range of issues related to gender equity and education are being lost in a singular focus on boys and reading to the detriment of all. Hopefully, the chapters that follow provide a timely and a reasonably comprehensive overview of studies investigating a wide range of phenomena related to gendered literacy practices.

CHAPTER 4

Researching Gendered Discourse Practices

Our understanding of the ways in which gender bias and inequities continue to shape literacy practices in classrooms owes much to the systematic review of research conducted by Guzzetti, Young, Gritsavage, Fyfe, and Hardenbrook (2002). Unfortunately, this important work is often overlooked in the deluge of reports that focus exclusively on boys and literacy. Intent on raising an awareness of gender issues in learning and practice, the researchers undertook a careful analysis of findings within and across qualitative studies in gender and literacy. The researchers limited their review to qualitative or observational studies that investigated text or text-based activity with informants drawn from or situated in classrooms. While their review focused on more traditional literacies (e.g., reading, writing, and speaking), their synthesis of research findings provides answers to questions that are insufficiently addressed by the quantitative data supplied by international and national test scores. Guzzetti and colleagues (2002) include information about successful interventions and make recommendations for classroom practice. Throughout their review of the existing literature on gender and literacy, the researchers bring to light unanswered questions and provoke new avenues for future investigations. Their book *Reading, Writing, and Talking Gender in Literacy Learning* serves as a valuable resource in locating studies that form the basis of a number of the discussions contained in the next three chapters.

This chapter also references international studies on gender and literacy from a wide range of disciplines and includes reports of findings from quantitative and qualitative studies that fall outside of the themes explored in the Guzzetti and colleagues analysis. In particular, in a handbook of this scope, it is necessary to report on studies that focus on trends among females and males with regard to their engagement with information technology.

In addition, I have included a discussion of recent findings from studies investigating how heteronormativity is both reinforced and disrupted through literature discussions about books with discernible lesbian, gay, bisexual, and transgender (LGBT) themes and characters. These are included in the section on studies on gender and talk. In the quest to foster an understanding of why we continue to document gender differences in literacy practices, the reader also requires some introduction to psychological theories that attempt to account for the life-long process of gender identification and personality formation. At the conclusion of this chapter, I discuss how social structures invariably emerge from the process of gender identification and how the highlighted studies provide evidence that literacy practices continue to conform to repeated patterns of gendered power relations.

STUDIES IN GENDER AND TALK

Guzzetti and colleagues (2002) identified 30 studies conducted since 1993 that investigated gender relations in students' discussions of texts. Not surprisingly, 80 percent of the first authors of these studies were female. The theoretical frameworks used for analyzing data were largely drawn from sociolinguistics or some form of feminism, with feminist poststructuralism being the most common. Feminist poststructuralism asserts that gender cannot be understood outside of its social and linguistic construction. It is aimed at changing "the power relations that structure all areas of life, the family, education, and welfare, the worlds of work and politics, culture and leisure." Such relations "determine who does what and for whom, what we are and what we might become" (Weedon, 1987, p. 1). The systematic review of the studies on gender and discussion yielded five common themes that appear consistent with many of the findings of studies subsequent to the Guzzetti review. Guzzetti and colleagues (2002) describe these as follows:

1. patterns of gendered discursive practice

2. gendered talk in literature-response groups

3. the stability of gendered discursive practice across content areas

4. the difficulties and dangers of interrupting gendered discursive practices

5. the problem of essentializing or assigning fixed or "natural" characteristics or behaviors to a particular gender (p. 16)

Patterns of gendered discursive practice across eight of the studies conducted by literacy researchers were consistent with the marginalizing practices identified through a body of research conducted within the field of sociolinguistics. Guzzetti and colleagues listed call-outs, interruptions, teasing, and contradictions as the means that males often used to "impede or facilitate females' (and some males') abilities to develop and express their ideas" (p. 39). Studies by Guzzetti (1998), Alvermann (1993, 1995) and Evans, Alverman, and Anders (1998) documented female silencing through these types of gendered discursive practices. For example, in Guzzetti's (1998) study conducted in three high school physics classes, she observed that boys in the freshman physics class asked questions of the teacher and occasionally of one another. By contrast, female students in the same class put their heads down to sleep and woke only to do the assigned seatwork. In the junior and senior physics classes, both whole-class discussions and small-group lab discussions of mixed-gender composition were dominated by the boys. Boys maintained the conversational floor by interrupting girls, shouting out answers, and disparaging girls' contributions.

Interestingly, discursive behavior patterns among middle school and senior high school students' classroom talk doesn't look all that much different from those patterns documented in study of adult discussions. Gritsavage (1997) analyzed whose topics were initiated, whose talk held the floor, and whose topics were sustained among a group of seven adult participants in her graduate course on gender, culture, and literacy. Despite the fact that females slightly outnumbered males (4:3), the oldest male in the class dominated the discussion with regards to topics initiated and sustained and in holding the conversational floor. Moreover, the oldest male participant's share of the conversation was almost equal to that of the female professor. He managed to steer the topic back to his issues at least three times during a particular episode. He interrupted the professor twice and a female student once. Notably, Gritsavage reported that the oldest male student was the only student to introduce a topic unilaterally rather than collaboratively.

Both of the highlighted studies give us much to ponder. In reviewing these studies and others that document gendered discursive practices, one detects that males and females experience a very different sense of entitlement when it comes to conversational rights in mixed-sex groups. Earlier research originating in the United Kingdom also indicates boys' domination of classroom discourse (Spender & Sarah, 1980; Mahony, 1985). Mahony (1985) concluded that "male identity and in particular the social construction of male sexuality is crucial in the maintenance of male power and it is this which we have witnessed in the mixed sex classroom" (p. 70). But girls are not the only students being silenced in classrooms. She adds that nonmacho boys are at risk of falling victim to male power. Davies (2003) conducted a discourse analysis of 14-year-old students in both single-sex and mixed-sex groupings engaged in several speaking and listening activities during their English classes. Her research demonstrates how "[b]oys' use of sexist language and stereotypes is rarely challenged by other boys—potentially harming themselves as well as girls" (p. 118). It is worth noting that both boys and girls engage in policing gender boundaries.

Explore with Students

When reading a novel that is considered a children's classic such as Lucy Maud Montgomery's (1908) *Anne of Green Gables*, Frances Hodgson Burnett's (1905) *A Little Princess*, or Mark Twain's (1876, 1884) *The Adventures of Tom Sawyer* or *The Adventures of Huckleberry Finn*, examine with students the ways in which the characters police or transgress gendered expectations relative to the novel's setting (time and place). Encourage students to think about how gendered expectations have changed and the ways children today keep gender in check.

Davies (2003) also argues that examination of results presented in gendered sets offers a far too simplistic view that only serves to obfuscate a more complex picture. Her research demonstrates the ways in which performing gender can facilitate or inhibit learning. For example, the girls in Davies's sample consistently expressed their gender through the use of "friendly talk" that fulfilled both a social and educational function. Like Vygotsky (1962), whose writings have become fundamental to our understanding of the social construction of knowledge, Davies observed that "friendship talk" is conducive to the learning process. The all-girls groups "worked in a supportive climate in which they could experiment with words and struggle with ideas together" (p. 119). Girls were also more comfortable narrating anecdotes. Storytelling allows speakers "to construct versions of themselves, to entertain, and display linguistic expertise" (p. 119). It provided an opportunity for collaborative meaning making as the girls supported one another in taking center stage and participating in narration the to develop their understanding of each other and the themes presented.

Gender allegiance in the all-girls group was implicit, and at no time did any of the girls feel that she had to define herself as being worthy to belong. On the other hand, boys found it necessary to constantly define the "male culture" and "demonstrate their worthiness to belong" (Davies, 2003, p. 124). Boys often felt compelled "to choose whether to be accepted by their peer group and join in the 'macho discourse' or to work hard and become ostracized and have their behavior and language derided" (p. 124). Not surprisingly to most educators and many parents, in every all-male group the term "gay" was bantered about "in a negative and gratuitous manner to defame other boys and to regulate group membership" (p. 124). Constant attention was paid to establishing a hierarchy of masculinity—a pecking order to keep everyone in their place. Off-task comments were directed at establishing sexual credibility among peers, and frequent taunts were used to empower themselves at the expense of others. Davies concluded that the discourse of work and the way in which boys expressed their gender allegiances were hardly conducive to collaborative learning.

Teacher-researcher Lyndsay Moffatt (2006) studied the gendered discourse of her 26 grade 5 and 6 students in an urban Canadian elementary school through seven months of informal observations of the students during silent reading, "reading buddies." and a variety of lessons. At the end of seven months, the researcher followed up with 20-minute interviews inquiring into students' ideas about gender and reading. Moffatt found that while 22 of the 26 students reported hearing another student chastising a boy for "acting like such a girl," only 5 reported hearing another student police a girl's behavior with a comments like "you're acting like a boy." Similar findings documented by Best (1983) and Thorne (1993) provide an indication of how gendered norms are established and maintained in classrooms and the extent to which male codes of behavior are more rigorously policed among peers. Moffatt (2006) noted during interviews that students had definite ideas about what constituted the discourse of gender-normative behavior and that the majority of students identified print literacy practices and reading with normative feminine behavior. They believed that there were more girl readers than boy readers and that girls both read more and liked to read more than boys. Some students also noted how girls enacted print literacy by playing with gel pens, writing notes, and reading. Moffatt notes that none of the students identified any such examples of literacy enactment for boys. However, given the discussion on expanding notions of literacy, I would have appreciated more information about what it is that the students thought boys like to do and whether any of the activities reported might relate to nontraditional literacies enacted out of school.

In a more recent study of gendered discourse in literature discussion groups, Mollie Blackburn and Caroline Clark (2011) investigated the nature of talk about books containing lesbian, gay, bisexual, transgendered, and/or questing (LGBTQ) characters to identify the ways such talk was liberatory or oppressive. Their research examined 18 transcripts of talk about 24 different texts recorded in a literature discussion group of 22 adolescents and 10 adults (including the authors) over a three-year period. Participants identified as either LGBTQ or as straight LGBTQ allies, and discussions were held in a LGBTQ youth center across from a large university campus. The researchers found that reading the books yielded patterns reflective of both LGBT-inclusive and queering discourses. LGBT-inclusive discourse intentionally or unintentionally reinforced heteronormativity or combated homophobia by using talk to consider the impact of homophobia, construct allies, universalize experiences of queer people, and police gender norms. By contrast, queering discourses interrogated heteronormativity by using talk to consider the impact of heteronormativity, broadening notions of family, being open to diverse attractions, and interrogating homonormativity. In addition, queering discourses foregrounded the sexual by using talk to deal with the discomfort in discussing sex, study characters that depicted sex, and struggle with stereotypes related to sex.

The researchers concluded that literature discussions centering on LGBT-themed literature reflected a complex reciprocal process among texts, talk, and context in which no single mode of discourse among those identified and coded predominated. Borrowing from de Certeau (1984), who distinguishes between strategic and tactical ways of operating whereby strategies function in oppressive ways and tactics in liberatory ways, Blackburn and Clark noted that despite the claim that all group members were striving to be tactical in their desire to combat the oppressive aspects of heteronormativity, at times many fell into a reliance on language and literacy practices that invariably reflect ready-made intentions. The researchers indicate that a participant's move to universalize the experiences of queer, for example in suggesting that the love story in a particular text might draw in a homophobic reader to "get past it ... being about gay people" (p. 245), might actually be tactical insofar as it demonstrates a potential for working against homophobia. The authors concluded in this case that the move to universalize queer experiences to heterosexual normative behavior is not solely strategic or oppressive even though it banks on what I have come to call the "just like us" discourse that can characterize a lot of social justice education.

GENDERED DISCOURSE IN ELECTRONIC SPACES

Rebecca Luce-Kapler (2006) noted the possibilities of using electronic text to work through female identities with a group of grade 11 students in an advanced English class that focused on women writers. She chose Shelley Jackson's (1995) *Patchwork Girl: A Modern Monster*, an e-literature text based on the premise that Mary Shelley, author of *Frankenstein*, herself made the monster and that the monster was a woman who travelled to the United States. In the process of engaging with e-literature, readers are required to actively construct meaning and direct the reading by clicking on a matrix of links that connect to a myriad of media options including text, image, and sound. Hypertext authors offer readers an array of contingencies and emerging options—narrative fragments that in this case aptly come together in patchwork fashion. Readers get intimate with the writer's consciousness—her fleeting thoughts and ideas as to where the narrative might go. Keeping the fragments in play allows for what Luce-Kapler (2004) has identified as subjunctive, "what if," or "side-showing" spaces which in her earlier work with women's writing groups led women to experiment with new forms, to challenge patriarchal order, and to engage their subjectivities. In working with digital texts, Luce-Kapler (2006) reminds us that we need to pay attention to making the role of genre in writing less transparent so that writers might pursue more open-ended possibilities. For example, she recalls how her junior high students writing fantasy were unaware of how deeply entrenched they were in cultural patterns. As a result, most girls were content with writing fairytale princess stories while boys wrote more violent science fiction.

After reading *Patchwork Girl*, Luce-Kapler introduced the grade 11 students to wiki writing and to Storyspace, inviting them to write hypertexts of their own. This experience led most girls in the class to appreciate the value of hypertext as a writing genre, citing the creative possibilities not typically available in other ways in school. One gets the sense in reading Luce-Kapler's account that girls were able to enact their agency as writers as, in the words of one student, "unexplained and unquestioned avenues open up" (p. 13). There were several who remained resistant to hypertext writing and saw it as a vehicle for writing poetry and journals but did not see it as a viable alternative to more traditional and linear forms of narratives.

There is an increasing body of well-theorized research that students' use of hypertext writing and hypermedia composing (digital video) has been shown to enhance creative thinking (Liu, 1998), stimulate metacognitive skills (Braaksma, Rijlaarsdam, Couzijn, & van den Bergh, 2002), increase motivation, and provide writers with a broadened repertoire of resources and space within which to integrate individual and collaborative thinking and meaning making (Ranker, 2008). More research, however, is needed regarding how students enact gender in composing across multimedia in individual and group contexts. Also needed is research investigating the extent to which electronic text fulfills its promise of providing for gender-free communication and whether virtual learning environments allow for more equitable gender participation in discussions. Prompted by the preponderance of psychological literature documenting gender differences in oral communication, Sussman and Tyson (2000) investigated whether gendered power differentials are evident in online discussions among undergraduate students. The researchers analyzed archived electronic discussions ($n = 701$) on sex-typed topics (feminine, masculine, and gender-neutral) according to length, frequency of communication, and discourse content (fact versus opinion). While women communicated more frequently than men, men wrote entries with a greater number of words and demonstrated a slight trend toward more opinionated communications on topics in the masculine and gender-neutral categories. Sussman and Tyson concluded that cyberspace remains a male-dominated atmosphere where the gendered power differential persists in much the same way as it does for other modes of communication. Finally, reiterating an earlier concern relating to the use of technology, more research is needed to examine the extent to which girls and boys are encouraged to engage in multimodal discourse.

GENDER IDENTIFICATION AND PERSONALITY FORMATION

Evidence of female silencing figures prominently in many of the findings reported in studies investigating patterns of discursive practice. Female silencing is a psychological consequence resulting from an observed tendency among girls, particularly adolescent girls, and women to make decisions in the face of a moral situation based on the expectations of a male-dominated society rather than on their own feelings and beliefs (Gilligan, 1993). In studies investigating girls' psychological development, Gilligan and her colleagues (Brown & Gilligan, 1992; Gilligan, Brown & Rogers, 1990; Rogers, 1993) have documented that as girls approach adolescence they experience a crisis of voice and relationship. As Gilligan (2003) explains, "Women living in patriarchal families, societies, and culture are bound internally and externally by obligations to care without complaint, on pain of becoming a bad woman: unfeminine, ungenerous, uncaring" (p. 157). Accordingly, they navigate life through "a web of relationships" (p. 156) and respond in ways that reflect their perceived responsibility in these relationships.

On the other hand, for boys and men, a sense of separation and individuation has been the foundation for male gender-identity development and personality formation. Freud theorized that the development of masculinity begins with the process of boys' separation from their mother. From a Freudian point of view, the process presents a desirable crisis within the child insofar as both males and females have to resolve their largely unconscious desire to possess the parent of the opposite sex and reject the other parent. During this Oedipal phase of ego development, children between the ages of three and five resolve the crisis through identification with the parent of the same sex and temporary renunciation of the parent of the opposite sex. For boys, individuation from the mother has long signified the first step toward an autonomous self that exists as a rational man outside of relationships with the inner and outer world. In the life-long process of individuation, as the child matures, the parent of the opposite sex is later reclaimed as the symbolic object of sexual desire.

The Oedipus complex as it appears in classic psychoanalytic theory has come under considerable and varying critique from inside and outside the field of psychoanalysis. Many argue that Freud's Oedipus complex is not a given but simply summarizes what happens as a result of how human beings are socialized. Whether or not we subscribe to Freud's views or any of the ensuing variations or rearticulations, we cannot deny that much of what Freud wrote on the id, the ego, and the superego has directed Western understanding of psychological development. The Western focus on individuation and individual achievement as benchmarks of maturity and personal autonomy, as we see in Kohlberg's (1976) stages of moral development, has worked to characterize concern for relationships as a weakness. Gilligan (1993) argues that when women's sense of relational responsibility comes up against the demands of patriarchal social order, women's thoughts and feelings are driven underground. Ironically, in order to participate in relationships, girls and women have to reject their desire for inter- and intrapersonal connections, and when faced with morally problematic situations, they are forced to anticipate male modes of conduct and adjust their behavior accordingly. Gilligan and her colleagues (Brown & Gilligan, 1992; Gilligan, Brown, & Rogers, 1990; Rogers, 1993) claim that the tension between women's relational knowledge and patriarchal order gives rise to a psychological dissociation among adolescent girls that compels a loss of voice:

> Girls' initiation into womanhood has often meant an initiation into a kind of selflessness, which is associated with care and connection but also with a loss of psychological vitality and courage. To become selfless means to lose relationship or to lose one's voice in relationships. This loss of relationship leads to a muting of voice, leaving inner feelings of sadness and isolation. In effect, the young woman becomes shut up within herself. (Gilligan, 2003, p. 159)

For example, in many of the selected literacy studies discussed in this chapter, girls yield the conversational floor to their male counterparts and silence themselves completely in traditionally male-dominated settings such physics classrooms. To act otherwise often has dire consequences, subjecting girls to ridicule, naming calling, and ostracism by both boys and girls. I feel compelled to point out that while the studies examined within this chapter do much to document existing social structures within and outside of the literacy classroom and provide evidence of Gilligan's earlier claims, we cannot move in any equitable direction unless parents and educators are willing to collectively and consciously work to dismantle the patriarchal framework for interpreting gendered patterns of behavior. As Audre Lorde eloquently pointed out the problem in 1979 in her comments referring to the representational absence of poor women, women of color, lesbians, and women of developing countries at the Second Sex Conference hosted by the New York Institute for Humanities, even academic feminist circles are not immune to unconsciously or consciously subscribing to the very racist, patriarchal tools used in perpetuating the oppressive situations we seek to escape. Like the girls and boys in the studies who have internalized "old blueprints of expectations and response, old structures of oppression" (Lorde, 2007, p. 123), parents, educators, and researchers who investigate gender are likely to operate within the same social structures that gave rise to white, male, hegemonic power. Lorde's oft-cited caution, "the master's tools will never dismantle the master's house" (p. 123), compels us to reimagine how power and difference are defined within gendered relationships and cautions that "old patterns, no matter how cleverly rearranged to imitate progress still condemn us to . . . repetitions of the same exchanges" (p. 123). Recalling Paulo Freire's *Pedagogy of the Oppressed* 1970), Lorde reminds us,

> . . . the true focus of revolutionary change is never merely the oppressive situations which we seek to escape, but that piece of the oppressor which is planted deep within each of us, and which knows only the oppressors' tactics, the oppressors' relationships. (Lorde, 2007, p. 123)

Before moving on to examining how gender has influenced reading practices, I challenge readers to think about the relational realities documented in these classrooms in order to come to some understanding of the ways in which existing social structures govern the gendered behavior of both boys and girls, of which achievement patterns in literacy are but one consequence.

MOVING ON

In Chapter 5, we explore a number of themes emerging from studies investigating gender and reading. There is a particular focus on instructional methods and on reading preferences and practices. It is not surprising to most readers that girls and boys are socialized to take up and respond to texts and characters differently. It is important to come to some understanding of genre and the difficulty in pinpointing reading preferences according to gender.

CHAPTER 5

Researching Gender and Reading

The ability to read well is highly valued in our society and viewed by many as essential to economic and social advancement (Snow, Burns, & Griffin, 1998). Convinced that increasing demands for higher literacy go hand in hand with advances in technology and an ever-increasing competitive global economy, policy makers at the provincial, state, and federal levels are concerned about the consequences of falling short. This unwavering belief among those who hold the economic purse strings has a direct impact on the moral panic associated with the documented gender divide in reading achievement between girls and boys. Advances in technology and economic change have prompted a "feminization" of the work force (Arnot, David, & Weiner, 1999: Maynard, 2002) where the economies of industrialized nations depend increasingly on the service sector for jobs—jobs that are traditionally held by women. Accordingly, workplace culture favors more "feminine" or relational modes of interaction (Gee, Hull, & Lankshear, 1996), for example, working cooperatively and interacting in teams as opposed to the individual competition that has characterized male advancement. The economic shift implies the need for enhanced verbal skills, an ability to read and write from multiple perspectives, and the critical capacity to read and interpret a range of traditional and nontraditional texts.

Arnot, David, and Weiner (1999) paint a picture of a "crisis of masculinity" in which they argue that schools have failed to provide boys with the necessary skills to adapt to new circumstances. But the fault of the logic behind the "crisis of masculinity" movement (Arnot, David, and Weiner, 1999; Faludi, 1999; Kimmel, 2002) and many of the reading interventions it has spawned is that they are driven by an underlying desire to restore patriarchal hegemony "against femininities and other masculinities" (Weaver-Hightower, 2003). Arnot and colleagues write of the threat to the "conventional basis both of masculinity and its associated ideal of the male breadwinner" (p. 125) and the concomitant "negative repercussions for boys" (p. 126). Faludi speaks of patriarchal promises broken, and Kimmel (2002) of male disenfranchisement that leads to a masculine culture of lashing out, leading to a rise in domestic and public violence. I urge readers to think about how easy it is to simply succumb to an acceptance of males' unquestioned right to violence and react in fear that if patriarchal power is not restored then all hell will break loose. The problem as I see it is that patriarchy has left us little room to imagine other cultural possibilities, and that includes other possibilities for enacting masculinities both in and outside the literature classroom.

The following review of reading research is intended to provide parents and educators with insight into the influence of gender on reading. Guzzetti, Young, Gritsavage, Fyfe, and Hardenbrook (2002) reviewed 38 studies relating to gender and reading. The majority of authors were female (87%), and a large number of the studies focused on girls and reading. From their analysis of the literature on gender and reading, the researchers extrapolated four themes:

1. importance of text and method in literature response

2. gendered reading preferences and practices

3. oppression or constraint in instructional and social context

4. opposition, accommodation, and resistance in reading

What follows are brief summaries of key studies representative of each theme and my commentary as it relates to the ongoing discussion of gender and literacy.

IMPORTANCE OF TEXT AND METHOD IN LITERATURE RESPONSE

A Response to Davies' Study of Primary Children's Responses to Fairy Tales

Notably, the discussion in Guzzetti and colleagues begin with a critique of employing unreflective reader response. Davies's (1993) study of primary-aged school children's responses to feminist fairy tales and fiction "illustrated the power of traditional storylines to assert oppressive gender relations as natural and correct" (p. 173). Cherland (1992, 1994) in her studies of sixth-grade students in reader-response groups also found that both girls and boys approached reading and their response to the texts in gendered ways. Male students tended to invoke a discourse of action through reasoning and logic. They defined characters by what they did and sought meaning in the plot and action of the story. Girls, on the other hand, invoked a discourse of feeling, focusing more on human relationships and the emotional states of the characters.

Davies (1993) criticizes the practice of reader response, contending that identifying with a character through our own personal feelings and experiences serves to perpetuate gender stereotyping because of the extent to which our feelings and experiences are already constructed in large part by our gendered positions as male or female. That our gendered positioning influences the way we both approach and respond to texts is not in question. I do believe, however, that much of the criticism of reader response neither begins to consider the critical role of empathetic identification in animating moral imagination (Dewey, 1915; Krasny, 2007) nor the contention that empathy is an evolved biological capacity necessary to human understanding (Thompson, 2007; Thompson & Varela, 2001) and to communicating intersubjectively. While readers will inevitably connect with certain characters in gendered ways, this same capacity for empathy, or putting oneself in the place of another, is a necessary condition to assume critical perspectives. It is only through some form of empathetic projection that we are able to anticipate the thoughts and feelings of others.

For example, we need to reach beyond language to identify with the feelings and actions of the colonized to read the historical and fictionalized accounts of European expansion from a postcolonial perspective. Empathy, which relies on the evocation of imagery and affect, enables us to make associations and project these feelings and actions to similar narratives of those who fell victim to imperialist projects. Likewise, to read from a feminist perspective, both females and males are challenged to recognize and feel what it is that structures the experience of girls and women. Alternately, perspectives emerging from the more recent field of masculinity studies, which attempts to account for observed phenomena as they relate to men, codes of masculinity, gender, and politics, might find generative ground in Shyam Selvadurai's *Funny Boy*, a novel that recounts a gay youth's coming of age during political unrest in Sri Lanka. The human capacity for empathy enables us to take up the perspective of the other. We can engage empathetically with the experience of others through literature both as insiders and outsiders of a particular group (e.g., African American) or intersections of groups represented (e.g., adolescent, African American, Muslim female). In other words, teachers and students need to recognize in what ways they empathetically identify with particular characters and begin to use this recognition as a point of critical self-reflection.

Fictional and nonfictional reading allow readers to vicariously live through the experience of others, but it must be emphasized that I am in no way suggesting that the lived-through experience of the reader is synonymous with the actual experiences of real persons. Such vicarious experiences, however, do make possible opportunities for developing our repertoire of critical perspectives. How we engage that repertoire of perspectives remains an ethical issue. Readers will invariably respond to texts regardless of whether we, as educators and parents, think it is good practice or not.

Empathy is an emotional response to an evocative event and as such can bring forth accompanying feelings of fear, anticipation, pleasure, or happiness. Feelings grounded in our lived experience can serve in the arbitration of good and evil, right and wrong, but these feelings are subject to social forces and obligations. To my mind, the argument is not whether reader response is inherently good or bad but that unreflective reader response may limit the extent to which reading literature can advance our understanding of ourselves and others (Krasny, 2007). Like readers, authors, too, consciously and unconsciously adopt and employ certain perspectives in their writing. Critical perspectives are a response to the various ways in which people experience the world. In Chapter 6, we will look more closely at how literature has contributed both to the construction of gendered roles and, alternately, to the potential for social change.

Pace and Townsend's Study of High School and College-Level Students' Response to *Hamlet*: The Importance of Instructional Approach

Pace and Townsend's (1999) study, which documented how two classes undertook the evaluation of Gertrude's behavior in *Hamlet*, is insightful insofar as it advances the argument that instructional context is paramount to whether or not students can actively engage in the critical deconstruction of societal and cultural frameworks that shape our perceptions and textual understanding. The authors compared classroom talk in response to the study of *Hamlet* in a first-year college literature class and an 11th-grade literature class. In the first-year college class, the male teacher adopted a transmission model of instruction whereby he assumed the role of expert and looked for the "right answers" when it came to textual interpretation. The authors noted that as the semester progressed, students' voices became increasingly silent. The college classroom teacher clearly privileged the perspective of Hamlet over that of Gertrude and assumed the tradition of presenting the protagonist in canonical literature as representative of all human experience. Not surprisingly, the authors found that in the college classroom, students' voiced perceptions of Gertrude and Hamlet were grounded in gendered stereotypes to the extent that biases against women seemed to represent some universal truth.

By contrast, the female teacher in the 11th-grade classroom employed more open-ended methods and used modeling and critical questioning to solicit student responses to characters and the plot. Guided in large part by the teacher's language of encouragement—"you have to make up your mind as you go along" (p. 46)—and instruction that honored the ambiguous nature of the study of literature, the grade 11 students openly shared a variety of views when interpreting characters' actions. Students initiated their own inquiry and used text referencing, a strategy modeled by the teacher, as a means of supporting their responses. As a consequence, exchanges among students and with the teacher allowed for a more complex under-standing of human behavior that made more stereotypical responses to the text problematic.

GENDERED READING PRACTICES AND PREFERENCES

Despite the fact that studies investigating reading preferences of children and adults date back more than a hundred years, trends are more difficult to document that one might think (Purves & Beach, 1972; Sebesta & Monson, 1991, 2003; Zimet, 1963). For example, who could have antici-pated the *Harry Potter* phenomenon that held an entire generation of girls and boys enthralled on a global scale to guarantee Harry a permanent spot in the cultural psyche of both child and adult? There are, of course, any number of competing and compelling theories that attempt to explain the Potter phenomenon from a wide range of disciplines including psychology and marketing (Brown & Patterson, 2010: Patterson & Brown, 2009), cul-tural studies (Lanier & Schau, 2007), and literary and narrative studies (Lopez, 2008), but research to date on reading preferences alone cannot fully account for the unprecedented success of J. K. Rowling's boy wizard. As discussed in the chapter to come on adolescent and children's literature, the *Harry Potter* books do fulfill many of our traditional gender expec-tations. Of particular relevance to this discussion on gendered reading pref-erences, however, is that Rowling was asked by her publisher to use her initials in place of her first name "Joanne" in order to mask her gender as a woman. It makes one wonder whether Harper Lee's *To Kill a Mockingbird* would have reached such canonical heights if the cover of this remarkable work had borne this female author's more feminine first name "Nelle." Publishers, like advertisers, are keenly aware of how constructions of gender determine marketing strategies, and Rowling's publisher feared that a novel written by a female author would not attract their target audience of boy readers. If nothing else, Rowling's success dispels the myth that female authors cannot pen a novel of interest to young boys. The degree to which publishers shape children's reading interests and preferences and the extent to which the characters in Harry Potter conform or break with gendered expectations are discussed more fully in Chapter 6.

Zimet's (1966) review of early literature documenting children's reading interests concluded that children's reading interests are sociohistorically sit-uated; that is to say, "children's stories tend to reflect the times, which in turn tend to mold interests" (p. 124). For example, Browman and Templin (1959) report that the preferences of children from 1925 to 1939 were dif-ferent from the preferences of children from 1952 to 1955. This suggests that reading preferences are rather fluid and, like reading engagement, are subject to environmental factors. Zimet's (1966) justification for exploring children's reading interests speaks directly to this twenty-first-century discussion on gendered reading practices:

> Since it has ... been ascertained that children's interest reflect the cultural and biological sex-role expectations of our society, it would seem reasonable to conclude that children's books play a vital role in communicating attitudes and cultural values. (p. 124)

It was Zimet who first recognized that there were both broad consistencies and conflicting results across a variety of early studies investigating children's reading interests and preferences. Differences between findings were believed to be due to variables related to population samples. Zimet claimed that populations in the studies were not representative across socioeconomic, cultural, achievement, and grade levels, and hence different interest patterns emerged. In the 1960s, researchers were looking for broad generalizations from quantitative data, and Zimet's critique today would support the contention that when it comes to books "one size does not fit all." She concluded that while the findings regarding interests of boys and girls received the greatest amount of agreement, factors such as "the times, age, maturity, socio-educational background, story illustrations, and availability of books" (p. 128) also worked in tandem to determine reading interests. Early studies provide evidence to suggest that children tend to like narrative forms with lively action, humor, and nonsense (Purves & Beach, 1972), and that girls' and boys' reading preferences begin to diverge in the upper elementary school years (grades 4 to 6) (Landy, 1977; Lynch-Brown, 1977; Wolfson, Manning, & Manning, 1984). By fourth grade, boys exhibit a stronger preference for nonfiction, and girls show a greater preference for realistic fiction. But reading interests change as children mature, and variables other than gender are clearly at play. For example, Baraks, Hoffman, and Bauer (1997) surveyed grade 4 and 5 students and found that while boys more often preferred fantasy and girls realistic fiction, inner-city children demonstrated a tendency to choose fantasy and suburban children realistic fiction. Several studies in the 1980s (Bundy, 1983; Graham, 1986; Hawkins, 1983) provided evidence that among intermediate or middle-years students, both boys and girls display an interest in reading mystery and adventure. By upper intermediate or junior high years, girls' and boys' reading interests continue to diverge but converge when it comes to certain genres. Notably, grade 7 and 8 girls exhibit a preference for mystery, romance, animals, religion, career stories, comedy, and biography. Boys, on the other hand, prefer science fiction, adventure, history, and sports but share girls' penchant for biography, animals, and mystery with their female counterparts. During these early teen years, both girls and boys display a growing interest in nonfiction, historical fiction, romance, and coming-of-age tales that deal with issues and concerns related to adolescence

(Carlsen, 1967; Carter & Harris, 1982; Gallo, 1983; McBroom, 1981; Smith & Eno, 1961; Strang, 1946). By senior high years, many students tend to read adult tales, and generally, required texts and supplemental reading associated with most language arts curricula would reflect this trend in reading preferences, combining a blend of canonical works and contemporary fiction.

Early studies that tended to rely on instruments constructed according to preconceptions about what children would be interested in reading have come under critique. Researchers presented young readers with limited text choices representative of what they already believed would captivate a younger audience and therefore contributed to the adult construction of the field of "children's literature" and ultimate findings of their studies. For example, such studies would hardly begin to capture young girls' and boys' genuine interest in exploring sexuality in the pages of adult novels, soft-porn magazines (even my brothers learned to say that they read *Playboy* for the articles), tabloids and screen magazines provided in ample quantity by the local beauty parlor, and household medical dictionaries. Furthermore, Purves and Beach (1972) point out that studies that rely on responses to synopses of texts to determine children's interest may not have adequately represented the key qualities of the particular works surveyed. In that regard, Purves and Beach argue that the findings from such studies may be misleading and say more about a child's preference for particular literary devices or writing styles than the genre itself. To these critiques I add one of my own. Most works do not fall neatly into a single genre, and more and more, children's and adolescent literature reflects hybridity. *The Magic School Bus* series made popular in the 1990s provides an explicit example of hybridity of genre. The series combines multiple modes of representation to include both nonfiction and fiction texts. On any one page or double-page spread, the reader may encounter a traditional narrative text, speech balloons containing dialogue among fictional characters, scientific diagrams rendered as illustrations, and notebook pages with facts and experiments popping up as marginalia, all coordinated under the narrative umbrella of a field-trip adventure with Miss Frizzle aboard a magical school bus. We still have a lot to learn about how the introduction of multiple modes of representation in texts such as these may alter the way we read and process information. We can say, however, that in light of the findings on gendered reading preferences, the *Magic School Bus* would seemingly satisfy early childhood readers' shared preferences for lively action, humor, and even nonsense while at the same time addressing the diverging interests among girls and boys as they transition to the intermediate elementary years by combining fiction and nonfiction. The careful coordination of aspects of multiple genres may have served to broaden the series' appeal to capture the imagination of both boys and girls across a range of ages, and this, in turn, may account in part for the series' initial and continued commercial success.

Other examples of hybrids include historical fiction, fictional biographies, biographical fictions, docudramas, graphic novels, science fiction, and romantic comedy. Scholars working in genre studies argue that the novel itself can be considered a hybrid as it combines aspects of classic tragedy and comedy in a form that is appealing and accessible to the masses. The introduction to Jonathan Frow's (2005) *Genre* states:

> Genre is a key means by which we categorize the many forms of literature and culture. However, it is also much more than that: in talk and writing, in music and images, in film and television, genres actively generate and shape our knowledge of the world. Genre is a dynamic process rather than a set of stable rules. (n.p.)

Bakhtin (1986, 1981) in *Speech Genres and Other Essays* and in his essay "Discourse in the Novel" contended that cultural forms such as the novel are complex means of communication in which multiple "speech genres" collude to convey to an audience particular themes and the author's plan within the more relatively stable compositional forms available. A speech genre denotes a mode of communication, everything from newspaper headlines and grocery lists to formal letters and lyric poetry. Each has socially agreed-upon rules that evolve over time, with some becoming obsolete as new discursive modes take shape. Educational research focusing on gendered preferences is motivated in part by a concern that all children gain the experience and skills to construct meaning from a wide range of texts. As the options for print-based and visual media have increased, so too have the possibilities for multimodal discourse. In other words, we recognize that we are not just reading the word, both in the sense that any work is bound to reflect the sociocultural context within which it is produced and received but also in the sense that our discursive imagination has expanded to accommodate the "word" or message in a myriad of ways. The dynamic nature of genre as a means for categorizing literature and culture suggests two important considerations as they relate to identifying gendered reading preferences according to genre:

1. A genre can be widely comprehensive (e.g., fiction, nonfiction, novel, historical) or relatively precise (e.g., eighteenth-century English epistolary novel, medical journal article), and different researchers are bound to use different categories and subcategories to yield different results.

Children too, draw their own lines. Take for example, C. S. Lewis's *The Lion, the Witch and the Wardrobe* from the *Chronicles of Narnia*. What one child refers to as adventure another may claim as fantasy, and yet another a book about sibling relationships. Lewis himself had categorized his works as fairy tales, but many critics have been persistent in the claim that the *Chronicles* are mainly a Christian allegory.

2. Any genre can be represented by a variety of forms (e.g., printed text, picture book, webpage, e-book, graphic novel, comic book, multimedia clip, film, opera, dance, drama, interactive video game), and therefore it makes sense for studies documenting gendered reading preferences to account for demonstrated preferences for certain styles and forms.

For example, is reading history more appealing to either gender when rendered as a graphic novel, as in Art Spiegelman's (1973) *MAUS: A Survivor's Tale* or Chester Brown's (2003) *Louis Riel: A Comic-Strip Biography*? Survey studies to date investigating genre preferences tell us little about how much of a child's stated love of mystery and adventure may be tied to a weekly TV drama and not necessarily to his or her choice in books. Indeed, there is a growing contention that TV and popular culture texts may be more significant sources of learning for children than traditional print texts (de Castell, 2000; Luke, 1996; Stack & Kelly, 2006). Ethnographic interviews, on the other hand, may tell us the extent to which the TV drama provoked an interest in reading mystery and whether the viewer has extended this interest to reading traditional texts. One thing is clear, however: literacy researchers have to move beyond investigations of traditional print literacy if they are to capture gendered preferences for various genres across multiple representations and attempt to account for the intertextual influence of media discourses.

A third consideration relates more to the notion of "personal taste," which can be fleeting and highly subject to current educational trends, political sway, popular culture, product availability, and advertising campaigns that all combine to make reading a commercial and profitable industry and to demonstrate that personal taste may not be so personal (Luke, 1996; Zipes, 2001). Jacqueline Rose (1984) has argued the impossibility of children's literature because, in her view, it is ultimately a construct of adult writers, publishers, and caregivers. Renowned children's literature scholar Jack Zipes also makes a cogent argument against the existence of children's literature as a genre. In his chapter, "Why Children's Literature Does Not Exist," Zipes (2001) adopts a Marxist perspective in detailing the social constructs shaped by socioeconomic conditions. These conditions are different for different cultures and determine varying conceptualizations of childhood. However, in this increasingly global economy, Zipes's contention gives us pause to think about the homogenizing effects of the "Disneyfication" of childhood. Licensed T-shirts, toys, books, comic books, movies, and vacation dreams pervade a global market and continue to contribute to a growing standardization of what we perceive as childhood. Similarly, McVeigh's (2000) study of the Hello Kitty phenomenon demonstrates

the way in which an icon/product of popular culture/industry such as Hello Kitty teaches us how the purchasing and collecting practices of a group of people, refracted through the mass media (TV, newspapers, comics) and reflected off the surfaces of public space (advertising copy, signs, interiors of post offices, etc.), manufacture a massive field of desire (e.g., pursuit of being cute, cool, feminine, in-group status, nostalgia). (p. 227)

Hello Kitty's market endurance profits from gender construction across ages because, beyond its obvious "cool" appeal for younger girls, it plays to its "camp" appeal for older teens and young adults, making it the ultimate collectible.

While our social constructions of childhood may have inevitably led to a view of children and childhood as investments and commodities (Zipes, 2001), on the more positive side, the entire field of children's rights rests on some consensus of what defines childhood and the rights and protection it involves. Nevertheless, childhood will continue to remain a contested territory and, as such, requires our active attention to the conditions that contribute to gender boundaries that determine choice and potentially hamper optimum development. Toddlers and preschoolers are socialized into gendered patterns of play, social values, behaviors, attitudes, and language through an intertextual universe connecting television to movies, video games, toys, licensed sportswear and clothing, games, coloring books, bed linens, lunch boxes, even supermarket convenience food (Luke, 1996). Add to that the dream of theme parks, skating extravaganzas, mall appearances, and contest prizes, and we get some sense of the extent to which young children invest meaning and representation in gendered stereotypes.

MARKETING GENDER IN CHILDREN'S BOOKS

Let's take a look at an immediate example of how gender construction is inscribed in marketing through schools. A quick survey of selections offered by Scholastic's December 2010 Seesaw Book Club Winter Sale (http://www .scholastic.ca/clubs/seesaw/) targeting early childhood readers and their parents and distributed nationally to U.S. and Canadian schools easily bears witness to a commercially constructed gender divide in children's publishing. Books on offer include *Lego City Adventure: Reading for Takeoff*, with a distinctively male uniformed Lego figure pictured alongside *Barbie in a Fashion Fairytale*; *Tangled*, a Rapunzel tale based on the latest Disney animated feature; *Megamind*, a book featuring the comedic "super villain" from the Disney/DreamWorks hit; and *Fancy Nancy* in a tutu boasting a "Holiday Hardcover with Glittery Cover." Two white covers with titles *Thanks to My Hockey Dad* and *I Love My Hockey Mom* stand out from an overrepresentation of shades of blue and pink but nevertheless spell out gendered expectations for children. The brainchild of Jason Howell, head coach of a novice hockey team, with the support of self-described "teacher/ hockey mom" Jennifer Sutoski, the books record seven- and eight-year-olds' reasons why they love their hockey moms and dads. The highlighted text in the Scholastic online and print circular reads, "thanks dad for playing end-to-end hockey in the driveway" and "I love my hockey mom for hugging me when I lose." The one cover depicts mother and child encircled in a pink rink, and the other, father and child in a more lively red. The cast is further set with the message that, ultimately, females nurture and appreciate:

> *For all the hockey moms who appreciate the simple needs of children to have fun and love and be loved.*

while males take action and need appreciating:

> *For all the hockey dads and all the things they do that are appreciated but not always acknowledged.*

The commercial potential of the works (at the at the time of writing, the books were sold out on Amazon.com) is likely to spawn similar titles such as "I Love My Soccer Mom" and "Thanks to My Soccer Dad" to sentimentalize mom for chauffeuring the team around in a minivan and dad for paying for pizzas. In *I Love My Hockey Mom*, a child actually thanks his mother for skipping work to attend games. The inclusion of the child's candid remark aimed at the reader's funny bone overlooks those mothers (and fathers) working two jobs to pay for the latest in equipment and struggling to meet registration costs on a payment plan. Recalling Zipes's assertion that children's publishing reflects the social constructs associated with particular socioeconomic conditions, we see how gendered stereotypes are projected within the values of the middle-class buying public where children's participation in organized sports is seen as the norm.

GENDER NORMALIZATION AND SCHOOLS

In my research investigating the construction of national identity in literature (Krasny, 2010), I have frequently looked to Foucault (1972) to explain how literary texts construct and sustain our conceptualization of normativity. As such, I argue that the ways we enact literacy constitutes an "axis of subjectivity" that determines, in some part, our sense of personal freedom and the set of practices we perform on ourselves. The same theoretical framework can be extended to account for the self-regulatory literacy practices in and out of schools that normalize gendered behaviors to position many girls and boys on the periphery of engaged participation, effectively confounding individual efforts at self-actualization. Wayne Martino and his colleagues (Lingard, Martino, & Mills, 2009; Martino & Pallotta-Chiarolli, 2003; Martino, Kehler, & Weaver-Hightower, 2009) have focused their attention on the ways hegemonic masculinities are legitimized in schools. For example, Martino and Pallotta-Chiarolli (2003) describe how boys negotiate their place (and situate others) in a hierarchy of masculinities through a system of surveillance.

Accordingly, "normalizing regimes of practice" (p. 4) entail "not looking like a fairy, not being too dumb, not being too smart, . . . fitting in the right groups" (Grant, 16 years, in Martino & Pallotta-Chiarolli, 2003, p. 4). Drawing on Foucault (1978), they work to uncover "the forms of power, the channels and discourses it permeates in order to reach the most tenuous and individual modes of behaviour" (p. 11). In other words, they use Foucault's framework to account for how adolescent boys relate to themselves and others as gendered subjects in maintaining heteronormative and hegemonic masculinities. Compulsory heterosexuality is a natural outgrowth of such policing actions, the normalizing effects of which we will read in Chapter 6, which have yet to be successfully countered by the collective body of contemporary young adult literature with lesbian and gay characters.

Elizabeth Dutro (2001) argues that gender is a central tension in children's choice of books. As early as kindergarten, boys' book selection is policed by other boys in ways that prevent boys from exploring gender boundaries through reading practices. According to Dutro, girls on the other hand were comfortable in their choice of *Lyle, Lyle, Crocodile* (Waber, 1973), *Frog and Toad Are Friends* (Lobel, 1970), *Where the Wild Things Are* (Sendak, 1963), and *Pinocchio* (I imagine a Disney picture-book version, given the age group), all of which, to my mind, were *not surprisingly* about males. In this case, the canonical status of both the works and their male protagonists may tend to make popular currency, rather than gender, the determining factor in these girls' book selections. But if one questions why boys won't select books about girls, then one also has to critically question why girls will select books about boys with less resistance. One also has to ask how instructional contexts have contributed and at times exacerbated the problem of the gender divide in literature selections. Dutro's (2001) study examined how a class of fifth graders read and discussed popular series books including *The Babysitters Club*, *Goosebumps*, *The American Girls*, and the *Matt Christopher* sports books to document how children circumscribe and enforce gendered reading boundaries. Dutro collaborated with the classroom teacher in implementing literature circles based on Harvey Daniel's (1994) *Literature Circles: Voice and Choice in the Student-Centered Classroom*. Her findings demonstrated that gender was always "an overt issue in the children's choices and discussion of popular series fiction," that children's actions sometimes contradicted their words insofar as boys might confide that they would like to read a book about a girl but these same boys would reject books about girls when voicing their choice more publicly, and that "[b]oys are more apt than girls to closely guard the gendered boundaries of their reading (in public)" (p. 384).

Dutro's (2001) findings should not in any way be surprising because, for the most part, popular series fictions are constructed in such as way as to profit from gendered expectations of readers and to convey simple, formulaic plots that do little to encourage critical thinking over passive consumption. The observed tendency of boys to police gendered reading behaviors more closely than girls speaks to the extent to which the consequences for transgressing patriarchal boundaries are evidently more severe for boys than for girls. The teacher in the study presented the grade 5 students with the choice of four books: *Karen's Big Sister* (Martin, 1999), a Babysitters Club Little Sisters book; *Addy Learns a Lesson* (Porter, 1993), an American Girls Book; *Super Hoops: In Your Face* (Herman, 1996), a book about basketball; and *Roger Friday: Live from the Fifth Grade* (McKenna, 1994), a book about the adventures of a group of school children. The teacher drew individual students' names from a can to determine who would make each choice in turn. Students' book selections established their membership in a particular literature circle. While Dutro's (2001) study reports on how students construct and adhere to gendered boundaries in book choice, she has failed to note that the instructional practice of providing students with such a dichotomous choice of reading materials literally handed boys with more power a ready opportunity to actively and overtly use the event to maintain their established pecking order throughout the observed book selection, and I shudder to think how the tension heightened as students made their choices in order to negotiate their status in the class. Dutro (2001) describes how boys "squirmed" as three girls selected the sports book while shooting them "smug smiles" and how certain boys intimidated other boys with threats to keep them from choosing the basketball book in an attempt to keep them out of their idealized group.

> Three girls in a row . . . walk deliberately to the front of the room and, throwing smug smiles at the boys at the front table, choose the basketball book. As the pile of basketball books grow shorter the boys' anxiety levels rise. They start squirming in their seats and whispering to each other, "Oh, man, I can't believe she took that book." As Keith, J. J., and Matthew—who are less popular, less athletic—approach the table of books, a few of the boys at the front table whisper threateningly to them under their breath, "You better not pick that basketball book, boy; you better not do it." It works. Not one of those boys chooses the sports book even though I am sure that Keith, at least, would have liked to. (Dutro, 2001, p. 378)

I want to emphasize that I am certain this is not what Harvey Daniels (1994) means when he writes about literature circles offering voice and choice in the classroom. The study demonstrates the instructional strategy is only as good as its implementation. Because the students themselves did not nominate the texts for study, they are hardly representative of a student-centered literacy curriculum, and I am dismayed at the thought that the selected works represented the mainstay of a purported literature-based program. Establishing literature circles as a more democratic means of literacy instruction takes considerable time that includes working with students in laying some ground rules and supporting them in their facilitation of groups and book nominations.

As a researcher and educator, I admit to having serious concerns about how Dutro and the teacher set the conditions for observation. While it may not have been their intent to create an instructional context that would pit student against student in this way for the sake of observation, I would have expected them to intervene and put a stop to it. As I have indicated, there is little to be learned from the highly contrived book selection event apart from what we already know. With merely titles and pastel-colored covers to guide them, students could have been making selections among any gendered commodity—birthday cakes, toys, or T-shirts—as a means determining membership in groups, and we likely could have watched the same social dynamics unfold. Having conducted literature circles with adults and children of all ages for more than a decade, I can report that I have never witnessed the kind of ruthlessness in which students' book choices were reportedly policed in this study. Educators and researchers need to work together to ensure that investigations do not compromise instructional integrity or perpetuate unnecessary emotional harm. The study constructs book selection as an activity independent from the actual book study in literature groups, and the less-than-complex plots and character portrayals in the books invite rather superficial and predictable gendered responses. Most of all, while I think that series books can satisfy the need to read for many (certainly, my childhood reading is marked by *Nancy Drew*, the *Hardy Boys*, and the boarding school adventures in Enid Blyton's *The Naughtiest Girl* series), I believe the thematically light and formulaic structure hardly merits the extensive time and effort on the part of students and teachers that goes into making literature circles a hallmark of more egalitarian instruction. The works might invite quick deconstruction, but students' responses didn't indicate that they were read in that manner or even invited to do so. While I found the results of Dutro's (2000) study rather predictable given the manner in which book selection was structured as a class activity, the students' responses unintentionally went a long way to illustrate how limited popular series are in challenging taken-for-granted stereotypes. Literature study should aim to engage students at this age in the discussion of complex and increasingly abstract themes (which can include gender) and in describing how various literary elements (i.e., character, plot, setting) interact to convey those themes. Even younger children are able to generate deep discussion about socially relevant themes derived from literature that can include race and gender. If in doubt, just take a look at Vivian Gussein Paley's (1997) *The Girl with the Brown Crayon* that documents an entire kindergarten curriculum based on Leo Lionni's fables. Paley's unorthodox curriculum provides rich literary terrain for discovery as children engage in questioning and debating the characters' traits and actions with persistent connections to their daily lives.

While I find Dutro's (2001) study limited in providing insight into gendered reading practices beyond how easy it is to perpetuate gendered book selection among students, I find studies focusing on the psychological functions of romance reading among girls and women more intriguing and insightful. Their detailed analysis offers readers a chance to explore how such idealized narratives provide female readers a symbolic gratification (Radway, 1984)—that is to say, to address "basic psychological needs . . . that have been induced by the culture and its social structures but that often remain unmet in their day-to-day existence" (pp. 112–13). Cherland's (1994) year-long ethnographic study of girls' fictional reading and identity construction introduces readers to how romance reading might function as a form of resistance for young girls—a kind of release from patriarchal expectations—and offer an escape from the "constant demands of being good" (p. 173). Similarly, Janice Radway's (1984) earlier study of the Smithton readers, a group consisting largely of middle-class, married mothers, demonstrates how reading romance novels allowed these women to "thwart cultural expectations" (p. 211), even for a short time. Unfortunately, despite readers' resistant aims, it is difficult not to conclude that popular romance ultimately reconciles women and girls to patriarchal values (Krasny, 2012).

While much has been written on girls' reading preferences, in particular, their continued fascination with the romance novel, it is only recently that researchers have undertaken the study of boys' reading preferences. Martino (2001) investigated the impact of masculinities on boys' reading preferences and involvement in literacy in one Catholic, coeducational Western Australian high school. He surveyed 42 boys to document the ways particular versions of masculinity inform adolescent boys' reading preferences and involvement in literacy. Martino identified three groups to correspond with patterns in the way boys responded to survey questions. Group 1, which accounted for 18 of the 42 surveyed (42.8 percent), consisted of those boys who rejected reading and claimed that it was boring, setting reading against more preferable activities including watching TV or playing sports. Nevertheless, many of the boys in this group did claim that they enjoyed reading magazines related to sports and surfing. Group 2, which accounted for 12 of the 42 surveyed (28.6%), consisted of those boys who did not refer to reading as "boring" but expressed a preference for reading only certain kinds of texts, mostly stereotypical subgenres of action, fantasy, science fiction, horror, and humorous stories. Many within this group stated their preference for nonfiction texts over fiction. Martino concluded that the boys' desire for reading particular kinds of magazines and fictional texts corresponds to "the ways in which particular regimes of masculinity operate in their lives such that their involvement in particular literacy practices outside of school confirms a culturally sanctioned version of masculinity" (p. 2). Group 3, which also accounted for 28.6 percent of the 42 boys surveyed, enjoyed reading or saw it as an escape. According to Martino, while a number of these boys still expressed a preference for the stereotypical subgenres, they did not value nonfiction over fiction, and five noted that reading fiction provided a form of escape.

In analyzing his findings, Martino suggests that boys in Group 1 employed a dualistic logic and a gender regime in which masculinity and femininity are viewed as polar opposites. Martino cites "Damien's" response as being representative of a number of boys in this group:

> I don't really like reading novels. I like reading mags (Playboy) but in today's society there are so many other things of leisure to do. I still read about two or three books a year, but I mean when a book comes up against TV or computer or kicking the footy with friends, mate! It has no chance. I read computer, surf, porn, footy and fishing mags because they're quick and interesting to me. (cited in Martino, 2001, p. 4)

Martino points to the frequency with which boys from both Groups 1 and 2 referred to a preference for reading pornography as one example of how the deployment of heterosexuality plays a part in their engagement with literacy practices outside of the officially sanctioned curriculum and asks us to consider "Neil's" response, in which such choices are consistent with heterosexual masculinity:

> I like reading magazines like sport and surfing and of course like any male would, except if you're gay—girlie mags aren't that bad either. I enjoy those texts because they're interesting and some are enjoyable to find out about sport and that kind of stuff including girl of the month. (cited in Martino, 2001, p. 4)

Martino concludes that the boys in Groups 1 and 2, who tended to organize their reading around practices and interest such as sport, TV, and computer-related activities and to devalue fictional reading, is tied to the ways these boys have learned to police and enact forms of hegemonic heterosexual masculinity. Among those boys in Groups 2 and 3 who indicated that they enjoy reading fiction, most expressed an interest in the subgenres of science fiction, action/adventure, fantasy, crime fiction, thrillers, and humorous stories.

MOVING ON

More recent research into gendered reading preferences indicates that boys' stated preferences are closely tied to performing masculinity. Girls are less likely to be guided by gender allegiance than boys in expressing an interest for certain genres and in making their selections, although this is not to say that gender does not play an important role in structuring girls' reading choices. Reading romance, for example, has held a special fascination for girls, and some would argue that it allows girls to read as a form of resistance as they are able to assume even temporarily the chance to enact the kind of life society has taught them is theirs to live but which, in actuality, is a far cry from routine reality. Purves and Beach's (1972) review of early research related to gendered reading preferences revealed that many of the studies appearing before the 1970s were methodologically flawed and often incorporated the researchers' own biases about children's range of interests as it relates to the list of selected passages or book titles from which children were to indicate their preferences. Zimet's (1966) early review of the research also pointed to inconsistencies in the findings that she believed could be accounted for in part by variables related to population samples. She concluded that while one could discern some broad consistencies regarding gendered reading preferences, by and large, taste is a rather fickle thing insofar as it is socially and historically situated and, I would add, further conflated by the fact that genre is rather malleable—a dynamic process rather than a set of stable rules (Frow, 2005). Overall, given the research at hand, one can say with relative confidence that children's reading choices are subject to the convergence of any number of influences, resulting in reading patterns and practices that are highly gendered, becoming increasingly more so as children move into adolescence (Hall & Coles, 1999).

One cannot ignore the overwhelming degree to which children's choices are already largely determined by adults. As books are published by adults for an adult buying public, Zipes (2001) cautions against the homogenizing effects of globalization as a rampant form of cultural colonization and cites the Disneyfication of childhood as a major means of deployment.

CHAPTER 6

Reading Gender in Children's and Adolescent Literature

In my former role as a language arts curriculum coordinator, I was involved in the division-wide implementation of a national arts program that established sustained partnerships between teachers and artists with the aim of enhancing student achievement in core subject areas and fostering creative thinking and problem solving. The integration of music, dance, drama, creative writing, visual arts, and film making provided students with opportunities to work collaboratively and to exercise judgment about qualitative relationships. They learned how to think through a particular medium, plan, strategize with others, and assume multiple perspectives. Storytelling was seen as a vehicle to assist students in conflict resolution. The program provides ongoing professional development for artists and educators, and in one particular storytelling workshop, I was struck by both the featured story and the audience's response. What follows is my attempt to recreate the story and the event.

A talented and well-known storyteller began the tale of three Cossacks who rode late into the night until it was time to lay their heads down to rest. Fearful that they might come under attack, each agreed to take turns standing guard while the other two slept. The first Cossack to stand watch was Ivan. Ivan was a rather talented wood carver, so to pass the time he decided to carve a figure of a woman from a block of wood. When he was finished, he gazed at his creation and was pleased at how beautifully he had fashioned her face. There wasn't much time to admire his work, for it was now his riding companion's turn to stand guard. Ivan lay down to rest, and the second Cossack to stand watch was Taras. Taras, it turned out, was a skilled weaver, and to pass the time he took to weaving the beautiful figure of a woman the finest of cloth. Once he had clothed her, he stepped back to admire his handiwork, but by this time his guard duty, too, had ended and it was time for the third companion to take his turn. The third Cossack to stand watch was Petro. Unlike the first two, who took pride in their handiwork, Petro's talent was his ability to captivate audiences with his speech. Struck by the beautiful creature before him, to pass the time he set about to teach the figure to speak. By the end of his watch, the beautiful figure had come to life and now spoke and sang in the most melodic voice.

It was at this time that the first two Cossacks awoke. It came as no surprise that all three men immediately fell in love with what they each saw as their creation. They soon fell into arguing about who should marry the beautiful woman. Ivan argued that it was he who gave her form and therefore he should have her as his bride. Taras argued that it was he who dressed her and made her beautiful and therefore he should have her as his bride. And Petro argued that it was he who gave her voice and therefore he should have her as his bride. They argued for hours until they all agreed that they should ask the wise man who lived at the top of the mountain (where else?), and they would abide by his decision. The Cossacks mounted their horses and were each satisfied to share their mount with the beautiful woman for at least part of the way up. When they reached the top of the mountain, they found the sage in his hut of mud walls and thatch. They immediately set out to ask the wise man: "Oh, Wise One, please tell us, who shall have this beautiful woman's hand." Ivan shouted: "Wise One, it is I who gave her form." Taras called out: "But Wise One, it is I who made her beautiful!" And finally Petro spoke up: "But Wise One, it is I who gave her the gift of voice." The old sage looked past the three men and gazed directly at the young woman. At this point in the story, the storyteller turns to the predominantly female audience of educators and asks, "And what do you think he replied?"

The storyteller had no sooner got the question out when virtually the entire audience shouted forth excitedly, "He lets her choose! He lets her choose!" At this point, the storyteller turns to me and asks, "Karen, what do you think he will say?" I found myself dumbfounded and tongue-tied—first at a story that I realize the entire room appeared to have accepted as heralding a woman's right to speak and second at the prospect of actually voicing my opinion among the happy crowd and possibly offending the storyteller. I mumbled something about whether there is interest in knowing my thoughts from a feminist perspective and registered some distress on the storyteller's face before he continued with the predictable conclusion. The woman in the story doesn't choose any of the eager suitors, and the reason seems totally immaterial and I have forgotten it. What I heard was that man gave woman life, voice, and the freedom to live. Even her right to choose was granted by the old man of the mountain. The story also reinforced that woman's desirability defines her worth and that her desirability is a function of her beauty. It is not that I am any more evolved a feminist than the women around me who cheered on the ending. Some feminists would argue that my response was not radical enough, choosing to write about it later rather than risk further offending the storyteller or making my fellow delegates uneasy. Where the audience, swept up by a compelling performance, heard a tale of liberation, I heard good intentions gone awry. Entire civilizations have invested much in the belief that woman draws life from man. This is a clear example of Audre Lorde's (2007) reminder that "old patterns, no matter how cleverly rearranged to imitate progress still condemn us to . . . repetitions of the same exchanges" (p. 123). In evaluating adolescent and children's literature, one must be mindful of the structures that maintain "old patterns"—archetypes and stereotypes in even the most contemporary works of fiction that relegate females to the rank of what Simone de Beauvoir (1952) referred to as the second sex or, as we shall also see, that work to define the perceived boundaries of gendered expression among culturally diverse populations.

Explore

Most everyone can remember a book that has had an impact on her or his life. Often this story is connected to a pleasurable experience. It may have been a book read to you as a child or possibly the first book you learned to read. It may have been a book that provoked interest or inspiration. Recall a special book that sticks out in your mind and jot down the title and record two reasons why the book is important to you. If you can locate a copy, set it aside. After reading this chapter, critically reflect on your selection. What new perspectives do you bring to this old favorite?

SPEECHLESSNESS AS METAPHOR

Sandra Gilbert and Susan Gubar (1979) contend that aphasia, or speechlessness, constitutes one of the defining literary metaphors of nineteenth-century feminine repression (p. 58). In light of Brown and Gilligan's (1992) documentation of silencing among adolescent girls, it is not surprising that this social phenomenon should manifest itself in contemporary literature written for young people and adults. In her book *Waking Sleeping Beauty: Feminist Voices in Children's Novels*, Roberta Seelinger Trites (1997) cogently argues that twentieth-century narratives that depict female investment in subjectivity, that is to say, in claiming power within oneself to grow and celebrate, tend to focus on the protagonist's articulateness. As Trites points out, as a metaphor, speechlessness "has certainly had an active life in twentieth-century women's narratives, as novels such as Margaret Atwood's *The Handmaid's Tale* (1986) and films such as *The Piano* (1993) demonstrate" (pp. 47–48). Pointing to feminist writers from Virginia Woolf to Adrienne Rich, Elaine Showalter (1981) calls for a feminist critique that would concentrate on women's access to language, one that examines "the available lexical range from which words can be selected, on the ideological and cultural determinants of expression." "The problem," as she sees it, "is not that language is insufficient to express women's consciousness but that women have been denied the full resources of language and have been forced into silence, euphemism, or circumlocution" (p. 193).

Trites (1997) highlights a number of texts written for children and young adults that can provide "an important counterbalance to traditional depictions of female passivity" (p. 47). She points to the works of three feminist writers for children—Patricia McLaughlin, Mildred B. Taylor, and Munlong Ho—whose novels carefully construct the female characters' recognition that their voice only exists in dialogue with others. For example, 10-year-old Cassie, the protagonist in Mildred B. Taylor's (1981) *Let the Circle Be Unbroken*, experiences speechlessness in response to her confusion over her identity or difference from others within her rural Mississippi community during the Depression. While Cassie is depicted as an articulate girl willing to voice her opinion, she is subject to continual reminders from those around her to keep silent. In one instance, Cassie is invited by her parents to come along to support an elderly friend's efforts to register to vote. Cassie's mother is adamant: "We decided you should go because it's important that you see this. But, Cassie, I expect you to keep that mouth of yours shut. I don't want to hear one word out of you all the while we're in that office, do you hear me? I'll do the talking" (pp. 353–54). Cassie remains quiet throughout, but the reader is privy to the dialogue within as Cassie formulates her comments in response to the event.

Cassie's vocal expression also comes at the expense of her older brother Stacey's constant interruptions. Cassie's frustration is exacerbated by her parents' tolerance of her brother's interruptions. She catches herself editing her expression in response to the clear message that her brother's voice is valued more than hers. Her unspoken comments such as "I started to say something, but decided I'd better not" (p. 49) and "I wisely kept quiet" signal to the reader the frequency to which Cassie is forced to repress her voice. Nevertheless, Cassie never doubts her inner voice. As Trites (1997) explains, Cassie comes to some understanding of the social dynamics that have perpetuated the silencing of an entire people and how that silencing, in turn, creates the frustration that would have her brother aggressively exert his control over her. The novel provides us with a sense of how the interrelationships among age, gender, class, and race have come to shape the sibling relationship between Cassie and Stacey and how through it all Cassie is determined to maintain her voice.

Novels typically demonstrating the female path to vocalization reflect a self-reliance and a refusal to silence their inner voices, which ultimately leads to strengthening their public voice (Trites, 1997). The climax of *Let the Circle Be Unbroken* comes at the point when Stacey accepts Cassie's voice and actually expresses his desire for her to talk to him. It is at this point that

Cassie is aware that she exercises her agency in dialogic relation to others, that is to say, that her agency can have an effect on others and, in turn, the opinions and responses of others will affect her subjectivity. While I agree with Trites's assertion that Cassie's aphasia or voicelessness is never complete because her inner voice is never silenced, I would argue, too, that her feminine silence is never fully transformed insofar as her outward expression is legitimized through her male brother's acceptance. Sounds familiar—remember the folktale of the three Cossacks. It is as if he has given her permission to speak. The act of granting Cassie the chance to speak her mind compromises to no small degree the engaged subjectivity that would fully transcend feminine silence. Taylor has circumscribed the temporal and spatial contours for her realistic fiction. Providing a neat and tidy solution is simply not in keeping with the complex existence of being an African American girl in Mississippi during the Depression. As Trites (1997) aptly points out, for Cassie, identity is tied to recognizing "the sources of her marginalization" (p. 51). In my view, it is not the author's job to deliver complete transcendence but to offer up to the reader the chance to confront and work through those difficult moments of silence. Yet providing ample opportunities whereby students feel confident to express their views in response to texts like these is not without problems. Possible pathways to providing greater access to voice in the classrooms and schools are discussed in subsequent chapters.

FEMININE SUBJECTIVITY IN THE *KÜNSTLERROMAN*

According to Marianne Hirsch (1979), the *Bildungsroman*, or coming-of-age novel, is characterized by the story of an individual's growth and development within the context of a particular social order. It usually encompasses the *Entwicklungsroman*, or a novel that focuses on the education of the self. As a literary genre, it constitutes a unique conceptual framework that contributes to how we think about, imagine, and experience the world (Bell, 2009). Hirsch identifies some general criteria that would seem to apply in varying degrees to all *Bildungsroman*. First, the process of psychological and moral growth entails a quest in which the protagonist searches for a meaningful existence within society. Second, the hero or heroine is spurred on a journey by some loss or restlessness that takes her or him away from home or family comforts. Third, the protagonist's maturation process is represented in the novel as a long and arduous journey, one in which the protagonist's needs and desires come into continual clash with an unyielding social order. And finally, the protagonist locates her- or himself within the existing social order as she or he comes to embody societal values.

The genre dates to 1795 with the publication of Goethe's *The Apprenticeship of Wilhelm Meister*, yet earlier works written by Fielding and others exemplify the thematic features found in Goethe's defining work. Examples of the *Bildungsroman* include Henry Fielding's (1749) *The*

History of Tom Jones, a Foundling, Jean-Jacques Rousseau's (1761) *Emile: or On Education,* Charlotte Bronte's (1847) *Jane Eyre,* Charles Dickens's (1850, 1861) *David Copperfield* and *Great Expectations,* Lucy Maud Montgomery's (1908) *Anne of Green Gables,* and Marjorie Kinnan Rawlings's (1938) *The Yearling.* J. D. Salinger's (1951) *The Catcher in the Rye* remains a popular *Bildungsroman* on the high school canon, and more contemporary titles that correspond to the *Bildungsroman* include Khaled Hosseini's (2003) *The Kite Runner,* Miriam Toews's (2004) *A Complicated Kindness,* and David Mitchell's (2007) *Black Swan Green.*

Elizabeth Abel, Marianne Hirsh, and Elizabeth Langland (1983) have noted several differences in the female protagonist's growth when compared with that of her male counterparts in coming-of-age novels. Most significantly, the female's potential for growth and development is tied to her relationships with others. And perhaps no less striking a difference, where the male protagonist of the *Bildungsroman* goes forth into the world, the female protagonist's journey is often one of retreat.

Many female *Bildungsromane* fall into the specialized category of the *Künstlerroman* whereby development is marked by growth as an artist. Trites (1997) describes how the heroine's self-identification as an artist is balanced or negated by a love relationship and points to Jo March of Louisa May Alcott's (1868) *Little Women,* who abandons her self-perception as a writer to marry Professor Bhaer. Most intriguing, Trites identifies within the genre of the children's *Künstlerroman* a subgenre, the feminist *Künstlerroman,* in which growth is demonstrated through the protagonist's identification and desire to be a writer. The degree to which the protagonist engages in writing in self-defining ways varies in these works, and Trites contrasts Lois Lowry's (1979) *Anastasia Krupnik,* for whom writing represents only one of a number of activities, with Louise Fitzhugh's (1964) *Harriet the Spy,* who serves as the prototypical protagonist of the feminist children's *Künstlerroman.* Harriet is among those characters for whom language is "primary to their self-creation, and they live through words, ultimately recognizing that they are powerless without them" (p. 65). As Trites explains, writing in her notebook as she does while spying on people, Harriet objectifies the world and locates her place within it. For example, we read that Mrs. Plummer is "BORING" (Fitzhugh, 1964, p. 45) and Franca Dei Santi is "DULL" (p. 57). More telling, in reference to the Robinsons, Harriet records: "SOME PEOPLE THINK THEY'RE PERFECT BUT...I'M GLAD I'M NOT PERFECT—I'D BE BORED TO DEATH" (p. 68). Her life comes to a screeching halt when her notebook is taken from her, leaving her quite powerless: "Without a notebook she couldn't play spy, she couldn't take notes, she couldn't play Town, she couldn't do anything. She was afraid to go and buy another one, and for once she didn't feel like reading" (p. 257). Harriet, like Emily in Jean Little's (1970) *Look through My Window* and Bridie McShane in Mollie Hunter's (1972) *A Sound of Chariots,* knows that language and writing are the vehicles through which she can claim her subjectivity. It is the means through which these girls maintain their voice and reject the silencing imposed by their respective cultures (Trites, 1997). Harriet's eventual integration comes at the point when she is able to imagine herself as others might see her and she comes to the realization that she is the target of her classmates' secretly formed The Spy Catcher Club.

Of particular relevance to this discussion on gender and literacy is the observation that the protagonist of the feminist children's *Künstlerroman* need not be female. I was immediately intrigued by Trites's (1997) discussion of Beverly Cleary's (1983) epistolary novel *Dear Mr. Henshaw* as it was a book that I had taken up with a group of grade 4 and 5 students some years ago. As part of a second grade assignment, Leigh Botts writes a letter to his favorite author, Mr. Henshaw. The author responds with a number of questions for Leigh, and the two begin a correspondence that documents Leigh's struggles with his parents' divorce, his father's lack of availability, and his anxieties about being the new kid. Mr. Henshaw convinces Leigh to record his thoughts and feelings in a diary, and the novel changes from a letter format to a diary. Like many of the protagonists in the feminist children's *Künstlerroman*, Leigh eventually takes his writing public—a sign that he is successfully integrating into the wider world around him.

Trites is careful to point out that not all novels written about a child writing are a feminist children's *Künstlerroman* and cites Sheila Greenwald's (1980) works as novels in which girls use writing as a way into romantic relationships. Where writing is the primary means of claiming subjectivity for Harriet and Leigh, it comes a distant second to gaining a boy's attention for Franny Dillman in *It All Began with Jane Eyre: Or, the Secret Life of Franny Dillman*.

PERFORMING MASCULINITIES AND CROSS-DRESSING POSSIBILITIES

While Trites identifies the possibility of writing a feminist *Künstlerroman* about a male character, literacy researcher Helen Harper (2007) describes how female protagonists enact masculinities in selected young adult novels about girls. She concludes that while the characters in these works were limited in their portrayal of masculinities, the novels under study offered readers "more complex renderings of gendered identity in the lives of female and male adolescent characters, addressed the effects of enforced traditional masculinity, and ... disrupted the connection between sex and gender [to] allow for engagement with alternative notions of masculinity" (p. 508). Harper contends that while a growing number of studies investigate the representation of masculinity in children's books in general (Bean & Harper, 2007; Nodelman, 2002; Stephens, 2002), girls' books can tell us a lot about masculinity from a relational standpoint. Citing Connell (1995), she reminds readers that in Western thought, the terms *masculinity* and *femininity* have meaning only in relation to one another. As they are organized as highly polarized opposites, Harper (2007) argues that a literary focus on femininity indirectly speaks to the construction of masculinity and, conversely, reading books about masculinity invariably tells us something about the construction of femininity. Harper's arguments are buoyed by Judith Halberstam's (1998) book *Female Masculinity* and Jean Bobby Noble's (2004) more recent *Masculinities without Men?* What is important to note is that female enactments of masculinities in literature are not limited to imitations of conventional or traditional masculinity but make room for a range of rich possibilities that include both lesbian masculine subjectivities—and Harper names "the drag queen, butch, stone butch or transgendered man" (p. 510)—and heterosexual female masculine subjectivities such as the tomboy and the female-to-male cross-dresser.

Harper's textual study of masculinity focused on five highly popular young adult novels written about girls: *Speak* (Anderson, 1999), *The Breadwinner* (Ellis, 2000), *Luna* (Peters, 2004), *Accidental Love* (Soto, 2006) and *Stargirl* (Spinelli, 2000). The titles are typically found in middle-years and secondary classrooms and in elementary and secondary school libraries and are easily obtained through public libraries and bookstores. Harper explains that the works featuring female protagonists ranging in age from 12 to 17 years focus more squarely on adolescence, and therefore sexuality and the body figure more prominently in these young adult narratives than in children's literature. Harper performed a close reading of each novel, making careful note of when traditional or feminine or alternative masculinity was in play. She paid particular attention to instances of male-to-female cross-dressing and female-to-male cross-dressing and of more subtle expressions of alternative, feminine, or traditional masculinity in each narrative. Her analysis aimed to uncover how these various performances of masculinities functioned in the novels. Harper's analysis revealed the ways in which the nature and deployment of masculinity varies from novel to novel, as does the degree to which the performance of masculinities is made explicit.

Harper's (2007) analysis of Deborah Ellis's *The Breadwinner* reveals the complexity and range of enacting Taliban masculinity. Ellis's protagonist Parvana temporarily disguises herself as a boy to achieve certain ends. During the Taliban rule, females entering public spaces had to be accompanied by a male relative. With her father imprisoned and her brother killed by a landmine, no adult male relatives remained to attend to seeing the women in Parvana's family to market. Parvana assumes a male identity to be able to secure food for her family and actually earns money by hiring herself out to read and write for illiterate citizens—a job her father once performed. As Harper points out, like most female-to-male literary cross-dressers, Parvana successfully assumes a masculine identity and, in this case, achieves more than she originally set out to do. She comes to know and enjoy her newfound freedom and responsibility, which is in stark contrast to the cloistered life of

Afghan girls and women. The experience lends her an uncharacteristic brav-
ado that allows her to be outspoken and a little wild—a change that does
not go undetected by her mother. Harper explains, however, that in *The
Breadwinner* gender remains limited to anatomy insofar as it is Parvana's pre-
pubescent body that makes possible the successful performance of masculinity. Accordingly, the "mature and maturing female body is seen as betraying
the possibility of male performance" (Harper, 2007, p. 515), as we see in
Parvana's cross-dressing friend Shauzia, who begins to worry that if her body
continues to change too much she will no longer be able to pass as a tea-boy.
Despite the precariousness and desperation of the girls' circumstances, Harper
argues that their experience allows readers to consider, if only for a moment,
the nature of gender as a performative act open to change. Harper identifies
other performances of masculinity in the novel that serve to demonstrate
how gender is organized according to political ideals. The extreme violence
of Taliban masculinity, vividly depicted as a young Talib man proudly holds
up a rope strung with four severed hands, is juxtaposed with the Western
ideals embodied by Parvana's father. Educated and modernized, Parvana's
father is seen as an avid supporter of his wife's work and daughter's schooling.
He is portrayed as a victim of Taliban violence and persecution. As Harper
notes, it is hard not to see such juxtapositions as reinforcing colonizing
notions of Western educated masculinity as being superior to other forms of
masculinity enacted elsewhere.

One of the novels in Harper's study of masculinities in books about girls
focuses on the explicit cross-dressing of a 17-year-old transsexual male,
Liam, who identifies as female. Cross-dressing in *Luna* presents more complexity in gender performance than Parvana's strategic performance of masculinity in *The Breadwinner*. The aim here is not mere disguise but Liam's
desire to live life as a woman. It is a story of transition and not temporary
accommodation. In contrast to Parvana's performance of masculinity,
Liam's constant shifts between female and male throughout the novel
emphasize "how masculinity can and cannot be enacted or enforced"
(Harper, 2007, p. 515). As an adolescent male, Liam is intelligent and over-
achieves in the sciences, a real computer geek. His father persists in his
attempts to get Liam to perform according to his ideal of a male by trying
out for sports, restoring an old car, and taking an interest in girls. Despite
Liam's desire to please his father, he is not interested in any of these activities
and is left desperately unhappy, with thoughts of suicide. As Luna, however,
the character takes on an entirely new persona, one clearly more expressive
and feminine. Luna openly laughs and enjoys wearing women's clothing and
makeup and longs to attend prom dressed as a girl. As a young child, Liam
played with dolls, insisting that he play Mommy and his sister the role of
Daddy. As Harper (2007) explains, Liam's dual performances serve to reify
the conventional bifurcation between masculine and feminine gendered
norms and expectations whereas his sister Regan, through whose perspective

the story of Liam's transition is told, functions to blur the polarization of these norms. Regan wrestles with her inability to perform conventional femininity as well as Luna but has no interest whatsoever in becoming male. Her negotiation of her own femininity and heterosexuality is repeatedly presented in contrast to Luna's decidedly feminine performance. Regan is interested in boys and in dating but is a bit of tomboy. She openly rejects the more domestic arts and is not particularly adept at being neat or fashionable. Her "faded carpenter pants and whatever shirt" she can pull "from the heap on [the] floor" present a stark contrast to Liam's "long-sleeved shirt ... pressed and buttoned to the chin; tucked into his khaki Dockers, which were ironed with military precision" (Peters, 2004, p. 6). Despite the seemingly radical shift from Liam to Luna, it is Regan who is less confident about enacting her brand of femininity.

As Harper (2007) points out, cross-dressing in children's literature is fairly common, referring to examples such as the wolf in *Little Red Riding Hood* and Toad in *The Wind and the Willows*. The same might be said for popular film and theater. In the next section, on gender representation in multicultural literature, readers are reminded of Disney's (1998) adaptation of the story of Mu lan, the legendary cross-dressing Chinese young woman who disguises herself as a male warrior to assume the place of her father in the fight against invading Huns. Many, too, will recall the stage and film adaptation of Isaac Bashevis Singer's short story "Yentl the Yeshiva Boy." In *Yentl* (1983), Barbra Streisand cross-dresses as a male named Anshel in order to pursue Talmudic studies and debate Jewish law. In Shakespeare's plays, female-to-male cross-dressing characters often function to restore order and harmony. For example, in *Twelfth Night*, the young noblewoman Viola is shipwrecked and disguises herself as the page Cesario in order to support herself in a foreign land. Her deception moves this comedic tale of unrequited love toward a double wedding celebration. Cross-dressing is also the means of restoring balance in Andy Fickman's 2006 film based on Shakespeare's *Twelfth Night* titled *She's the Man*. Teen actor Amanda Bynes plays Viola Hastings, who assumes her brother Sebastian's identity in order to play on Illyria's boys' soccer team and to exact revenge on Cornwall, the rival high school that recently cut its girls' soccer team, on which Viola once played. A double wedding celebration is replaced by a soccer victory in this "tween" version, and the survival and safety that motivates Viola in *Twelfth Night* gives way to a more explicitly stated, although somewhat debatable, feminist agenda in *She's the Man*.

Beyond restoring harmony and balance, female-to-male cross-dressing in Shakespeare's plays works to challenge traditional male authority. The Renaissance was a period of transformation in which society wrestled with an onslaught of new ideas. Women's total surrender to male authority was being compromised by the idea of partnership (Johnová, n.d.). The stage became the site of social experimentation where Shakespeare and other playwrights of the time could grant their comedic heroines attitudes and actions that may still have been unacceptable in a wife but not totally unimaginable. Cross-dressing allowed female characters to assume rights and engage in active behaviors openly defiant of moral codes, and it was expected that the audience would play along and join in the deception, well aware of the irony of male actors playing a female-to-male cross-dresser. From a twenty-first-century perspective, it may be difficult to see how Shakespeare's cross-dressing heroines could signify a change in women's status, and indeed the potential threat to social order posed by female-to-male cross-dressing was undermined by the fact that cross-dressing women usually become a boy of lower status; restoring balance at the end means that Shakespeare's heroic comediennes, concerned with love and relationships, come to abandon their masculine behaviors to accept male authority. Nevertheless, the female-to-male cross-dressing characters in Shakespeare's comedies explore physical and verbal freedoms previously beyond the bounds of cultural plausibility in ways that allow them to achieve their ends, whether it be their own preservation or the right to choose their own husband.

What we learn from these stories is that females are often allowed to pass as males, but male-to-female cross-dressing is deployed often as farce with far less successful results. In this regard, one can say that literature mirrors society's differential tolerance for females' and males' behavior that deviates from gendered norms. But as Harper argues, this discrepancy demonstrates that female-to-male cross-dressing can serve to debunk "a unitary notion of masculinity tied exclusively to male bodies" (p. 511). Harper's study of masculinities in books about girls further demonstrates the legitimacy of employing masculinity as a lens through which to read and analyze texts. In the conclusion of this chapter, I take up the cross-dressing possibilities embodied by Shyam Selvadurai's award-winning *Funny Boy*. Unlike Liam/Luna, whose transition from male to female is structured to provide a compelling backdrop to Regan's story of sibling sacrifice, Selvadurai's cross-dressing Arji is the subject of his own story.

GENDER REPRESENTATIONS IN MULTICULTURAL LITERATURE

Edward Said's (1978) *Orientalism* drew our attention to the long-held assumptions underlying the Western falsification, eroticization, and romanticizing of Middle Eastern and non-Western peoples and cultures. The scope of Said's *Orientalism* extends to encompass the manner in which multicultural literature written for children often persists in the promotion of gendered stereotypes. In addition, multicultural texts, both old and new, are largely produced and marketed within an Anglo-American market and as such tend to offer little insight into how gender might be performed differently in other cultures. Parents and educators need to be aware of the implicit messages that are being conveyed to children and adolescents with regard to what it means, for example, to be an Arab boy or South Asian girl. Like Said, who admittedly grew up entertained by many a Hollywood film depicting Arabs such as *Ali Baba and the Forty Thieves* but found no resemblance whatsoever between what was pictured on screen and life around him, many of my students identifying as Muslim or Jew, Aboriginal, Arab Canadian, South Asian Canadian, East Asian Canadian, Caribbean Canadian, Afro-Canadian, Indo-Canadian, or Eastern European Canadian often find fault with the gendered representations in children's and adolescent literature marketed as multicultural. Many perennial favorites and even more contemporary titles include problematic features that reinforce stereotypes, distortions, and homogenizations of gendered roles within diverse cultures.

Among the worst culprits are the pseudofolktales such as Arlene Mosel's (1968) beloved *Tikki Tikki Tembo*. By virtue of the fact such works are Western fabrications of other cultures' traditions and stories, they naturally fail at conveying any depth of human experience. Apart from the delightful onomatopoeic and rhythmic quality of the prose, *Tikki Tikki Tembo*, according to one of my students, is an attempted creation of an original folktale that mocks the Chinese language and misleads children into believing that this legend explains why Chinese people have short names.

Nodelman and Reimer (2003) contend that power is distributed unequally in society through the categories of gender. Arguably, this gendered power differential may be more prominent in multicultural texts. Nodelman and Reimer suggest the practice of reading against the text to notice assumptions about gender with regard to what children's literature suggests is appropriate gendered behavior. Readers should ask themselves questions about the characters and the outcomes of their actions. In other words,

> what kinds of "subject positions"—conventional ways of being human—are available to characters and what happens to characters in different "subject positions"? Also what emotions and desires are relevant to each kind of character and what kinds of personal attributes, attitudes and possessions are necessary for a character to be recognized as a particular kind of "subject." (p. 159)

For example, Margaret Chang (2001) writes there are two basic stereotypes of Asian women familiar to Westerners—the victim of oppression suffering from backward traditions and the "exotic seductress" (p. 81), often portrayed as the shy, oversexualized, doll-like beauty. Asian men, on the other hand, are often depicted in film and literature (including comics) as martial arts experts, sinister villains, or geeks rather than complex emotional characters (Chiu, 1997). More often than not, East Asian men appear in literature and film "as isolated figures apart from family and social settings

[and] in a limited number of occupations such as laundry worker or farmer, or only in a Chinatown setting" (Heller, Cunningham, & Heller, 2000). Two notable and welcome exceptions appear in Robert Munsch's (1994) picture book *Where Is Gah-Ning?* and Riki Levinson's (1988) *Our Home Is the Sea.*

Where Is Gah-Ning? is a story of about a Chinese Canadian family who lives in Northern Ontario. While the father holds a stereotypical job as a Chinese restaurant owner, he is not isolated from his family and is depicted in his red apron chasing after his rather unruly and energetic young daughter (shattering another stereotype of the quiet and obedient Asian girl), who escapes the boredom of her rural home several times, lured by Kapuskasing's promise of something new and exciting. In true Munsch fashion, this book does not purport to have the spiritual depth and cultural insight of a book like David Bouchard's (2001) *Buddha in the Garden* but it does offer young readers insight into a girl's diasporic identity in a minority setting. Despite a fascination of what lies beyond her rural town in Northern Ontario, Gah-Ning has an understanding that she is connected to the town by the family business and her grandmother's gravestone. As one student and part-time librarian pointed out, there are certainly not enough picture books about people who live in rural Canada, let alone one about an East Asian family. We are glad to see one that represents both and manages to expand our conception of life in the north and the gendered experience of Chinese Canadians.

One is encouraged to find a growing number of picture books depicting current and realistic representations of East Asian men and boys who do not in any way come to resemble the one-dimensional, oversimplified characters with bright yellow skin and thin slanted eyes wearing traditional clothing, a queue in their hair or with conical hats, as in Kurt Wiese and Marjorie Flack's (1933) picture book classic *The Story about Ping.* Riki Levinson's *Our Home Is the Sea* is set in modern-day Hong Kong and tells the tale of a young boy's journey home from school to his family's *sampan.* The book provides young children with a glimpse of busy Hong Kong life and the boy's yearning to be a fisherman just like his father and his grandfather despite his mother's wishes that he become a schoolteacher. The sparse text comes alive in the rich details of Luzak's textured oil paintings to give us the impression that the boy's love of the sunlit sea as his home is something much more than patriarchal legacy.

Chang (2001) is concerned that appropriations of traditional Chinese stories about girls and women invariably entail "the wish to impose modern feminist values" (p. 82). According to Ann Scott MacLeod (1998), the authors of European and American historical fiction for children want to grant their heroines freer choices than their cultures would have in fact offered. Hunter (1984) contends that imposing Western values on Chinese gendered identity is not a new phenomenon. Protestant missionaries in the early years of the twentieth century were uncomfortable with traditional Chinese gender conventions that would allow some girls to be educated like boys or to dress like boys. Authors like Pearl S. Buck, who came from a missionary family and grew up in China, interpreted Chinese life for American readers. Buck's famous novel *The Good Earth* (1931), together with the 1937 film—which cast Luise Rainer in the role of O-lan, the backward yet patient and enduring wife, and lesser known Tilly Losch as the concubine Lotus—did much to establish in the minds of Westerners the Chinese female stereotypes of the long-suffering victim of oppression and the exotic seductress. *The Good Earth* tells the story the rise to wealth of Wang Lung, a poor Chinese farmer, and it still remains on many middle school and high school reading lists. I, myself, can vividly recall Luise Rainer's trusting face looking wide-eyed up into the camera after viewing the film in a middle school classroom in the 1970s. The fact that none of the starring roles were actually played by Chinese actors didn't seem to bother anyone, although at the time, I did recognize among the cast Key Luke, the overexcited eldest son of Fu Manchu–moustached Charlie Chan. It is all a bit disconcerting now to realize the extent to which these gendered stereotypes invade my memory, but there is educative value in interrogating these and other works with students and coming to some understanding of how they are representative of and contributed to imperial domination.

Buck's novel and the subsequent film also make misguided assumptions about gendered acts presumably aimed at declarations of physical attraction. Chang explains that by having Wang Lung cut off his queue to please the sultry Lotus, the author has missed completely the fact that the long braid is a symbol of oppression forced upon ethnic Chinese by their Manchu conquerors. Placing the act within the context of Wang Lung's temptation works to satisfy a Western audience of readers but, according to Chang, leaves the Chinese with the impression that both the book and film versions of *The Good Earth* form "a well-meaning but simplistic portrait of their country, about as Chinese as the actors chosen to for the major roles of the film, Europeans or Americans all" (p. 81).

While some may think that *The Good Earth* is simply one more colonial narrative and that present-day publishing is committed to turning out more accurate portrayals of non-Western cultures, one need only peruse the dramatic detail of Marianna Mayer's (1995) picture book that retells Puccini's 1926 opera *Turandot* to confirm the extent to which we continue to be fascinated with an imagined China replete with "exotic decadence" (Chang, 2001, p. 80). For those of you unfamiliar with the opera, the story of Turandot, as Chang notes, is probably of Persian origin and was first staged as a play in eighteenth-century Italy. It tells the tale of Turandot, a cold-hearted Chinese princess who demands that her suitors correctly answer three riddles or die. Calaf, an unknown prince who falls madly in love with the princess, answers the riddles correctly, but Turandot recoils from any thought of marrying him. He decides to challenge her to guess his name by dawn. If she does not, she must marry him; if she does, Calaf faces execution. The princess decrees that no one shall sleep until the suitor's name is known. The story is one with which I am thoroughly familiar. I was raised on opera and long before a mobile-phone salesman on *Britain's Got Talent* made *Turandot*'s most famous tenor aria, *Nessun Dorma* ("None shall sleep"), a YouTube favorite, I had firmly acquired the image of Calaf kneeling before the calculating princess as the audience hears for the first time the aria's theme exploding with emotional impact. There is often little about the staging and costumes of Puccini's operas that is not over the top, and one can say the same about Winslow Pels' oil-and-pencil illustrations for Mercer's picture book. Chang (2001) notes that Pels perpetuates the Western fantasy about Chinese women as "compellingly seductive and cruel" ... "but one that bear little resemblance to the real aristocratic maidens depicted in Chinese art for centuries" (p. 80). The text features close-ups of Turandot looking like a vamp wrapped in pearls, arms covered in tattoos, and draped over a tiger. While Mercer is careful to make clear in the book's afterword that the story and Puccini's opera is of Western origin and in no way reflects Chinese imperial succession, Chang (2001) discovered that the picture book nevertheless found its way into an American Library Association *Book Links* article featuring teaching activities to complement the study of Laurence Yep's (1977) authentic portrayal of a Chinese American girl in *Child of the Owl*. The unfortunate insertion by the quarterly's editor suggested including Mayer's *Turandot* because "it is set in Peking ... [and] we don't include enough musical connections" (cited in Chang, 2001, p. 80). The editor's tacit acceptance of the highly exoticized portrayal of female Chinese aristocracy and the misguided assumption that the story is of Chinese origin provides us with some indication of the uncritical zeal to find multicultural books that "educate."

According to Hunter (1984), the Chinese see gender identity as a role that can change in response to extreme circumstances. This is a possibility that eluded the folks at Disney in their attempt to depict the legendary heroine Mu Lan as a paragon of *feminist* virtue as she dresses as a warrior to take the place of her conscripted father in the Emperor's army. Mu Lan, who eventually returns home and resumes her role as a woman once her military obligation is fulfilled, is consistent with other stories of the period. For example, the legend of kung fu master Wu Mei tells the story of a girl born to an aristocratic family and educated as if she were a boy. The ease with which the legendary Mu Lan and Wu Mei shed and reclaim their roles as women is likely tied to their aristocratic class. To my knowledge, there are no stories of lesser classes engaging in the same practice. When her family loses their position at the fall of the Ming Dynasty in 1644, Wu Mei makes her way to the Shaolin monastery, becomes a nun, and using her superior skills in the martial arts instructs boys and girls in the skills of kung fu. Wu Mei is the subject of Emily Arnold McCully's (1998) picture book *Beautiful Warrior*. McCully developed her own interpretation of classic

Chinese art to create, in Chang's (2001) opinion, "vigorous, lively heroines, unusual but consistent with their time" (p. 83). Chang explains that by contrast, when Disney's (1998) Mulan gazes into her mirror and sings, "When will my reflection show who I am inside?" she is expressing what Hunter (1984) some years earlier referred to as "a Protestant culture of feeling" rather than "a Chinese culture of role" (p. 261). Disney's discernibly profeminist heroine was heralded by some critics as a welcome departure from the studio's formulaic female characters. The problem is that Western appropriations of multicultural folklore often fail to either recognize or acknowledge culturally different ways of performing gender. As Chang explains, while modern Western women are more likely to want Mu Lan to hang on to her sword, generations of Chinese weaned on the ancient Chinese poem see Mu Lan's actions of shedding her female role and then reclaiming it as unquestionably appropriate. Asian American writer Katherine Kim (1998) sees the "free-spirited personality and forthright manner" of Disney's Mulan as an attempt to make the legendary heroine more palatable to Western audiences, going so far as to characterize her as "a banana—yellow outside, white within." As she explains, with "her anglicized name, her perfect unaccented English and her wild gesticulations, it is easy to see she is not a Chinese woman warrior, but an Asian-American feminist" (n.p.). Kim ultimately found that the Disney release (1998), which highlighted Mulan's "irresistible spirit" in the face of her "tradition-bound society" (n.p.), positions the West as superior to the East and found the film "one-dimensional and stereotyped throughout" (Kim, 1998, n.p.).

TRANSGRESSING HETERONORMATIVITY IN CHILDREN'S AND ADOLESCENT LITERATURE

Any discussion of gender in children's and adolescent literature needs to address the question of whether young people, both gay and straight, can find the imaginative spaces to explore gendered options for themselves in the books they read. We have seen, in the case of Cleary's *Dear Mr. Henshaw*, that a boy can be the protagonist of a novel in which language is the means through which he can claim his subjectivity and locate himself in the wider world. While literature is an important vehicle for disrupting and challenging taken-for-granted assumptions about gender, it has a long way to go in offering a wider range of possibilities for young people growing up who are desperate to locate themselves outside of the overdetermined male/female binaries. In this section, I discuss the portrayal of gay and lesbian characters, highlight works that might transgress heteronormativity, and interrogate some of the mainstream offerings.

As I have pointed out, literature can provide both moral terrain and rich narrative possibilities that allow us to existentially explore our options for life. Consider the following testimony taken from Adam Mastoon's (1997)

The Shared Heart: Portraits and Stories Celebrating Lesbian, Gay, and Bisexual Young People:

> I read Edmund White, Bret Easton Ellis, George Whitmore, James Baldwin. I read them all for the sex. . . . But while I was looking for one thing, I found another: a series of experiences, a set of emotions that echoed my own, beyond sexual desire. I found characters who were lonely like I was, sad like I was, and some characters who were happy living lives I was not even sure were possible. (p. 68)

Clearly, this young man was fortunate to have found stories that gave him hope, but as I write this, I am reminded of mothers I have encountered while working in schools who could no longer hold back their tears, secretly confiding their despair at bearing witness to their children's pain of growing up "different" and desperately wanting them to feel good in their skin. Responsible educators can no longer ignore how educational practice has exacerbated homophobia and conceptualizations of normalcy by subscribing to a structural view of identity where sexual diversity is lost in thinking and acting according to the either/or of heterosexual/homosexual binaries.

There is considerable evidence from a range of educational researchers demonstrating that curricular contexts emphasizing LGBT inclusivity often take the form of isolated lessons limited in time and scope (Blackburn & Clark, 2011; Clark & Blackburn, 2009; Britzman, 1995; Linville, 2009; Martino, 2009). Rather than advancing an understanding of self and identity as emerging from a multiplicity of conscious and unconscious interactions (Slattery, Krasny, & O'Malley, 2007), an approach that concentrates its LGTB focus on a single day in an awareness campaign or study of a single literary text tends to reinforce prevalent ideologies by structuring the reading and discussion of LGBT-themed literature as an intervention—a response to widespread homophobia. Interventionalist efforts typically adopt the "just like me" approach aimed at erasing difference, all the while positing heterosexuality as the normative default. Mollie Blackburn and Caroline Clark (2011) point out that a commitment to LGBT inclusivity often carries with it the unintentional results of "restricting the range of discussion possibilities and representation available to students" (p. 223). As Deborah Britzman (1995) explains, education aimed at responding to homophobia and at merely correcting for the representational absence of lesbians and gays to queer students, who are seldom if ever allowed to be fully present in the classroom, fails to interrogate our normative conceptualizations of sexuality and gender identity. All of this begs the question, what kinds of possibilities for being lesbian, gay, bisexual, or transgendered are represented in young adult and children's fiction? Moreover, is there a way to queer reading practices such that all students might read beyond and across gendered binaries in ways that would allow them to name and explore the complexities of sexuality? Furthermore, can such practices draw their attention to the sociocultural and sociopolitical influences that have contributed to their sexual and gendered behaviors and identities? This section of Chapter 6 addresses the first of these questions as I attempt to account for patterns of LGBT representation in young adult and children's fiction. A more fulsome discussion of queering reading practices and their potential to uncover sexual subtexts in canonical and contemporary literary works that can lead to disrupting normative ways thinking about gender and sexuality is featured in Chapter 7 on policy and classroom practice.

Paulette Rothbauer's (2002) recent review of Canadian young adult fiction revealed that lesbian and gay characters are barely present. Among the books with lesbian and gay characters, very few make it onto published bibliographies of young adult fiction, with the notable exception of Diana Wieler's (1989) *Bad Boy*, heralded as the first Canadian young adult novel to feature a young gay man, and Catherine Brett's (1989) *S. P. likes A. D.*, as story about a young woman's attraction to another girl. Admittedly, I have read neither but for several years running, my third-year university students enrolled in my section of Teaching English/Language Arts in the Intermediate/Senior Years have nominated and elected to read Marion Dane Bauer's (1994) *Am I Blue: Coming Out from Silence*, an edited anthology of young adult fiction devoted to lesbian and gay themes as a literature circle selection, and I am given to believe that it continues to maintain considerable currency in public high schools. The anthology's mainstream status is due in no small part to the fact that it has assembled works from celebrated young adult authors including Lois Lowry (*Number the Stars*), Jane Yolen (*The Devil's Arithmetic*), Gregory Maguire (*Wicked*) and Francesca Lia Block (*Weetzie Bat* series). The 18 short stories range from Block's offbeat "Winnie and Ted," in which a teenager comes out to his girlfriend on a road trip to San Francisco, to Jacqueline Woodson's "Slipping Away," a poignant tale of one girl's discovery that there are some things a friendship cannot endure. Apart from the title story—a fantasy in which a fairy godfather comes to the aid of a gay-bashing victim—the majority of the works are realistic fiction that attempt to capture the complex emotions associated with the recognition of sexual difference in an adolescent world in which conformity is often severely policed. In a review for *School Library Journal*, Christine Jenkins (1994) writes: "As with most short story collections the overall quality is uneven but the best stories are memorable. They speak of survival and hope; they say like the man on the beach in Giblin's story, 'You are not alone' " (p. 144).

But despite the apparent ease with which the teacher candidates in my third-year education course laid their hands on a copy of *Am I Blue?*, locating the more than 100 English-language titles published specifically for a young adult audience with lesbian or gay characters is no easy task (Jenkins, 1998; Rothbauer, 2002). Novels about homosexuality are still difficult to access, and many reviewers are reluctant to signal the presence of lesbian and gay characters, often choosing to downplay it in the titles (Fuoss, 1994; Rothbauer, 2002; Rothbauer & McKechnie, 1999). Jenkins (1998) identifies John Donovan's *I'll Get There, It Better Be Worth the Trip*, published in the United States in 1969, as the first novel for young adults to include a homosexual encounter between two boys. Rothbauer's (2002) survey of Canadian young adult literature yielded the following titles since the publication of Wieler's *Bad Boy* and Brett's *S. P. Likes A. D.* in 1989. The collection is significant insofar as it provides us with important insights into how lesbians and gays are generally represented in young adult fiction.

Published in 1992, William Bell's novel *No Signature* features a gay character as the protagonist's best friend. Bell's novel was followed in 1994 by Martha Brooks' *Traveling On into the Light* and features a gay father and his partner. Gay characters appear in both Bernice Friesen and Linda Holeman's 1995 collections of short stories, respectively *The Seasons Are Horses* and *Saying Goodbye*. David Boyd's *Bottom Drawer* that focuses on homophobic violence was released in 1996. Diana Wieler contributed yet another title in 1997, as the third book of her RanVan trilogy, this time depicting a relationship between gay men, one of whom is HIV positive. Mary-Kate McDonald's (1998) short story collection *Carving My Name* contains a story of a gay male, and a young gay man comes out in Carol Matas's *Telling* in the same year. Another tale of a gay male with AIDS-related illnesses is the subject of Glen Huser's (1999) novel *Touch of the Clown*, and Wendy Lewis's (2000) *Graveyard Girl* is the story of unrequited love of one girl for her female best friend. Rothbauer's survey of Canadian young adult fiction with lesbian and gay characters concludes citing the publication of three young adult novels with gay male characters: Teresa Toten's The Game (2001), Shelley Hrdlitschka's Dancing Naked (2002), and Sarah Withrow's Box Girl (2001).

The brevity of Rothbauer's list of 15 works summarized above and published over a period of 12 years is a quick indication of the underrepresentation of lesbian and gay characters in Canadian young adult fiction. Moreover, the nature of the representations reflected in the collection reveal that of the 15 titles, two of the six lesbians represented are central protagonists of their own stories—Stephanie in *S. P. Likes A. D.* and Tish in Wendy Lewis's short story "You Never Know," although Tish's sexual orientation is never made totally clear and, according to Rothbauer, her infatuation could easily be dismissed as a crush. Among the 20 gay males appearing throughout the collection dating from 1989 to 2001, Rothbauer identifies Diana Wieler's Tulsa Brown in *Bad Boy* as the only complex characterization of a young gay man, but even his characterization operates in a supporting role as the novel is largely about Tulsa's best friend A. J., whose actions are precipitated by his homophobic feelings. Rothbauer concludes that while lesbian and gay characters do exist in Canadian young adult literature, consistent with the larger subgenre to which these 15 Canadian works belong, the fictional lesbian and gay characters "are present and are visible to the mainly heterosexual protagonists" (p. 23). Citing Jenkins (1998), she adds lesbians and gays are seldom the focus of their own stories and continue to be "portrayed as outsiders who live (often somewhat precariously) within the heterosexual mainstream" (p. 320). Individual titles within the collection are not without merit but together combine to emphasize the literary limits imposed on lesbian and gay life.

Almost half of the 15 titles in Rothbauer's survey contained elements of a "coming-out narrative" where disclosure had "serious, risky, and often negative consequences," projecting "fear, confusion, and self-loathing on the part of the lesbian or gay character; and disbelief, resistance, intolerance, harassment, and abuse on the part of family members, friends, and peers" (p. 23), leading to some form of self-acceptance, acceptance by some other, or total rejection by others. There is one death from AIDS-related illness and two suicides. As for love and passion, Rothbauer counts a meager two kisses; the only sexual encounter between characters of the same sex occurs in *Bad Boy*, but it no way signals a love story. In her opinion, there is little life-affirming or uplifting, and sadly, young adult readers searching to find themselves in a story that celebrates their life will not find what they are looking for within the pages of these works. In addition to expanding life's narrative possibilities, fiction with lesbian and gay characters should allow those whose sexual identity falls within heterosexual bounds the opportunity to develop some understanding and connection (beyond pity) to the experiences and lives of persons who are lesbian, gay, transgendered, and bisexual. Here again, many of the young adult works with lesbian and gay characters published to date fail to hit home.

HARRY POTTER, SEXIST?

In an interview with H. J. Cummins (2000) for the Minneapolis *Star Tribune*, renowned children's literature scholar Jack Zipes was asked what he thought of the Harry Potter series, and he replied that he thought them to be formulaic and sexist. His remark caused immediate furor, and he soon found himself deluged by media requests for further interviews. Harry Potter is by far the biggest phenomenon in the history of children's literature to date and is arguably the biggest phenomena in modern-day publishing. At the time of its release, *Harry Potter and the Goblet of Fire*, the fourth volume in J. K. Rowling's series, had the biggest advance order ever, including the 350,000 sold on Amazon.com. It had the biggest printing ever, with 3,800,000 copies in the United States alone, and the *New Yorker* heralded it the biggest takeover ever of the *New York Times* bestseller list by a single writer. When it hit the bestseller list, the preceding three Potter books were still in the rankings. A literary phenomenon of this magnitude should make us wonder if indeed the degree to which the characters conform to traditional gender roles does play a role in making it such a cultural commodity.

According to Zipes (2002), what the Harry Potter books have in spades is predictability. An article in the *New Yorker* pointed out that J. K. Rowling made use of virtually every convention used in fairy tales described in Vladimir Propp's 1928 *Morphology of the Folk Tale*. One by one, the series demonstrates some function in Propp's grammar of action.

> At the beginning of the story, Propp says, the villain harms someone in the hero's family (The evil wizard Voldemort murdered Harry's good-wizard parents...). The hero is branded. (Voldemort's attack left Harry with a scar in the shape of a lightening bolt on his forehead). The hero is banished. (Harry is forced to go live with his loathsome aunt and uncle, the Dursleys.) The hero is released. (Harry is finally informed that he is a wizard, and goes off to live at Hogwart's School of Witchraft and Wizardry). The hero must survive ordeals, seek things, acquire a wise helper. All of which Harry does. (*New Yorker*, July 31, 2000, p. 74)

So now that we have more or less confirmed Zipes's claim that the Harry Potter books are formulaic, what about sexist? Does the comfortable predictability of J. K. Rowling's books owe something to traditional gender role expectations?

According to cultural critic Christine Schoefer (2000), the Harry Potter books are a bit of a sacred cow, and any critique is going to be met with the kind of resentment that greeted Zipes on a local radio show where 90 percent of the callers were parents attacking him for demeaning J. K. Rowling's works, which they felt had done wonders for their children. Like Schoefer, at first, my children and I were captivated by vivid images of Diagon Alley, the Sorting Hat's deliberations, and the sheer inventiveness of Quidditch. I didn't even care much that the action progressed in lock-step fashion according to Propp's structural grammar. I trusted that at home and at school, my sons had access to and read from a wide range of literature with complex plots and challenging themes. But like Schoefer, I could not ignore the sexism. In her commentary appearing on Salon.com, Schoefer writes:

> Harry's fictional realm of magic and wizardry perfectly mirrors the conventional assumption that men do and should run the world. From the beginning of the first Potter book, it is boys and men, wizards and sorcerers, who catch our attention by dominating the scenes and determining the action. Harry is supported by the dignified wizard Dumbledore and a colorful cast of male characters. Girls, when they are not downright silly or unlikable, are helpers, enablers and instruments. No girl is brilliantly heroic the way Harry is, no woman experienced and wise like Professor Dumbledore.

But what about Hermione, you ask? Surely the smartest student at Hogwarts is able to exercise her agency and claim her subjectivity in meaningful ways that could speak to young female and male readers. But time and time again, despite the thoroughness with which Hermione approaches every task and problem to be solved, her efforts are thwarted, diminished, or fail miserably, often with humiliating consequences. This I found to be particularly troublesome in the first three books where Hermione is still struggling to prove her worth to Harry and Ron.

Hermione is able to exercise accepted forms of agency typically associated with being a girl, most notably by following the rules. Yet events in the *Harry Potter* books demonstrate the irony that while we live in a world in which men make the rules and maintain the system of power, it is men who do not want to play by the rules, and they are seldom held accountable to the same standard as women (de Beauvoir, 1949; hooks, 2000, Kristeva, 1974; Mayes-Elma, 2006). Take for example, in Chapter 9 in the first book, *Harry Potter and the Sorcerer's Stone*,[1] when Hermione tells Harry and Ron that they cannot sneak out of their dorm room to carry out their plan to duel Malfoy because it would be against Hogwarts rules. She confides that she thought about telling on them but decided otherwise. To this, Harry replies, "It's really none of your business" (Rowling, 1997, p. 154). This castigating remark is significant insofar as it determines Hermione's actions in the troll incident that follows.

The troll incident in Chapter 10 in the first book proves most revealing in demonstrating to readers how power is distributed unequally between genders and in setting the bounds for female agency. Harry's victory over the 12-foot troll wandering the hallowed halls of Hogwarts marks his first achievement at the school of wizardry. To summarize, as the prefects lead students back to their dorms, it dons on Harry that Hermione does not know about the troll. Against strict regulations, Harry leaves the group and heads off with Ron to warn her. They come upon the troll and unwittingly lock the monster in the girl's bathroom with Hermione. Together the three of them manage to knock out the troll. Any contribution Hermione may have made to the conquest is negated when at the sight of the troll she "sinks to the floor in fright . . . her mouth open with terror" (Schoefer, 2000). As Schoefer (2000) comments, "Like every Hollywood damsel in distress, Hermione depends on the resourcefulness of boys and repays them with her complicity" (n.p.).

With the hierarchy of power established, we also learn that not only do boys and girls play different roles in Harry's narrative, but they are treated differently by others when it comes to breaking the rules (Mayes-Elma, 2006). When Professor McGonagall finds all three with the troll and begins to scold them, rather than admit to simply being in the wrong place at the wrong time, Hermione abandons her agency, which up to this point has

---

[1]Originally published in Britain and marketed and distributed outside the United States as *Harry Potter and the Philosopher's Stone*.

been so steadfastly invested in maintaining the rules, and lies to win the reluctant approval of Harry and Ron. She tells Professor McGonagall that it was she who sneaked out of her dorm to find the troll when it was actually Harry and Ron. Generic readings of the book such as that found on SparkNotes.com mark this action for students as the point that the "know it all" and "bossy" Hermione is finally rendered more sympathetic to the reader (SparkNotes, n.d.). To my mind, all of this sympathetic acceptance comes at a cost. Hermione's actions illustrate Gilligan's (2003) claim that adolescent girls are socialized into a kind of selflessness associated with care and connection but also with loss of psychological strength and resilience. She provides the perfect example of the female silencing associated with making decisions in the face of a moral situation based on the expectations of a male-dominated society rather than on one's own feelings and beliefs (Gilligan, 1993). Professor McGonagall expresses her disappointment at Hermione's supposed transgression and scolds her: "Miss Granger, you foolish girl, how could you think of tackling a mountain troll on your own" (Rowling, 1997, p. 178) and takes five points from Hermione's house. To the actual rule-breakers, Harry and Ron, Professor McGonagall warns: "You were lucky," and then adds in a tone of admiration, "but not many first years could have taken on a full-grown mountain troll. You each win Gryffindor five points" (p. 178).

This double standard for girls and boys regarding rule following and rule breaking pervades the *Potter* books and arguably provides an apt literary illumination of the findings discussed in earlier chapters that teachers interact differently with boys and girls. Earlier in Chapter 9 of *Harry Potter and the Sorcerer's Stone*, we see how Harry is actually rewarded for his blatant disregard for the rules. Harry's flying class is ordered to stay on the ground while Madam Hooch accompanies the injured Neville to the hospital. But Harry takes off on his broom after Malfoy in an attempt to recapture Neville's magic ball. As usual, Harry is caught in the act by Professor McGonagall. He is at first reprimanded and ordered to follow her. But rather than face a punishment, Harry is introduced to Oliver Wood, captain of the Gryffindor Quidditch team. The next morning, his rebellious disregard for the rules earns him a Nimbus Two Thousand and an invitation to Quidditch practice, further emphasizing that when it comes to breaking the rules, there are clear-cut boundaries for girls and boys (Mayes-Elma, 2006). By contrast, on the rare occasion that women do enact their agency in rule-breaking ways, they are made to feel remorseful and ashamed as Hermione is after she is caught leaving her dorm to help rescue Norbert. She is so overtaken with guilt and shame that this overachiever actually withdraws from her classes.

Lesser female characters tend to fare far worse than Hermione and are frequently shown to be caught up in their emotions as we "watch them 'shriek,' 'scream,' 'gasp,' and 'giggle' in situations where boys retain their composure" (Schoefer, 2000, n.p.). Even the sturdy and authoritative Minerva McGonagall consistently defers to Dumbledore. He, too, has been granted the power and vision to break the rules whereas Professor McGonagall's agency is restricted to enforcing them. Despite her cool and austere appearance, she is not above losing composure at Harry's return from the chamber of secrets, clutching her chest and gasping while Dumbledore, calm, cool, and collected, simply looks on and beams.

Intelligence may provide another way for Hermione and Professor McGonagall to enact their agency. Nevertheless, as Schoefer (2000) notes, while Hermione can successfully cast spells for the boys, she invariably screws up one of her own and winds up hiding in the lavatory with cat fur on her face. There are bounds, too, to a female character's agency to resist (Mayes-Elma, 2006). Female characters frequently allow male characters to dictate what will happen and are quick to back down. For example, Hermione wants to discuss responses to their exams with Harry and Ron. Rowling makes it clear that she enjoys doing this and that Harry and Ron are aware of how she finds this debriefing a satisfying conclusion to the all the studying, but neither boy is willing to oblige. Hermione does not question them or push them further but rather agrees to doing what they want to do, which is sit and relax under a tree.

In short, the Harry Potter books offer little in the way of challenging traditional gender constructions. Ruthann Mayes-Elma (2006) argues that female characters are caught in a pattern of "resist and retreat" (p. 104), demonstrating that maintaining patriarchal power requires women to back down. Women and girls are afforded agency, but that agency is enacted within the bounds of traditional institutions of family, school, and now, as we know it, the wizarding community.

MOVING ON

In Chapter 6, I attempted to offer readers an introduction to how traditional gender roles are represented and challenged in adolescent and children's literature. Chang's (2001) historical analysis of classic and contemporary works marketed to an adolescent and children's market should caution parents and educators to examine carefully with children the gendered stereotypes projected in many of the multicultural selections. Their educative value may lie in their potential to tell us more about Western imperialism and perceptions than in actually providing us with authentic accounts of the gendered experience of others viewed as different from ourselves. James Banks (2002) argues for a multicultural education that illuminates some of the inconsistencies:

> Theory, research, and ideology in multicultural education are both linked to and divergent from past educational reform movements related to race and ethnic diversity. Examining the historical and social contexts from 1911 to

2000 [identifies] ways in which the research and knowledge constructed about race and ethnic groups mirrored and perpetuated these contexts. (p. 16)

Yet the idea of multiculturalism as coming to terms with difference relating to gender, social class, and ethnic, racial, or other cultural characteristics is not without contention. In selecting multicultural texts, parents and educators need to be aware of the risk of what Stanley Fish (1997) describes as engaging in "boutique multiculturalism" (p. 379) exemplified "as ethnic restaurants, weekend festivals, and high profile flirtations with the other" (p. 378).

Children and adolescents coming to terms with sexual identity and difference will find little in the vast body of children's and young adult fiction that deviates from a heterosexual script or that poses a challenge to cultural plausibility. Overwhelmingly, lesbian and gay characters are seldom the protagonists of their own story but rather function as a catalyst for the protagonist's actions and do not appear in relation to a wider queer community (Rothbauer, 2002). Working in Toronto, my students and I frequently play host to some well-known authors, and for the past several years we have been fortunate to welcome Sri Lankan diasporic writer Shyam Selvadurai. Like Bauer's (1994) anthology *Am I Blue*, Selvadurai's novel *Funny Boy* was consistently chosen year after year by my third-year undergraduates as one of our literature circle selections. The novel is the coming-of-age story of Arjie, a Sri Lankan youth who works through his sexuality amid the members of his extended upper-middle-class Tamil family and the political tension in Columbo in years leading up to the 1983 riots. The title *Funny Boy* references his father's fear that Arjie will turn out "funny" if he persists in donning a *sari* and playing the female role in his favorite game "bride-bride." But more significantly, "funny" hints at Arjie's sexual "inbetweeness" where cross-dressing play is an important and early means of exploring that "inbetweeness." The strict gender roles enforced by his family leave Arjie "caught between the boys' and the girls' worlds, not belonging or wanted in either" (Selvadurai, 1994, p. 39). Selvadurai deftly situates Arjie's struggles against the trauma of wider social and political conflicts. In his complex portrayal of his protagonist, sexuality is read as but one aspect of Arjie's identity as the youth must also come to terms with his ethnicity and fleeting middle-class privilege as the family is forced to immigrate to Canada. Selvadurai's (1994) critically acclaimed novel is not marketed as young adult literature and therefore was not part of Rothbauer's (2002) analysis. The novel, however, is accessible reading for high school students and offers some redemption for the frequent unanswered victimization, marginalization, and fear-inducing narratives documented in Rothbauer's study.

In closing, I wish to follow up on Schoefer's (2001) stated confusion over J. K. Rowling's creative ability to "conjure up a unicorn shedding silver blood" and "a marauder's map" but her failure to leave us with a "bold and lovable heroine" (n.p.). Similarly, we can wonder why writers like Marianna Mercer and illustrators like Winlow Pels cannot turn their attention and unquestionable talent to providing young readers with a work that breaks the bonds of conventionality to challenge taken-for-granted stereotypes. It may seem unfair to single out particular authors and illustrators as the children's book market is largely a cultural (and profitable) commodity governed by major publishers (Zipes, 2001) and—let's face it—conventionality sells. But as a number of literary scholars and critics, including Jack Zipes (2001) and Roger Sutton (1999), editor of *The Horn Book*, have noted, the problem is not that, like so many works written for children and adults, the *Harry Potter* books provide "readable, saleable, everyday... prose" (Weldon, cited in Allison, 2003) or that Rowling's writing appears governed by "clichés and dead metaphors" (Bloom, 2003); it is that somehow the *Harry Potter* phenomenon has come to represent for many the world of children's books. Referencing an article by British children's literature critic Brian Alderson, Zipes (2002) argues that the fact that the overwhelming phenomenon of Harry Potter should detract "from the profound accomplishments of Joan Aiken and other writers such as [William] Mayne, Rosemary Sutcliff, Ursula LeGuin, and Janni Howker" (p. 187) is absurd.

Parents and educators looking to introduce children and youth to fantasy that challenges sexism might do well to pick up *Tehanu* (LeGuin, 1990), the fourth book in Ursula Le Guin's *Earthsea* series, in which her heroine Tenar questions the labels placed upon her by the male-dominated society and female identity is negotiated against the narrative of the dragons, which begins at the point when dragons and humans were one. But if witches and not dragons are on order, those looking for historical fiction might cast fantastical brooms and Horcruxes aside and select Carol Matas's (1994) *The Burning Time*, a revisionist tale of witch hunting in seventeenth-century France that signals a feminist rejection of victimization. Trites (1997) points to other feminist novels that show that a female protagonist can enter into a heterosexual relationship and remain empowered. She offers ups Cynthia Voigt's (1985, 1990, 1993) fantasy trilogy including *Jackaroo*, *On Fortune's Wheel*, and *The Wings of a Falcon*; Virginia Hamilton's (1987) *A White Romance*; Katherine Paterson's (1995) *Lyddie*; Mildred B. Taylor's (1990) *The Road to Memphis*; and Minfong Ho's (1986) *Rice without Rain*. The protagonists in these novels demonstrate that feminist resistance means using their voice in dialogue with others to act upon their own goals and would give Hermione Granger serious pause to rethink her relationship with Harry and Ron.

CHAPTER 7

Policy, Practice, and Research: How Schools and Communities Take Action

As major social institutions, schools reflect and reinforce the social structures of the larger society (Weiss & Fine, 1993). If parents and educators are to take action, first and foremost they need to pay close attention to the ways schools and schooling have served as vehicles of cultural transmission to uncover and correct for the systemic practices that have worked to stream girls and boys into different areas of study, provide for inequitable teacher attention, reinforce perceived differences between girls and boys, and condone varying degrees of sexual harassment (Beck & Murphy, 1996; Sanders, 2000). We need to recognize how faculty, staff, and students consciously or unconsciously use language in ways to police gender and how such actions may lead to serious consequences. One might think that feminism has secured gender equity a permanent place on school agendas, but in a study by Ginsberg, Shapiro, and Brown (2000) documenting a Philadelphia school district initiative to promote gender awareness through education, one teacher voiced her exasperation as follows:

We start with gender, and within minutes, we are pursuing arguments about race. We start with gender again and immediately head in the direction of teenage violence. We mean to start with gender next time, and we talk about social class. But gender is the piece which is mentioned less often by name in the staff room, in professional development workshops, in the newspapers or in the classroom. (p. 164)

Of the many quotes I have read on gender equity in education, I thought it best to launch the discussion on how parents and educators can take action with the frankness of this teacher's comments. The teacher's stated observation is significant in two ways. First, it signals the extent to which gender equity (not merely boys and reading) remains a missing piece in discussions of educational and school reform. In fact, the moral panic expressed in countless media headlines on boys and reading may prove relatively restrictive in promoting a more comprehensive view of gender construction and the price exacted on both sexes. Second, despite the teacher's obvious frustration that the mere mention of gender as a topic for discussion is readily hijacked by seemingly more pressing issues, the inevitability of such an occurrence points to the extent to which *gender is embedded in complex issues related to "race," "teenage violence," and "social class."* In other words, gender awareness is an integral piece toward building a fuller understanding of broad social issues, yet the interrelationship between constructions of race, ethnicity, and gender is often overlooked.

Environmental and sociocultural factors related to constructions of gender, race, and class work in combination to shape how children experience their learning environment differently. The amount of environmental and sociocultural stimulus a child receives inside and outside of school can have serious consequences for student participation and achievement (Sanders, 2000; Valentine, 1999; Matthews, 1987). The differences in the ways girls and boys experience school may be amplified or altered when race and socioeconomic status also come into play. Educational researchers investigating student performance show that students' aspirations, parents and teachers' expectations, and teacher-student interactions are all influenced by gender, race, and socioeconomic status and, in turn, contribute to differences in performance (Grant, 1984; Delpit, 1988; Orenstein, 1994). By and large, the teacher remains key in communicating different expectations to girls and boys in the classroom, suggesting that the promise of school reform is contingent on teachers having opportunities to develop a deeper knowledge and understanding of gender construction in order to make conscious and informed changes to their behaviors (Sanders, 2000). In other words, day-to-day interactions with students are more likely to have more sustainable effects than one-time school-wide or district-wide gender-equity interventions.

The nature of teacher-student communication and its contribution to a gender-differentiated learning environment in schools is well documented (Sadker & Sadker, 1994; Stanworth, 1981, 1990; Walkerdine, 1981, 1990). Orenstein (1994), in preparation for her seminal work *School Girls*, noted that gender equity registers low on a scale of priorities in communities of color. In reference to gender equity, one teacher interviewed in Orenstein's study declared, "We have other more important things to think about here" (p. 150). Yet the findings from research investigating how race and ethnicity and gender shape classroom dynamics in mixed-race/mixed-gender groups provide evidence that white males are most likely to receive teacher attention, males of color the second most likely, and white females the third. *Females of color are the least likely to receive teacher attention,* and not surprisingly, given what we know about female silencing, many become increasingly invisible as they move through high school (Irvine, 1986). Consistent with Gilligan's (2003) claim that adolescent girls are socialized into a kind of self-lessness associated with care and connection but also with loss of psychological strength and resilience, Sanders's (2003) review of the research found that in predominantly white classrooms with few girls of color, girls of color either fell into the role of "little mothers" and helped the teacher reinforce classroom and school rules or, alternatively, withdrew into silence. Yet adolescent females of color in racially segregated, inner-city schools appeared to assume greater agency and voice, but such psychological assertiveness usually took place outside of the classroom.

THE INFLUENCE OF TEACHERS AND TEACHERS' ORGANIZATIONS ON POLICY AND PRACTICE

While day-to-day teacher-student interactions are likely to have more sustainable effects than one-time school-wide or district-wide gender-equity interventions, teachers also have to feel supported in building gender-equitable learning environments through sustainable inquiry into the policies and discourses that circulate what James Paul Gee (2005) refers to as "situated meanings" (p. 96). Situated meanings relate the political, economic, and social conditions that guide us to the particular questions and answers that direct our decision making. Ensuring gender-equitable rights for students is undoubtedly an uphill climb in schools where the organizational structure, institutional discourse, and approved curriculum materials continue to reflect sex-role stereotyping. By now it should not surprise readers that the history of educational research informing policy making on gender-equitable schooling owes much to feminist research, but readers may be less aware that effectively linking research to policy and practice is due in no small part to feminist scholars working in faculties of education and to interested educators working in schools (Coulter, 1996). Rebecca Priegert Coulter (1996) documents the noticeable effects of feminist research on educational policy in Canada. She argues that while sex-role socialization theory has been highly influential in shaping government policies and pedagogical practices, educators also have drawn on a wider body of research. Her historical review demonstrates how educational research and gender-equity policy making have been linked through the dedicated work of teachers and their organizations. It serves as a clear illustration of the *long-term, coordinated* efforts and networks needed to forge new policy and implement change. For example, during the 1970s, the earliest initiatives on sex-role stereotyping in textbooks in Canada were informed in part by a study conducted by the Ad Hoc Committee Respecting the Status of Women in the North York System. The results of the committee's investigation, published as an interim report by the North York Board of Education (1975), were supported by findings from similar studies conducted around the same time (Batcher, Brackstone, Winter, & Wright, 1975; Cullen, 1972; Women in Teaching, 1975). Relying primarily upon quantitative methods to document stereotypes and the number of times women appeared in stories and illustrations and in what type of roles, all studies pointed to the bias in textbooks. The North York study of basal readers for use in grades 1 to 3 also revealed "shocking evidence of various other kinds of rigid stereotyping and of racism" (North York Board of Education, 1975, p. 16). As a result of this and related studies, policy was developed and by 1987, all Canadian provinces had established guidelines for textbook selection including an evaluation grid to aid teachers and curriculum specialists in eliminating sex bias in educational materials (Julien, 1987, p. 53).

Coulter (1996) describes in detail another notable example of teachers working for change. While the women's movement successfully put women's inequality on the Canadian political agenda (Vickers, Rankin, & Apelle, 1993), attention tended to focus on issues such as employment, poverty, child care, violence against women, and reproductive rights. Coulter points to the irony emerging from the suggestion made by government and other institutions that the response to these and other issues of gender equity might be found in education. As Coulter goes on to explain,

> Eschewing structural or systemic explanations, governments identify sexism as being simply a "wrong" attitude and target education, especially the schooling of children, as the means to change this attitude. As a result, governments often pass weak legislation or develop "soft" gender equity through education policies, designed to offend no one. (p. 443)

Coulter nevertheless acknowledges the importance of passing laws and policies, even if at first they appear relatively inadequate, for they provide "a necessary legitimation for educators to raise gender issues in the schools and offer teachers an opportunity to work out the practical meaning of equity" (p. 443). Beyond individual implementation efforts on the part of many women, laws and policies can provide the groundwork for teachers working in small groups or networks and with their school boards, associations, or federations. I contend that such legislative efforts also foster a specific type of gender literacy by providing linguistic frameworks lending political shape and form to school- and classroom-based initiatives. Coulter rightfully argues, "It is teachers, through their practice, who provide many of the real links between research/theory and policy" (p. 443).

Coulter cites Lise Julien (1987), who earlier concluded from her survey of the women's issues in education and the policies and practices at the elementary and secondary levels that teacher federations are the most active agents in equipping teachers with the knowledge and tools to understand, develop, and implement gender-equity policies. She then points to the British Columbia Teachers' Federation (BCTF) Status of Women Program to further illustrate the critical role of teachers working together to effect change. Beginning in 1969 in response to the women's liberation movement, a group of female teachers in British Columbia came together to share concerns about sex discrimination in education. They formed a grassroots group called Women in Teaching and in 1970 they wrote to the BCTF executive to draw their attention to the report of the Royal Commission on the Status of Women issued in the same year. As a result, the BCTF established a task force on sex discrimination in school systems that subsequently spawned the BCTF Status of Women Program in 1973. As Coulter explains, the BCTF had two primary aims. The first focused on finding and educating local teachers who would build the Status of Women Program in each school district. The second aim was "to help solve sex discrimination in the education system" (Shuto, 1974, p. 2). In this regard, the work of the BCTF program, like much of the work of the AAUW directed at education in the United States, squarely focused on curriculum, classroom interactions, and teacher attitudes, emphasizing the links among sexism, racism, and classism as being at the root of women's oppression.

Through its organizational efforts and commitment, the BCTF Status of Women Program garnered considerable media attention as women's programs and groups were burgeoning in anticipation of 1975 as the International Year of Women. During this time, the BCTF Status of Women Program increased its network and influence by providing professional development activities in the way of teacher in-services and workshops and conferences for students and teachers, developing classroom materials, presenting briefs to school boards, and getting Status of Women representatives onto local board executives. Most importantly, the BCTF Status of Women Program made a concerted effort to integrate women's issues into all division of the federation so that women's issues were not seen as isolated and of concern only to the members of the task force. There is no doubt that the influence of the BCTF was felt elsewhere (Grove, 1984, p. 13), and in 1976 the BCTF Status of Women Program brought together delegates from all of the Canadian Teacher Federations at the conference Challenge '76: Sexism in Schools. The conference served as a nationwide forum on education designed to discuss issues of gender equity and to develop organizational strategies for action. The strategies were later shared through a series of Canadian Teacher Federation (1976, 1977) publications. While decades later the emphasis on sex-role stereotyping in education has given way to fostering a more complex understanding of how the content and practice of schooling are subject to structural inequalities and how gender is situated in relation to race, class, ethnicity, and sexual orientation (Novogrodsky, Kaufman, Holland, & Wells, 1992), in Canada and elsewhere in the world, teachers and their organizations continue to be a driving force behind gender-equitable practice and policy.

Explore

Acquaint yourself with gender-equity policy in your school. How is such policy reflective of legislation past and present? What coordinated efforts are in place to ensure that that the gender-equitable rights of faculty, students, and staff are respected and maintained? When was the last time gender was a topic of discussion in faculty meetings? What was the focus of the discussion?

LINKING GENDER TO SEXUALITY TO COMBAT HOMOPHOBIA IN SCHOOLS

While teachers' federations in Canada and national associations such as the AAUW in the United States have done much to highlight the contribution of feminist research and bring issues of gender equity in educational practice to the point of political action, the material consequences of our success in linking policy to practice continues to be felt in schools and classrooms. In "What's There to Fear: Calling Homophobia into Question," feminist and gender-studies scholar Didi Khayatt (2006) delivers a cogent argument for dealing with gender *in conjunction* with sexuality if we are ever to begin to disrupt homophobia in schools. Khayatt introduces her cross-cultural analysis of hegemonic masculinities by highlighting an interaction she had with a student while teaching French in a small town in Northern Ontario some 30 years ago. Not satisfied with Khayatt's response to his constant attempts to disrupt class by hailing her attention to gain permission to yet again leave the class to go to the bathroom, the student turned to a classmate and in a voice just loud enough for her to hear, whispered: "She's in a bad mood because she probably did not get fucked last night" (p. 134). The male student exercised his considerable social power among classmates in a verbal play to negate Khayatt's institutional authority and reduce her to a sexual subject. At the same time, the student demonstrates the knowledge that to evoke sexuality in terms of getting "fucked" reestablishes (lest any woman forget) gender dominance.

Khayatt's (2006) analysis of hegemonic masculinities across diverse cultures reveals that the real and *imagined* act of penetrability is what casts aspersions on an individual's masculinity. Her focus on the interplay between gender and sexuality forces us to think about the gender in relational terms. In brief, Khayatt suggests,

... because gender is perceived as an essentialist bi-polar category with masculinity as impenetrable and femininity as penetrable, the phallic penetration of a man by another man, orally, but especially anally renders both of them "feminized," that is, potentially capable of penetration. (p. 140)

Khayatt explains that the mainstream articulation of gender through sexuality (i.e., the act of penetration, here represented in the vernacular use of "fuck") reinforces gender domination and homophobia whereby any discursive analysis that would allow for categories of gender or sexuality as "unsettled, fluid, shifting, and with permeable boundaries" (p. 140) invariably poses a perceived threat to an established social order premised on stable and separate categories of masculinity and femininity in which masculinity is imbued with considerable social power in relation to femininity. In Khayatt's view, any attempt in schools to deal with the subject of sexuality needs to be tied to an analysis of masculinity and, by extension, femininity. Further and more pointedly, she contends,

... as long as in schools we are teaching boys about "tolerance" toward "homosexuality" without ever broaching the subject of what exactly is threatening about "queer" sexuality, without making the connection between the anxiety about being penetrated and their fear of having their masculinity questioned or being perceived as "feminized," we are maintaining the status quo. (p. 141)

Like Khayatt, I agree that despite a widespread acknowledgment of issues in education related to gender, we cannot move forward on changing attitudes toward sexual orientation unless educators are prepared to explore notions of gender in conjunction with the more difficult topic of sexuality. Critical discourse analysis continues to prove insightful in examining the ways sexuality is evoked as a means of maintaining the social power invested in hegemonic masculinities.

USING CRITICAL PEDAGOGY AS A LENS FOR EXAMINING GENDER-EQUITABLE PRACTICE

Constructions of gender so pervasively shape our behaviors that it often becomes difficult to detect gender bias in the classroom and our complicity in maintaining those structures. Ministries of education, local school districts, and the community at large need to support teachers in providing them with the necessary professional learning opportunities to reflect upon and critically analyze their interactions with girls and boys across a variety of instructional contexts. Teachers also have to exercise the wisdom, compassion, and courage to act and respond appropriately when they witness or hear reports of sexual harassment or assault. Teacher-student interactions can contribute significantly to the "hidden curriculum," or the more implicit and often unintentional transmission of norms, values, and attitudes embedded in learning experiences.

Curriculum theorists and educational philosophers have a long history of inquiring into the socializing effects of the hidden curriculum as it is enacted through formal schooling. Notably, curriculum theorist Philip Jackson (1968), in his landmark work *Life in Classrooms*, made a convincing and influential argument that we need to begin to understand the socializing and culturally reproductive function of schools. Shortly after, the work of Brazilian educator Paulo Freire in the 1970s and 1980s alerted us to the extent to which the hidden curriculum determines our expectations for students, schooling, and society as a whole. His book *Pedagogy of the Oppressed* (1970) legitimized critical pedagogy, with its organizing principles of equity and social justice, as a counter movement to the culturally transmissive educational curriculum that largely served to maintain the status quo and perpetuate an inequitable division of labor. This Freire and his colleague Donald Macedo referred to as the "banking system" of education (Freire & Macedo, 1987). At the same time, in the United States, Jonathan Kozol's work was gaining both critical attention and practical currency among educators and the public at large. Kozol's (1992) *Savage Inequalities: Children in America's Schools* established the author as one of the most important educational polemicists of the latter twentieth century, a reputation that he has extended into the next century with the publication of *The Shame of the Nation: The Restoration of Apartheid Schooling in America* in 2005. This recent work takes a hard-hitting look at increasing segregation of black and Hispanic children in urban American schools and the devastating effects of a neoliberal agenda on the education of poor children and children of color. Throughout the years, Kozol's arguments have drawn considerably from comparisons between rich and poor school districts, notably the alarming disparity in annual per-child spending in support of K–12 schooling. A number of curriculum theorists have contended that the consequences of unequal spending have been exacerbated by voucher systems and No Child Left Behind. While I am advocating for the adoption of critical pedagogy with its guiding principles of equity and social justice as a lens for examining gender constructions in schools, I am also cautious about the fact that historically the feminist voice has been left wanting, and the work of many prominent critical pedagogues has failed to consider the inequities that exist among the oppressed or to acknowledge how gendered knowledge and experience are transmitted.

In "Why Doesn't This Feel Empowering: Working Through the Repressive Myths of Critical Pedagogy," an article published in *Harvard Educational Review*, Elizabeth Ellsworth (1989) provoked legitimate concerns about the assumptions embedded in the discourse of critical pedagogy. She argued critical pedagogy operated mostly at the level of abstraction and the literature to date, while providing students and educators with the language to enter into philosophical debates on freedom, justice, and democracy, was of considerably less use in helping students and educators "in thinking through the ways [classroom] activities were political" and "how the practices [prescribed] actually alter specific power relations outside or inside schools" (p. 303). Ellsworth calls upon both teachers and students to acknowledge their longstanding investment in various political agendas and describes how rational discourse practices associated with critical pedagogy, which purport to empower, give voice, and foster dialogue, can ultimately lead to the reproduction of relations of domination. She asks the question: "What diversity do we silence in the name of 'liberatory' pedagogy?" Indeed, a number of literacy studies speak to the dangers of attempting to interrupt gendered discursive practices (Alvermann, 1995; Alverman, Commeyras, Young, Randall, & Hinson, 1997; Alvermann, Young, & Green, 1997; Evans, Alvermann, & Anders, 1998), inciting Alvermann and her colleagues (1997) to caution "easy to think about, difficult to do" (p. 73). Ellsworth's experience with working through critical pedagogy with her college-level students suggests that there is real benefit to be derived from disengaging from the abstraction of theoretical language and notions of what we "should be" and what "should be happening" and focus, instead, on context-specific classroom practices. Gender dynamics in the classroom are shaped by multiple factors—race/ethnicity, religious and cultural values, socioeconomic status, teacher beliefs, politics, age, instructional method, even gender composition in terms of female-male ratio. Rather than letting theory dictate normative responses, we need to pay attention to the lived experience, partial narratives, social commitments, and positions of privilege in classrooms as we debate issues related to gender. Whether discourse is conducted face to face or electronically, those with the most power determine who occupies the conversational floor most often, who gets to voice an opinion, whose comments are most validated, and whose are most dismissed. Interventions to change gendered discourse practices are inevitably attempts to alter power relations (Guzzetti et al., 2002).

LINGUISTIC STYLE AND POLICY DECISION MAKING

Deborah Tannen's (1995) article "The Power of Talk: Who Gets Heard and Why" explains in clear detail how women and men are socialized throughout childhood to employ different linguistic styles that work to subordinate women and their contributions in the corporate arena and wherever important policy decisions are being made. Schools and organizations serious about forging policy in support of gender-equitable learning and working environments need first to understand that often the forum for making such decisions is itself fraught with inequitable power relations, and members of the decision-making body would do best to begin by coming to some understanding of the linguistic, sociological, psychological, and anthropological factors that have contributed to our expectations of gendered patterns of expression and how these practices influence the ways in which ideas are considered, what weight they are given, and to whom credit is bestowed.

By and large, girls have been socialized into conversational rituals that emphasize the *rapport dimension* of relationships, whereas boys have been socialized into rituals that emphasis the *status dimension*. While not all girls and boys grow up to subscribe wholly to either role or are as successful at negotiating within these dimensions, there tends to be penalties exacted on those who deviate from the norms as we have seen with adolescent girls who assert themselves intellectually (Guzzetti, 1998) and boys who act in ways that appear to transgress dominant versions of masculinity (Martino & Pallotta-Chiarolli, 2003). It is not surprising that girls learn to downplay the ways in which they excel and emphasize instead the ways that they are all the same in order to avoid sounding too sure of themselves and risk being ostracized for thinking themselves "too good." Boys, on the other hand, are expected to play toward their high status in the group, with one or two boys being seen as the leader or leaders. Giving orders or taking center stage by telling stories and jokes are ways of maintaining the high-status role (Tannen, 1995). Tannen argues that these lessons learned in childhood carry over into the workplace and come to characterize boardroom discussions and meetings, with men speaking in ways that position themselves as one-up (Holmes, 1986; Tannen, 1995; Tracy & Eisenberg, 1990/1991). For example, men are more likely to exhibit confidence, boast, and engage in verbal opposition. They are quick to avoid asking questions, inviting unwanted critique, paying routine compliments, or engaging in anything that might be construed as a lack of competence and power (and yes, Tannen adds that this perceived threat to independence is why men are less likely to ask for directions when they are lost). By contrast, women frequently apologize, mitigate criticism with praise, and exchange compliments. In short, "[w]omen are likely to downplay their certainty; men are likely to minimize their doubts" (p. 142). But these conversational rituals may be more conventional than literal, and colleagues engaged in policy-making deliberations have to be mindful that *indirectness* is often the name of the game in decision making.

Tannen explains how indirectness operates as another linguistic signal in human communication that can vary according to power and status, cultural practice, and gender. Women are more likely to be indirect than men when telling others what to do, which, according to Tannen, is due in part to "girls' readiness to brand other girls as bossy" (p. 146). Men, on the other hand, are more indirect than women when admitting fault or weakness due to "boys' readiness to push around boys who assume the one-down position" (p. 146). But indirectness characterizes a lot of the requests by those in power. For example, consider a teacher's request, "Do you think we can get that tidied up by recess?" Likely, the expectation here is that the students will get to cleaning straight away and that the collective "we" does not include the teacher. All of these linguistic rituals shape the way policies are negotiated, and it may help to recognize our positionality within particular discourse communities. An awareness of the differences in conversational style enables us to see the potential of unequal access. Tannen contends that the critical skill for managers—or within the context of this discussion, parents, educators, students, and administrators—is to ensure that all people with something valuable to contribute get heard.

GENDER EQUITY, SEXUAL HARASSMENT, AND THE LAW

Parents and educators might begin with knowing the law and the extent to which present legislation has worked to eliminate sexual harassment and has laid the foundation for gender equality in schools and other educational institutions. In the United States, Congress enacted Title IX of the Education Amendments of 1972 with the aim of eliminating sex discrimination in federally funded educational programs. In 2001, members of the AAUW conducted a study to investigate sexual harassment in secondary schools. The study was designed to compare the present-day frequency and kind of incidents of sexual harassment—everything from unwanted comments to forced sexual activity—with the results obtained from their earlier 1993 study. The AAUW researchers came to the overwhelming conclusion that the widespread occurrence of sexual harassment continues to operate at high levels in American schools. Despite the good intentions of Congress, sexual harassment in schools continues to be tolerated and in some cases condoned. Results from both the 1993 and 2001 studies showed that 80 percent of students experience some form of sexual harassment at some time during their school lives. Students most often experience some form of sexual harassment for the first time between sixth and ninth grade, but some students report instances occurring before third grade (AAUW, 2004). Working through gender issues in schools demands that parents, students, and educators actively recognize how language is used to marginalize and exclude. In the 2003 National School Climate Survey conducted by the Gay, Lesbian, and Straight Education Network (GLSEN), 91.5 percent of LGBT students reported hearing frequent homophobic remarks at school (Kosciw, 2004). The prevalence of homophobic remarks in schools is likely reflective of the inability or unwillingness on the part of faculty and administration to address the problem. Almost 83 percent of LGBT students in the same survey reported that faculty "never" or only "sometimes" intervene when they overhear such remarks. Boys and girls targeted by bullying and harassment are prone to anxiety, distress, confusion, loss of self-esteem, depression, and loss of concentration on schoolwork. In extreme cases, consequences of sexual harassment perpetrated in schools can lead to psychosomatic symptoms, avoidance of school, and suicide (Olweus, Limber, & Mihalic, 1999).

SETTING SCHOOL POLICY ON SEXUAL HARASSMENT

The 2001 AAUW study did, however, reveal one notable difference in the eight years since its original survey that is, at the same time, both hopeful and disconcerting. According to the AAUW report, students in the 2001 study were more likely to say that their schools had a policy or distributed literature on sexual harassment. On the one hand, this finding indicates that schools are aware that sexual harassment is a problem and have taken some action in the form of implementing policies, and furthermore that students appear to be aware of these initiatives. On the other hand, it is distressing to know that while students and teachers now seem to know about the policies and supports in place, incidences of sexual harassment in American schools have not declined over the eight years between studies, and considerable evidence exists to show that many incidents remain unreported. Somewhere along the line, the language of policy is not translating into practice. Taking action demands a dedicated effort to understand why this is so.

In response to the 2001 survey, the AAUW Foundation convened a task force of educators, researchers, and experts to develop a resource guide addressed to parents, students, schools, and school districts as they move forward to tackle the problem of sexual harassment. In *Harassment-Free Hallways: How to Stop Sexual Harassment in Schools*, an AAUW (2004) task force provides strategies for assessing strengths and weaknesses with regard to existing sexual harassment policies, developing user-friendly sexual harassment policies based on existing models, understanding individual rights and responsibilities, reporting and responding to reports of sexual harassment, and fostering an attitude of leadership on the issue of sexual harassment in schools. While the guide spells out a student's rights and provides a suggested protocol for reporting, many students still fear the genuine risks associated with reporting sexual harassment or abuse. The recent events surrounding the suicide of 18-year-old Rutgers freshman Tyler Clementi drives home the devastating and cumulative effects of sexual harassment and the callous ease with which acts of sexual harassment and bullying are committed against LGBT students. In citing reasons for not telling school personnel about being harassed or assaulted, nearly a third (31.8%) of respondents in the GLSEN survey (Kosciw, 2004) reported that experience had taught them that nothing would be done to address the situation, and among those who said that faculty or staff at their school would not intervene, many believed that their inaction was due to the faculty or staff's own anti-LGBT bias. The report cited a number of the students' comments including the following:

Teachers and staff don't see my being bullied for being a lesbian as a big deal. They see words such as "dyke" and "queer" as common teenager slang, and even use the terms themselves on occasion. Most teachers refer to students as

"acting gay" when students do something stupid . . . so telling a teacher makes
no sense because they don't care. (female student, 11th grade, Nevada). (p. 35)

I didn't feel like it needed to be brought up. Besides, my principal was
homophobic, and didn't want to be bothered with what he called "faggots."
(male student, 10th grade, Georgia) (p. 35)

The AAUW recommends that every school and school district have its own
policy prohibiting all forms of sexual harassment and that policies be clearly
written in a style accessible to all members of the school community including students, parents, faculty, staff, and other individuals who spend time in
the school or on school grounds (e.g., support personnel, volunteers, visiting
artists, etc.). Schools and school districts should consult a school board
attorney in drafting a sexual harassment policy to ensure that it complies
with state or provincial and federal laws. The success of any policy requires
effective leaders willing to monitor implementation and revisit and revise
policy in response to identified deficiencies. While Title IX forbids any discrimination or segregation by gender of students in school programs,
courses, or activities, in practice, and despite a documented awareness
among educators and students, it is clear that policy alone is insufficient in
combating sexual harassment in schools.

For most transgendered youth, schools remain an unsafe place. A recent
survey by Egale Canada (2009) reported that trans students experience verbal and physical harassment, assault, teasing, social exclusion, and property
theft more than any other student group. As a result, trans students drop out
of school at higher rates than any other group, and many resort to drugs in
order to cope with increased stress. Trans youth of color often struggle
against the additional challenges of systematic racism. According to Egale
Canada's climate survey, 95 percent of trans students felt unsafe at school
and 90 percent reported being verbally harassed because of their gender
expression. Compounding the fear of harassment from peers is teachers'
perceived indifference and lack of action, with 50 percent of trans students
surveyed reporting that staff never intervened when homophobic or trans-
phobic comments were made. Egale Canada makes an important point
regarding policy. Schools should not wait until they "get" a trans student
in order to begin creating supportive policies and learning environments.
It is likely that a school already has trans students but faculty and
administration are unaware because these students fear "coming out" in an
environment they perceive to be unsafe and unwelcoming. Many trans youth
begin experimenting with gender in high school years. They potentially face
widespread discrimination and risk family rejection and even homelessness.
Arguably, schools can provide a safe and stable environment. To this end,
Egale Canada suggests that individual staff need to support trans students
through supportive classroom interactions and by being available to talk
about gender and preferred name. Above all, teachers need to be vigilant

about signs of stress and incidences of harassment. Trans youth see princi-pals as responsible for establishing a school culture committed to gender diversity and enforcing a "zero tolerance" approach to harassment and for ensuring adequate supervision of hallways and locker rooms.

MOVING ON

In this chapter, discussion focused on gendered literacy practices that shape discourse in institutional settings. While schools will invariably reflect the social structures of the larger society, they can also be sites of change. To this end, teachers and their organizations have played a critical role in link-ing research to practice. Feminist inroads into lobbying for educational change during the rise of the women's movement in the late 1960s and throughout the 1970s put gender on the table in ways that have made it pos-sible for twenty-first-century educators and researchers to continue to work toward policy respectful of gender diversity. Deborah Tannen's linguistic analysis of how power and status are established through differing styles of communication makes policy makers aware of how patterns of gendered discourse function in ways that can disadvantage certain stakeholders from participating fully in the decision-making process. Within the context of schooling, it is important that students, too, have opportunities to make their voice heard when developing policies related to the creation of equi-table learning environments—everything from establishing classroom rules and instructional routines to setting school and district policy. Chapter 8 features the story of Avondale Middle School, where grade 8 students employed their critical literacy skills to revise and redraft the current policy on sexual harassment to demonstrate how classroom practice can be linked to social action.

CHAPTER 8

Taking Action in the Classroom

It can be argued that the current emphasis on standards has left teachers and students looking for "right answers" to problems of literary interpretation. But classrooms, of literature and otherwise, should be important sites of collaborative inquiry that rely on integrating multiple perspectives to solve problems or to come to some understanding about a particular cultural artifact, whether book, music, film, art, or event. Teachers and students need to work together in building their knowledge and understanding of the social construction of gender identity and how it shapes their lives and their relations with others. Critical literacy practices are associated with taking social action. They demand that we be able to draw from a repertoire of perspectives to make certain evaluative judgments. In the examples that follow, students and teachers were involved in critical literacy practices that allowed them to uncover unconscious bias to critically think through gender as a social construct. In the Avondale Middle School example, students rethink their beliefs about sexual harassment to draft actual school policy. Following this middle school example, I relate my experience reading E. L. Konigsburg's (1993) novel, *T-Backs, T-Shirts, COATS, and Suit* with a former grade 4 class to demonstrate how literature can provide the means for developing among young readers an understanding of how gender structures many of our choices. The novel study led to intertextual connections relating to popular television and dress codes. Finally, I conclude with Laraine Wallowitz's example of her senior high Women's Studies class in which she and her students assumed a feminist lens in order to interrogate gender construction in canonical texts and cultural media. Finally, readers are introduced to my more recent study with Farra Yasin (2010), in which writing and illustrating comic strips was the vehicle for middle school students in a multicultural suburban school in the Greater Toronto area to explore their gendered subjectivities in relation to other aspects of their identity.

WORKING THROUGH THE PROBLEM OF SEXUAL HARASSMENT THROUGH CRITICAL LITERACY PRACTICES: THE AVONDALE MIDDLE SCHOOL EXAMPLE

Reading and writing policy statements require a specific set of literacy skills. Recalling Ellsworth's (1989) insistence that educators and students need to work through their understandings of critical social issues within the space of specific classroom practices, giving students the opportunity to rewrite existing policy or draft classroom policies on sexual harassment within the context of regular classroom instruction allows students to educate themselves on the issue of sexual harassment and exercise leadership in creating gender-equitable learning environments. *Harassment-Free Hallways* (AAUW, 2004) documents the experience of students enrolled in an eighth-grade criminal law class at Avondale Middle School in Michigan in 1998 who were troubled by the fact that several students suspended for sexual harassment did not fully understand how their actions constituted sexual harassment. Under the guidance of their teacher, students were to identify an existing problem in their community, find out what policy exists to address the problem, and determine whether the policy was effective. Students concluded that there was a policy on sexual harassment but it was ineffective insofar as it did not educate students about the range of behaviors that can constitute an act of sexual harassment, and in their view, it did not go far enough in preventing harassment from occurring in their school. As a result, the students revised the existing policy to incorporate definitions of mild, moderate, and severe forms of harassment and stricter sanctions for those who engage in sexual harassment of students.

Notably, complaints of sexual harassment declined since the student-revised policy was adopted from 40 in 1998 to just several in 2001–2002, and the teacher responsible for the project has since collaborated with a California school district in developing a video series to help schools take action on the issue of sexual harassment. According to the AAUW task force report, the Avondale students' policy has been adopted by the Michigan State Board of Education and remains a national model. The Avondale experience demonstrates how student leadership can play a critical role in drafting policy on sexual harassment and other important issues affecting learning environments. The project epitomizes critical literacy practices insofar as the student-revised policy was prompted by a genuine need to address identified deficiencies in existing policy, and students' work had a direct effect on immediate and distant audiences.

Being proactive in the prevention of sexual harassment and discrimination means beginning with early education. Children at a very young age need to begin to develop the language and skills necessary to recognize what behaviors are unacceptable and to learn to speak up for themselves and others. As I write this, I know full well that this is easier said than done.

Many children may have learned appropriate language through antiharass-
ment programs and programs designed to protect children from physical
and sexual abuse, but children's relative lack of power makes them particularly vulnerable, and we need to recognize that they are not always in a position to protect themselves against more powerful adults and older children.
The peer group, too, can play a critical role in children's decisions regarding
a particular course of action regardless of what they may believe is right or
wrong. Bullying usually entails peer support and attention in executing acts
that individuals would not commit if left on their own.

USING LITERATURE TO WORK THROUGH AN UNDERSTANDING
OF GENDER AND IDENTITY: GRADE 4 STUDENTS READ E. L.
KONIGSBURG'S *T-BACKS, T-SHIRTS, COATS, AND SUIT*

Many teachers and students use literature and the arts as a gateway to
expand and examine their understanding of critical social issues. During
the 1990s, while teaching a grade 4 class in an urban Canadian school, my
students and I read together E. L. Konigsburg's (1993) *T-Backs, T-Shirts,
COATS, and Suit*. The novel proved to be the impetus for working through
issues of gender and identity as they relate to our investment in our outward
appearance and the clothes we wear. The novel opens with Konigsburg's
12-year-old protagonist Chloe in angst over a proposed summer pact with
her best friends that stated if any one of them was to have a "bad hair
day" that all three would have to jump in the local pool and totally immerse
themselves. Should she refuse, she would be shunned. As Chloe, a non-
swimmer, wrestles with the consequences of signing or not signing the pact,
she is released from the burden of choice when her stepfather sends the
young New Jersey suburbanite to visit his sister Bernadette in Florida, advis-
ing her to "give the unexpected a chance." From middle-class worries about
"bad hair days," Chloe is thrust into the daily grind of helping Bernadette
run a commissary food wagon supplying lunch to local workers. When
two new female commissary drivers don skimpy bathing suits known as
T-backs, they put a dent in Bernadette's sales and provoke outrage from a local
conservative alliance, COATS—Citizens Opposing All T-Backs. In addition to
losing sales, Bernadette undergoes mounting pressure from both the funda-
mentalists, who object to the wearing of T-backs as being indecent, and her
coworkers, who see her refusal to wear a T-back as a lack of solidarity.

In working through the fictional events of what might seem to most a
rather benign set of circumstances, both boy and girl readers found themselves trying to reconcile what they viewed as blatant sexism to sell with
the personal freedom to choose. They engaged in a number of discussions
in which they deconstructed sexism and gender bias in advertising, films,
and television including the one centering on the *Due South* trailer described
in Chapter 1. From their position as children from a predominantly white,

middle-class, urban neighborhood that was home to a number of gay and lesbian families and that prided itself on being socially conscious, reading the text yielded fairly sophisticated discussions about the body as the site of identity politics as these 9- and 10-year-olds identified the ways in which clothes become gender markers and how conforming to peer and societal pressures can pose a threat to one's sense of self. The students' responses reflected in large part, what Stanley Fish (1980) referred to as their "interpretive communities" (p. 167). In writing this account, I recognize that the place of reading and book talk in many of the students' homes had a direct influence on the students' willingness to exploit the novel's themes with gusto. In listening to their responses, I was reminded of the extent to which their social positioning and schooling to date had provided them with the language, confidence, and rhetorical strategies to air their views and enter into debate. I have also been assigned to classrooms where the students have much to say but have not yet had an opportunity to develop and exercise the "rules of play" when it comes to large-group and small-group discussion. These are routines that need to be worthy of teaching time and student input if discussions are to be productive in deepening students' understanding of critical issues and extend their comprehension of literary texts. Schools and classrooms that emphasize the importance of "keeping a lid on things" are bound to succumb to a transmission model of education whereby knowledge is merely transferred from teacher to student.

I made it a practice at the beginning of the year at Meet the Teacher Night and later in monthly newsletters or class overviews sent home during reporting periods to familiarize parents and caregivers with the literature to be taken up in class and the themes explored. I found that parents and caregivers appreciated being in the loop, and I believe that in being up front about potentially controversial themes I may have anticipated some of their concerns and addressed possible objections. This practice also allowed parents and caregivers to extend classroom discussions on the home front, and while I had no formal way of knowing who decided to take up which themes, many parents that year commented that the choice of Konigsburg's novel was a brave one and it had generated a lot of talk around the dinner table and during long car rides to and from music lessons and sports. The response to *T-Backs* from both boys and girls was encouraging and revealed that children are aware of how constructions of gender shape their lives and the lives of others.

It was not until years later than I came upon the research findings indicating that teachers tend to craft curriculum, including their choice of books for study, on the basis of what they think will appeal to boys (AAUW, 1992). To be honest, during the time I worked as a classroom teacher in both elementary and middle years, I made it a practice to select whole-class readings based on provocative themes and what I could sink a lot of myself into because I still see the importance of reading aloud to students in establishing common literary ground and modeling reading as a pleasurable enterprise. Admittedly, at the time, it didn't occur to me to actively correct for the representational absence of a protagonist of either sex, and I delighted in exploring with students the function of some of the lesser characters. When I sit down and make a list of all the young adult novels my students and I read together over the course of a given year, it would appear that as far as protagonists go, gender was fairly equitably represented. What was far more important was that the literary works provided ample opportunities for us to engage in what Dewey (1922/1983) called dramatic rehearsal as individually and collectively we worked through morally problematic situations presented in the texts and tested our solutions against those chosen by the author. I paid considerable attention to what my students chose to read independently and what they noted as favorites. I kept track through their reading logs and literary response journals and found that while students recorded series like *Goosebumps* and *Babysitters' Club*, by and large, they soon ran out of things to say about them and saved their more critical and detailed literary responses and discussion contributions for novels with more complex characters and multilayered plots. This of course depended on making such works readily available to students in large number. Over the years, classroom libraries aimed to house close to a thousand titles representative of a wide range of genres (and yes, nonfiction titles, magazines, cassette recordings, maps, and later compact disks were also on hand). We engaged in a great deal of informal book talk, and again, as the topic of "girl's books and boy's books" never surfaced, no one ever justified a book on the basis that it would be good read for either gender. I can clearly recall boys openly expressing an appreciation for the stoic resilience of Roald Dahl's *Matilda* (1988), the meticulous planning of Louise Fitzhugh's *Harriet the Spy* (1964), the eccentricity in E. L. Konigsburg's From the Mixed-Up Files of *Mrs. Basil E. Frankweiler* (1993), and, from an 11-year old boy looking back, a nostalgic fondness for Astrid Lingren's *Pippi Longstocking* (1950). Literature became a locus for delving into intra- and interpersonal experiences and for pursuing intertextual paths to other cultural texts and artifacts. Consistent with what Sumara (2002) years later would come to describe as literary anthropology, we (students and teacher) found ourselves engaged within "literary commonplaces" whereby we collected "past, present and projected interpretations of [ourselves] and [our] situations" (p. 95).

WALLOWITZ: "READING AS RESISTANCE: GENDERED MESSAGES IN LITERATURE AND MEDIA"

In "Reading as Resistance: Gendered Message in Literature and Media," Laraine Wallowitz (2004) describes how teaching feminism as a critical perspective enabled students registered in a senior high Women's Studies course to analyze the ways in which cultural constructions of gender shape the

experiences of males and females. She and her colleagues centered their curriculum around four essential questions: "How do women use language to
overcome obstacles? How has 'woman' as a cultural construct changed over
time? How do race and gender shape identity? How do literature and media
influence ideas of femininity?" (p. 26). The class read, viewed, and listened
to an array of texts including multicultural novels, short stories, historical
documents, oral histories, essays, scholarly articles, films, fashion, television, advertising, and other forms of media representations. Inspired by
Judith Fetterley's (1978) *The Resisting Reader: A Feminist Approach to
American Fiction* and in particular Jonathan Culler's (1978) chapter titled
"Reading as a Women," Wallowitz sought to introduce feminist scholarship
to students as a framework within which they might place their experiences
with both traditional and nontraditional texts. Guided by a "broadened
sense of the variety of texts that create and reflect notions of gender" and
Freire and Macedo's (1987) notion of reading the "word and the world" referenced earlier in this text in Chapter 1, Wallowitz and her colleagues set out
to uncover students' hidden assumptions about gender and how their
notions of femininity and masculinity derive from traditional and nontraditional texts such as TV, advertising, music, clothing, film, and art. To
this end, Wallowitz adapted an exercise from Martino and Mellor's book
Gendered Fictions and chose two short excerpts from a literary work
that did not include reference to either the protagonist's name or gender.
Students read the excerpts and were asked to decide whether the protagonist
is female or male by making assumptions based on such details as where the
character is located (indoors or outdoors), what the character is doing (passive or active), and how the character responds to the environment (victim
or hero). Students then shared their hypothesis with a partner, comparing
their preconceptions before engaging in whole-class discussion. The activity
yielded dialogue as to what constituted typical female and male behavior
and how texts construct gendered stereotypes. Wallowitz probed students
further to determine individual assumptions about gender and those that
were common to the class. She wanted to know where such assumptions
come from—TV, books, advertising—and whether students thought that literature perpetuates gender stereotypes or creates them. According to
Wallowitz, the exercise incited an interest in students, but they were not
yet convinced of the impact of textual influences on their understanding of
what it means to be female and male.

Wallowitz implemented another activity from Martino and Mellor's
book called Changing Gender in an attempt to get students to recognize
how readily they accept gender norms. The activity entails students reading
from a passage dealing with a relationship between a female and male character. The activity calls for switching the characters' genders and then asking
students to reread the passage, paying careful attention to how gendered
boundaries were crossed and to any discomfort or dissonance they felt as

readers. The situation created is somewhat akin to the earlier example of how the network switched up gendered behaviors between men and women in the *Due South* trailer in order to evoke a kind of humorous dissonance. In this case, students read characters who did not fit gendered expectations as abnormal, that is to say, a boy who is sensitive was considered a coward; a girl who is tough was considered a tomboy (Wallowitz, 2004). Throughout the exercise, students came to see how the text positions them as readers by reinforcing gender assumptions. Wallowitz extended these exercises by asking students to make experiential connections through the writing of personal narratives. Students began to realize the extent to which their gender identity is tied to the context in which they were raised by responding to such guiding questions as these: "In what ways were the gifts you received gendered? What did others assume about your interests and hobbies? Did gender assumptions confine your experiences? In what ways did you challenge gender stereotypes? How did others react? What do you think it means to be female and male in the environment in which you live?" (p. 28). Wallowitz followed up with reading gender in nursery rhymes and fairy tales to demonstrate just how we are bombarded by gendered messages from a very young age. Once again, she relied on an activity from *Gendered Fictions* to analyze Disney's *Cinderella* from a feminist perspective. In teaching critical perspectives, I usually recommend that educators work from the known to the unknown, and rather than introduce both a new theoretical lens and a new text, it is advantageous to apply new perspectives to work with familiar material and see it anew. In the exercise, students are asked to complete a graphic organizer in which they identify which characters exhibit traditional masculine qualities ("Who is active? Who is outside? Who is mobile? Who is demanding? Who desires?" [Martino & Mellor, 2000, p. 4]) and which characters exhibit traditional feminine qualities ("Who is passive? Who is inside? Who is static? Who is nurturing? Who is desired?" [Martino & Mellor, 2000, p. 4]). The activity helps students see that folktales function in such a way as to project values and express "a culture's taboos and anxieties" (Wallowitz, 2004, p. 29). For example, students are later asked to review their chart and think about how we read characters that do not fit society's constructions of femininity and masculinity. Do we admire them or dislike them? Think of the Wicked Stepmother.

As students gained an increasing awareness of the ways normative gendered behaviors are constructed and perpetuated in literature and media texts, they became more confident in their readings and began to engage in critical resistance. For example, in response to Nathaniel Hawthorne's "The Birthmark," one female student in Wallowitz's study made a comparison to the way eighteenth-century women are objectified in literature with present-day beauty standards and noted the extent to which the pursuit of impossible ideals prompted women of both eras to seek the aid of science and technology. The entire unit stands as an example of the curricular planning and attention necessary to developing students' critical awareness of how their ideas of femininity and masculinity are socially constructed "by the music we listen to, the books we read, the television we watch, and the stories we heard growing up" (p. 27). At the conclusion of the unit, students were asked to apply the knowledge gained about gender constructions to other texts. They were invited to choose among a number of suggested activities, including analyzing song/rap lyrics for gender messages, writing a children's book with a strong female heroine, or writing a review of a novel from a feminist perspective for Amazon.com.

GENDERED SUBJECTIVITIES IN ADOLESCENT COMIC BOOK WRITING PRACTICES

In North America, comic book reading and writing is generally perceived as an exclusively male domain. Perhaps nowhere is the stereotypical male reader of comics more vividly reinforced in the minds of North American viewers than in the currently popular sitcom *Big Bang Theory* produced by Chuck Lorre and Bill Prady. The routine life of Sheldon Cooper and friends Leonard Hofstadter, Howard Wolowitz, and Rajesh Koothrapali is punctuated by a Wednesday-night trip to Stuart's Pasadena comic book store. The cross-generational appeal of the series can be attributed in part to the fact that comic book aficionados, baby boomers, and gamers alike can tune in to find familiar ground in a nostalgic return to classic DC favorites, sci-fi memorabilia, and intertextual references to comics-inspired contemporary movies and video games. Stuart's comic book store represents for the show's characters a male (albeit not the mainstream ideal) inner sanctum in which any introduction of a girl is bound to wreak havoc, as we see when Leonard's love interest Penny visits the store for the first time and leaves with a confirmed date with Stuart. In a subsequent season, Amy Farrah Fowler's decision to accept a date with the lowly comic book shop owner on her maiden voyage to the store sparks jealousy in the heart of the obsessively unflappable Sheldon Cooper. Yet as teacher and researcher Farra Yasin points out, the North American perception of girls as outsiders to the comic book world does not hold the same sway in other countries or at other times in North American history. American comics historically derive from newspaper "funnies" that were intended to be read by men and women alike. Cartoon features, first in movie theatres and later on television, also fueled the publication of comics. Throughout the twentieth century in Europe, Herge's *Tintin* grew from a serialized children's feature in a Belgian newspaper to a series of comic books translated into 50 languages with recorded sales to date of more than 200 million copies. In contrast to the American superhero, the clean-cut Tintin, a Belgian reporter, travels the comparatively realistic world, aided by his trusty dog Snowy. While comics were overwhelmingly written about the superhuman or swashbuckling adventures of males, Tintin did not preclude a fan base of girls and women.

Yasin, also an accomplished comic book artist and self-professed fan of the genre, spent much of her childhood and adolescence writing and illustrating comics as means of actively exploring her identity through a critical lens to test racial and gendered boundaries. On occasion, she may have depicted herself as a male protagonist, but to Yasin this was the imaginative means to harness and experiment with the power invested in male identities. As a child growing up in the 1960s, my brothers, sister, and I voraciously read DC, Marvel, and Dell comic books. Morphing in and out of characters structured a lot of our play as we exercised our imagined powers to go forth and do good in the world. Guided by a belief that children's creative comic book writing and illustrating could potentially tell us a great deal about how children and adolescents navigate life and enact their subjectivities, in 2010 Yasin and I combined forces (we couldn't resist) to investigate the representation of identities in the comic book writing practices of 161 (94 female, 67 males) middle school students from nine classes in a multicultural suburban school in the Greater Toronto area. While many scholars have pointed to the need to expand our conception of literacy beyond traditional print literacy (The New London Group, 1996; Barton & Hamilton, 1998) and to the idea that comics could be an important means of engaging student in critical literacy practices (Cope & Kalantzis, 1996; Jacobs, 2007; Ranker, 2008; Schwartz & Rubenstein-Avila, 2006; Wilson, 2005), much of the literacy research on comics has focused either on the motivational potential of comics to engage readers or on readers' responses to works already in print. By contrast, our study demonstrated the potential of writing and illustrating comics as a multimodal means of representing adolescent identity. Our ethnographic investigation involved Yasin as a participant observer who assumed responsibility for instructing students in the drawing techniques used by comic book artists. Students were asked to individually create a comic strip to tell the story of a single event in which they are cast as the story's protagonist. Each comic strip was accompanied by a reflective artist statement that elaborated upon each student's artistic choices and thinking processes. In keeping with the school's commitment to cross-curricular planning, we met with interested teachers, the school's literacy team leader, and school librarian to develop the unit of instruction and to evaluate resources. The unit plan, structured into a series of five 40-minute lessons over a three-week period, was incorporated into regular language arts and visual arts instruction and reflected overall and specific outcomes listed in *The Ontario Curriculum, Grades 1 to 8: Language* (Ontario Ministry of Education, 2007).

Through an analysis of ethnographic fieldnotes (Emerson, Fretz, & Shaw, 1995) collected through participant observations and a close reading of students' writing, illustrations, and artist statements, we examined the extent to which students' active engagement in the creation of comics reflected the stated premise in the Ontario Ministry of Education (2007) curriculum guidelines that language is a "fundamental element of identity and culture" (p. 5). The resulting data offered rich insights into how these adolescents aged 11 to 14 constructed gendered identities within and across the three dominant themes of friendship, the body, and cultural imagination. For example, students' comics revealed their interest in having good friends, and 38 of the comics focused specifically on exploring friendship. Friends were conceived of as being helpful and supportive and as instilling a feeling of belonging in the world, but while both girls and boys expressed a desire for close friendships within which one can share experiences of a more personal nature—a BFF (Best Friend Forever)—only girls explored mixed-gender friendships in their comics. Girls, too, more than boys wanted to construct their comics with their friends as characters and were more likely to represent parity. For example, in several of the girls' comics, the artists chose to depict their friend in the exactly the same way as they depicted themselves. Two female students coordinated their efforts to create their comics to feature the same plot of instant friendship but told from their unique perspectives—one cast in the role of a pixie who absentmindedly falls in the mud and the other as the princess who stumbles upon her while trying to escape the loathsome "Dinky Dong." Both girls' and boys' comics spoke to what qualities they believed made for a good friend. One girl's comic pointed to the perils of being too boastful and antagonistic in an *Indian Idol* competition. Boys' comics that focused on friendship stressed desirable qualities such as being respectful and the ability to compromise. In one comic, a young male artist depicted himself as a cape-wearing pencil and his friend as a ruler. Pencil and Ruler have fallen out of favor because Ruler makes fun of Pencil's cape. In the last panel illustrating the situation a month after their disagreement, Ruler apologizes for making fun of Pencil's cape and Pencil abandons wearing the cape, suggesting that it is important to compromise in order to maintain friendships. In addition to this charming example, there were numerous other comics demonstrating that young adolescent boys can use their literacy skills to express their emotional life.

Michael Bitz (2004) instituted the Comic Book Project, a national after-school program that engages students in the creative production of comic books as a path to enhancing literacy and building community. The project began in inner-city New York schools involving more than 700 students. Bitz (2004) emphasizes how comic book writing allowed students to explore their identities and interpret life in the city, stating, "comics enable children to investigate meaningful dimensions of the world that are typically absent from traditional schooling" (p. 34). Bitz found that the majority of the comics produced by students centered on relations with peers and, in particular, gang relations and opposite-sex relations. Drug abuse also figured prominently in many of the comics. Many boys explored the pressure to join a gang and the negative consequences of belonging to one. Storylines often ended with a fight and the character's escape from the city. Girls, too, wrote about gang violence, often depicting how insults about body type, weight, and race often escalated to gang fights. Consistent with the young adolescents in the Yasin and Krasny (2010) study, the girls in Bitz's program also wrote about opposite-sex relations, but the themes were much more explicit and focused on the consequences of dating drug users. Bitz rightfully argues that the comics provided insights into the hopes and fears of urban youth.

MOVING ON

From these accounts of classroom practice, we see that instruction of critical perspectives need not be didactic. Actively involving students in subverting texts and reading as resistance to gendered norms proved a sure means of engaging them on a critical plain seldom encountered in the tiresome pretest/posttest scenario still associated with literature education. We have read how the introduction and application of critical reading practices to young adult literature and of a feminist perspective on traditional and nontraditional texts became part of students' personal metanarratives in the recognition of their own gendered identities. Returning to the concept of *Bildung* described in Chapter 6, I have long maintained that the act of reading makes an important contribution to the process of self-formation as readers explore and test the existential parameters of the text. It is within this type of instructional context that students and educators can challenge gender barriers rather than succumb to passive identification with stereotypes and classic archetypal structures of femininity and masculinity. I caution educators and parents that combating sex-role stereotyping by attempting to eliminate it entirely from children's reading selections assumes that the world is free from sexism, racism, and class bias. A more effective approach to equipping children with the knowledge and skills to combat these inequalities is to engage them in literary works that present female and male protagonists struggling with injustice and to name that which has to be changed. It means, however, that parents and educators recognize that the function of literature study extends beyond acquiring a set of basic reading skills. It is difficult to reconcile the constant lament of U.S. policy makers that a mere 3 percent of grade 8 students achieve "Advanced" levels of reading comprehension on the NAEP (1992, 2007, and 2009) with their persistent investment in a standardized literacy curriculum that continues to establish the primacy of a hierarchy of discrete skills over critical engagement. The importance of acquiring the literacy skills required to unlock meaning and communicate in a linguistically dominated world is not in question here. I am, however, advocating for a more integrated approach to literacy that would refuse to relegate students identified as "lower performing" to drill and practice sheets and vocabulary-controlled reading materials that profess to be "high interest." If I appear passionate it is because I have long battled against the oft-times prevailing practice that would see enrichment and critical study as reserved for the already enriched. I chose instead to work with *all* students in building mutually supportive and cooperative learning environments as opposed to streaming kids into ability groupings.

Involving students in drafting school policy on sexual harassment asks students to consider carefully the ways that gendered discourse and aggressive enforcement of codes of masculinity and femininity can have negative and at times devastating effects. Hopefully, the Avondale Middle School example detailed in this chapter will serve as inspiration for other initiatives in which educators and students work together in the quest for more gender-equitable and safe schools.

CHAPTER 9

Gender Literacy: Some Parting Thoughts

I first proposed this book as *Gender Literacy* rather than *Gender and Literacy*. I wanted to convey that insofar as gender is socially constructed and performative, language remains a primary means through which we conceive of our gendered selves and through which we structure and perform our gendered relations with others. The project was intended to demonstrate to parents and educators how literacy practices largely determine our relational parameters and govern our bodies according to a descriptive account of the conditions that make the perception of gender intelligible to us. Returning to Judith Butler's (1990) insistence that "what qualifies as 'gender' . . . attests to a pervasively normative operation of power" (p. xxi), gender invariably entails a judgment as to the degree to which we conform to those norms. Language is used to regulate and reinforce a perceived hierarchy of gendered appearance and behavior. Linguistic representation can either reveal or distort the realm of possibility, and it is clear we remain caught "within the language of 'presumptive heterosexuality'" (Butler, 1990, p. xxx). We speak of a "real man's man," "a girlie girl," "Daddy's little girl," "a Momma's boy," "a tomboy," "a real lady," "a true gentleman," "a tramp," "a queen," and "a dyke," all terms and phrases that bear judgment and rank against patriarchal ideals. I want parents and educators to think seriously about the consequences of unquestioned compliance to gender norms and the disadvantages and limitations it places upon our youth. We have traditionally undervalued the feminine/female, consistently making it the object of our contempt and yet rather perversely have applied that same contempt in centering the blame on education and the prevalence of female teachers for boys' failure to learn and relate in ways that would allow them to adapt to more feminized work environments. The result has been quick-fix solutions based on accommodating traditional forms of masculinity that are unlikely to lead to any sustained change in boys' attitudes toward literacy (or women) or toward developing the kind of work habits and relationship skills that have been stereotyped as feminine—skills that have now come to characterize the global workplace.

Throughout this book, I have advocated for a sociocultural approach to understanding the relationship between gender and literacy (read "literacy" and not exclusively "literacy achievement"). I wrote in the hope that parents and educators would develop a deeper knowledge and understanding of gender construction and that reading this book would provoke them to critically reflect on their own assumptions and investments in those constructions. I paid careful attention to my claim of writing "in a style accessible to both parents/families and educators," but at the same time I recognize the need to push readers beyond the popular and all-too-accessible rhetoric that has moved national education agendas into a moral panic. I wrote in the belief that there is real value in providing parents and educators with language that can lend theoretical shape and form to their arguments. While differing achievement levels between girls and boys in various disciplines are a legitimate concern, understanding gender in terms other than biological might lend considerable insight into how enacting normative codes of femininities and masculinities contributes to those differences. Furthermore, it is important to see in what ways our investment in correcting for those gendered differences is politically and economically motivated so that we are more mindful of what it is we are actually asking for our children. The importance of providing for gender-equitable learning environments cannot be underestimated for there is a growing body of evidence to support the claim that in schools where gender difference is *less* emphasized, that is to say, where schools have not entered into "boy-friendly" practices but rather maintained high expectations for *all* students, both girls and boys achieve highly (Keddie & Mills, 2008; Lingard, Martino, Mills, & Bahr, 2002, 2003; Younger, Warrington, & McLellan, 2005).

In closing, I offer parents and educators additional resources in the way of organizations, programs, and recommendations for reading for those who wish to follow up on specific issues relating to literacy and gender. While many of the organizations specifically relating to gender are national in scope, many programs listed are regional but nevertheless offer helpful ideas and extensive online resources that may inspire interested working groups to establish similar programs elsewhere. National organizations are either funded in whole or part by federal governments or are supported through corporate and charitable donations, and therefore may express certain opinions that may not necessarily reflect the views of either this author or those of the publisher. The organizations and associations referenced here seek to address critical issues related to gender and/or literacy in meeting the educational needs of all students. It is highly advisable that educators, parents, and administrators carefully review any resource listed before using it with students as some may contain sensitive content and may not be appropriate for all ages. In reviewing the resources listed, schools may wish to engage support personnel, such as curriculum coordinators, psychologists, social workers, or equity officers, or invite persons working in human rights and gender-equity organizations external to the school board to facilitate workshops or study groups focusing on program implementation or helping stakeholders come to a deeper understanding of gender and literacy. An annotated bibliography of recommended reading is followed by a list of literary works cited throughout the book. It is my sincere hope that parents and educators will take up some idea presented in *Gender and Literacy: A Handbook for Parents and Educators* and that it will lead them to further inquiry and appropriate action.

ORGANIZATIONS AND ASSOCIATIONS

American Association of University Women

www.aauw.org
AAUW
1111 Sixteenth St. NW
Washington, DC 20036, USA
Tel: (202) 785-7700
Toll free: (800) 326-AAUW
E-mail: connect@aauw.org

The American Association of University Women (AAUW) is a nationwide network that reaches an international audience. AAUW's expertise in monitoring critical issues affecting women and girls is actively recognized by the United Nations with the Economic and Social Council. The AAUW boasts more than 100,000 members, 1,000 branches, and 500 college/university institutional partners. The AAUW mission aims at the advancement of equity for women and girls through advocacy, education, philanthropy, and research. As indicated throughout this handbook, numerous AAUW reports have led to an identified need for more gender-equitable learning environments and have laid the foundation for subsequent studies in gender and education.

American Library Association

www.ala.org
American Library Association
50 E. Huron Street
Chicago, Illinois 60611, USA
Toll free: (800) 545-2433
Rainbow Project: http://glbtrt.ala.org/rainbowbooks/

The American Library Association (ALA) publishes a number of periodicals related to libraries, collections, and information technology, among them *American Libraries, Booklist,* and *Book Links* and *Book Links Online,* available through paid subscriptions, in which one will find reviews regular reviews of young adult and children's books and articles pertaining to literacy. In addition to the advancement of literacy and promotion of intellectual freedom through an a awareness of challenges to library materials, the ALA is host to the Rainbow Project, a joint initiative of the association's Gay, Lesbian, Bisexual, and Transgendered Round Table and the Social Responsibilities Round Table subgroups. The Rainbow Project prepares an annual bibliography of quality books with significant and authentic GLBTQ content written for children and adolescents from birth to 18 years of age.

Canadian Federation for Sexual Health

Gender Identity and Sexual Orientation: www.cfsh.ca/Your_Sexual_Health/
Gender-Identity-and-Sexual-Orientation/
Canadian Federation for Sexual Health
1 Nicholas Street, Suite 430
Ottawa, Ontario K1N 7B7, Canada
Tel: (613) 241-4474
Fax: (613) 241-7550

The Canadian Federation for Sexual Health is a charitable organization aimed at the promotion of sexual and reproductive health and rights in Canada and internationally. The featured link marked Gender Identity and Sexual Orientation provides a helpful glossary of terms for those wishing to establish some common understandings.

Canadian Rainbow Health Coalition

www.rainbowhealth.ca
P.O. Box 3043
Saskatoon, Saskatchewan S7K 3S9, Canada
Toll Free: (800) 955-5129
Fax: (306) 955-5132
E-mail: info@rainbowhealth.ca

The Canadian Rainbow Health Coalition (CRHC) is a national organization that focuses on providing information and educational resources on issues related to GLBT health and wellness. There are suggestions for workshop presentations, and interested researchers working in the area of GBLT health are able to register in order to post their research to the CRHC database.

Center for Educational Pathways

www.edpath.org
Dr. Michael Bitz, Executive Director
Tel: (917) 674-0014
E-mail: bitz@edpath.org
The Comic Book Project: www.comicbookproject.org

The Comic Book Project is an arts-based literacy initiative hosted by the nonprofit Center for Educational Pathways. The project aims at engaging children into an alternate path to literacy by writing, designing, and publishing original comic books. The project website provides interested educators and parents with a step-by-step guide, videos of children at work, and a gallery of children's work.

Egale

www.egale.ca
Tel: (613) 230-1043
Toll free: (888) 204-7777
Fax: (416) 642-6435
E-mail: egale.canada@egale.ca

Egale Canada is a national organization committed to the promotion of equality and justice for lesbian, gay, bisexual, and trans-identified people and their families across Canada. With particular reference to K–12 schools, Egale's extensive website features articles on safe schools, LGBTQ students' rights, bullying, and the importance of gay-straight alliances. It also provides a link to Taylor and Peters's (2011) *Every Class in Every School: Final Report on the First Published Report Climate Survey on Homophobia, Biphobia, and Transphobia in Canadian Schools.*

Gender Identity Research and Education Society

www.gires.org.uk
Melverley
The Warren
Ashtead
Surrey KT21 2SP, UK
Tel: 01372 801554
E-mail: info@gires.org.uk

The Gender Identity Research and Education Society (GIRES) is a British charitable organization that advances a biological explanation for people who experience atypical gender-identity development, especially trans people. Its primary mission is to improve the circumstances for trans people and their families through the promotion of supportive attitudes, especially among those who can effect societal change including politicians, policy makers, clinicians, and government service providers (police, teachers, employers, and journalists). Their approach is based on research investigating both the biological origins of atypical gender identity and transsexualism and the ways society reacts to gender variance. The information provided sheds light on genetic factors influencing gender identity, but some readers may find that the scientific discourse has a tendency to pathologize nonheteronormative identifications.

International Reading Association

reading.org
International Reading Association
800 Barksdale Rd.
P.O. Box 8139
Newark, DE 19714-8139, USA

The International Reading Association (IRA) is a nonprofit, global network of individuals and institutions dedicated to worldwide literacy. IRA provides extensive resources for literacy professionals in the way of highly ranked peer-reviewed journals, professional books, online position statements, advocacy efforts, volunteerism, and regional and international professional development activities and events. The IRA is an established leader in setting strategic directions for literacy education in the United States, Canada, and countries throughout the world. To this end, the association publishes a series of position statements, available online or for purchase, that help shape public policy in education. The association's journals—*Reading Research Quarterly, Journal of Adolescent and Adult Literacy*, and *The Reading Teacher*—provide a valuable source of high-quality, well-researched articles on gendered literacy practices. The IRA has a network of reading councils throughout North America, which host a number of professional development events and local literacy initiatives.

National Council of Teachers of English

ncte.org
National Council of Teachers of English
1111 W. Kenyon Road
Urbana, IL 61801-1096, USA

Like the IRA, the National Council of Teachers of English (NCTE) is an established leader in informing policy related to literacy education in the United States and Canada. NCTE is committed to improving the teaching and learning of English and the language arts at all levels of education. It publishes a number of high-quality, peer-reviewed journals including *Language Arts, Voices from the Middle, English Journal, English Education,* and *Research in the Teaching of English,* among others, and provides professional development tailored to various career stages and to all levels of education from preschool to graduate school. Its online resource ReadWriteThink.org provides free access to classroom-tested lesson plans among which one can find lessons that foster students' awareness of gender construction in language, books, film, and other media.

PFLAG

www.pflagcanada.ca
1633 Mountain Road
Box 29211
Moncton, New Brunswick E1G 4R3
Tel: (506) 869-8191
Fax: (506) 387-8349
Toll free: (888) 530-6777 (English); (888) 530-6483 (French)
E-mail: execdirector@pflagcanada.ca

PFLAG is a Canadian charitable organization receiving corporate and private donations that assists Canadians struggling with issues of sexual orientation and gender identity. It provides resources to parents, families, friends, and colleagues who have questions or concerns. Canadian schools and youth groups may obtain free copies of *Challenge Stereotypes. Celebrate Your Potential. Be Yourself. Inspire Change* through the PFLAG website. A two-page classroom discussion guide is also available. The website provides helpful links for all educators. The PFLAG website also features videos of individuals sharing their stories of coming out or of their relationship to someone who is out.

Rainbow Resource Centre

www.rainbowresourcecentre.org
170 Scott Street
Winnipeg, Manitoba R3L 0L3
Tel: (204) 474-0212
Fax: (204) 478-1160
E-mail: info@rainbowresourcecentre.org

The Rainbow Resource Centre in a nonprofit organization committed to representing and supporting lesbian, gay, bisexual, trans, two-spirited, intersex, queer, questioning, and allied individuals, communities, and families by providing education and outreach services, accessible counseling, and other programs and services. This independent center has roots dating back to the 1970s beginning as a student group at the University of Manitoba. The organization currently provides public outreach and private consultation to health care providers, educators (K–12 and postsecondary), social service practitioners, and anyone wanting to build capacity and awareness and to learn about challenges facing gay, lesbian, bisexual, transgender, and two-spirit children, youths, and adults. The Rainbow Resource Centre offers workshops, presentations, and seminars facilitated by persons trained in adult education on a wide range of topics adapted to the needs of different audiences.

RECOMMENDATIONS FOR FURTHER READING

Suggested Reading for Chapter 1: Why a Handbook on Gender and Literacy?

Sex and Gender Identification

Fausto-Sterling, A. (2000). *Sexing the body: Gender politics and the construction of sexuality.* New York: Basic Books.

> Fausto-Sterling is professor of biology and women's studies at Brown University. In this collection of essays, she advances the idea that labeling someone a woman or a man is a social decision. She makes a clear and cogent argument that scientific research about gender is often affected by existing beliefs.

Public Health Agency of Canada. (2010). *Questions and answers: Gender identity in schools.* Ottawa, ON. http://orders.catie.ca/product_info.php?products_id=25670.

> This public document was developed in response to feedback from a national evaluation of Canada's *Canadian Guidelines for Sexual Health Education,* published in 1994 and revised in 2003 and 2008, that called for evidence and resources on specific issues. *Questions and Answers* is designed to address the most commonly asked question regarding gender identity of youth in schools with the intention of assisting educators, curriculum and program planners, school administrators, policy makers, and health professionals in their efforts to create a healthy, safe, and equitable school environment for youth struggling with issues of gender identity.

Gender and Play

Thorne, B. (1993). *Gender play: Girls and boys in school.* New Brunswick, NJ: Rutgers University Press.

Through daily observations in the classroom and on the playground, Thorne describes how a group of fourth and fifth graders construct and experience gender in school. Her investigation provides readers with clear insights into how the organization and meaning of gender is influenced by age, ethnicity, race, sexuality, and social class. The book includes practical suggestions for enhancing cooperative mixed-gender interaction.

Girlhood Culture

Orenstein, P. (1994). *School girls: Young women, self-esteem, and the confidence gap*. New York: Doubleday.
Inspired by a report by the AAUW, Orenstein set forth to examine the steep decline in the confidence of adolescent girls. She documents the obstacles they face at home, in school, and in our culture and their struggles with eating disorders, sexual harassment, and declining academic achievement.
Walkerdine, V. (1990). *Schoolgirl fictions*. New York: Verso.
Walkerdine's seminal work reveals that femininity and masculinity are fictions lived as fact. She challenges the assumption that girls readily take on roles and stereotypes by documenting their struggles to alter the identities created for them.

Culture of Boys

Gilbert, R., & Gilbert, P. (1998). *Masculinity goes to school*. Melbourne: Routledge/Kegan Paul.
The authors provide a balanced view of a wide range of issues surrounding boys and education. They make clear how popular constructions of masculinity pervade every facet of boys' lives at home, at school, and at leisure. The book offers a review of programs and approaches to working with boys in schools.
Salisbury, J., & Jackson, D. (1996). *Challenging macho values: Practical ways of working with adolescent boys*. London: Routledge/Falmer Press.
Two teachers working with inner-city youth in the United Kingdom challenge the culture of aggressive manliness with which most boys have grown up and uncover the key social forces that currently shape masculine identities. The book includes practical suggestions for changing boys' destructive patterns of behavior.

Literacy

Freire, P., & Macedo, D. (1987). *Literacy: Reading the word and reading the world*. South Hadley, MA: Bergin and Garvey.
This book furthers the argument first presented in Freire's (1970) *Pedagogy of the Oppressed* that, historically, education does not shape society but rather society shapes education. The authors reveal how literacy is linked to knowledge and power. Freire and Macedo's work is generally regarded as required

reading for anyone interested in understanding the potential and limitations of literacy as a vehicle for social change.

The New London Group. (1996). A pedagogy of multiliteracies: Designing social futures. *Harvard Educational Review* 66, no. 1, 60–92.

The authors expand readers' understanding of literacy and of literacy teaching and learning to account for increasing cultural and linguistic diversity in globalized societies. They provide a justification for a multiliteracies approach as a corrective to barriers arising from differences of culture, language, and gender.

Willinsky, J. (1990). *The triumph of literature/the fate of literacy: English in the secondary school curriculum.* New York: Teachers College Press.

In this work, Willinsky reveals how public schooling with its emphasis on literature education effectively curtailed the social agency associated with increased literacy rates among the working classes in the mid-nineteenth century. Willinsky's social and historical analysis demonstrates Freire and Macedo's (1987) claim that literacy is tied to material and political conditions.

Policy

Title IX: 25 Years of Progress. U.S. Government Archived Resources. http://www.ed.gov/pubs/TitleIX/title.html.

This 1997 report issued by the U.S. Department of Education and the Office for Civil Rights outlines the national agenda for prohibiting sex discrimination in federally assisted education programs. Title IX of the Educational Amendments of 1972 states that schools cannot deny any student participation in educational program or activity on the basis of sex. Title IX has been cited as a major obstacle to the establishment of publicly funded same-sex schools.

Suggested Reading for Chapter 2: Taking a Critical Approach to Interpreting the Research and Literature on Gender and Literacy

Orellana, M., & Gutierrez, K. (2006). The problem of English learners: Construction genres of difference. *Research in the Teaching of English* 40, no. 4, 502–7.

In this article, authors Orellana and Gutierrez challenge deficit constructions that characterize much of the research literature on English language learners. They argue that we need to reconceptualize the nature of the problems we name as such frameworks are likely to shape the work we do in cultural communities.

Smith, M., & Wilhelm, J. (2002). *"Reading don't fix no Chevys": Literacy in the lives of young men.* Portsmouth, NH: Heinemann.

Smith and Wilhelm document their work with a diverse group of 49 young men in middle and high school to provide readers with some understanding of how young men use literacy and the conditions that promote their active literacy engagement.

Sokal, L. (2010). Long-term effects of male reading tutors, choice of text and computer-based text of boys' reading achievement. *Language and Literacy: A Canadian Educational E-Journal* 12, no. 1, 97–115.

In this article, Canadian researcher Laura Sokal reviews existing literature on three popular interventions designed to correct for boys' reported under-achievement in measures of reading performance. By and large, the author concludes that there is little evidence to suggest that any of these interventions produce any sustainable effects.

Suggested Reading for Chapter 3: International and National Literacy Assessments

Organisation for Economic Co-operation and Development. (2009). *PISA 2009 results: What student know and can do: Student performance in reading, mathematics and science (Volume 1)*. http://www.oecd.org/document/53/ 0,3746,en_32252351_46584327_46584821_1_1_1_1,00.html.

Conducted by the Organisation for Economic Co-operation and Development (OECD), the Programme for International Student Assessment (PISA) is a triennial survey that both measures and compares the learning skills of 15-year-old students from participating countries. Data collected from this survey may be used to further our understanding about patterns of reading as well as the sociocultural factors that bear on students' literacy skills. The website is also host to published reports for past surveys.

Topping, K., Valtin, R., Roller, C., Brozo, W., & Dionisio, M. L. (2003). *Policy and practice implications of the Program for International Student Assessment (PISA) 2000: Report of the International Reading Association PISA Task Force*. Newark, DE: International Reading Association. http://reading.org/ General/CurrentResearch/Reports/PISAReport.aspx.

This report details some of the policy-level and practical implications of the PISA 2000 survey and situates questions of literacy differences between boys and girls in reference to conversations about the social construction of gender. Gendered differences in literacy are discussed in reference to prominent gender stereotypes in popular culture, the feminization of school environments, and the ways in which secondary-school language arts curricula have the potential to reinscribe gendered codes of behavior. Task force reports for subsequent PISA and Progress of International Reading Literacy Study (PIRLS) studies are also available on the IRA website.

U.S. Department of Education. *National Assessment of Educational Progress (NAEP)*. http://nces.ed.gov/nationsreportcard/.

Designed to collect information regarding student performance in a variety of subject areas, the NAEP draws attention to the ways in which different contexts for reading may contribute, in part, to the differences in what readers can do. The context of reading is divided into three different categories: reading for literary experience, reading for information, and reading to perform a task. NAEP findings are also analyzed in reference to sociocultural factors such as socioeconomic status, ethnicity, and gender.

Suggested Reading for Chapter 4: Researching Gendered Discourse Practices

Gilligan, C. (2003). *The birth of pleasure*. (Reprint). New York: Vintage.
  The phenomenon of female silencing guides Gilligan's work as she investi-
  gates the psychological consequences that women bear in male-dominated
  society. Drawing from literature as well as other fields, Gilligan demonstrates
  how the voices of women and girls are systematically silenced or ignored and
  the social relationships that are thus made possible or impossible.
Guzzetti, B., Young, J., Gritsavage, M., Fyfe, L., & Hardenbrook, M. (2002).
  Reading, writing, and talking gender in literacy learning. Newark, DE:
  International Reading Association.
  Generally concerned with raising awareness regarding the intersections
  between issues of gender, learning, and classroom practice, the authors of this
  text provide qualitative data and interpretations related to traditional concep-
  tualizations of literacy and gender. This text supplements the quantitative
  data contained in large-scale surveys and national test scores.
Guzzetti, B., & Bean, T. (eds). (2012). *Adolescent literacies and the gendered self:
  (Re)constructing identities through multimodal literacy practices*. New
  York: Routledge.
  This new edited volume explores how a dynamic range of literacy practices
  construct gender identities among today's youth. The contributing authors
  explore gender influences and identities in literacy and literature, in new liter-
  acies, and in issues and policies within local and global contexts.
Lorde, A. (2007). The master's tools will never dismantle the master's house. In A.
  Lorde, *Sister outsider: Essays and speeches* (pp. 110–13). Berkeley, CA: The
  Crossing Press.
  Lorde challenges those in feminist circles to acknowledge the absence of poor
  women, women of color, lesbian women, and women of developing countries
  in academic feminist circles. She invites feminist academics to grapple with the
  knowledge that their own work is not exempt or protected from the racist and
  patriarchal tools they seek to dismantle.

Suggested Reading for Chapter 5: Researching Gender and Reading

Cherland, M. R. (1994). *Private practices: Girls reading fiction and constructing
  identity*. London: Taylor and Francis.
  This ethnographic study offers insight into the relationship between literature
  and the social construction of gender. Offering a critical analysis of the ways
  in which gender is constructed, Cherland suggests that literature participates
  in cultural reproduction and provides some practical suggestions that may
  encourage the development of egalitarian relationships and a more socially
  critical standpoint.
Davies, B. (1993). *Shards of glass: Children reading and writing beyond gendered
  identities*. Cresskill, NJ: Hampton Press.
  Working within a poststructuralist framework, Davies's research with primary-
  school-aged children highlights the existence of traditional stereotypes and

considers the ways in which shared social discourses constitute the subjectivity of individuals. Centered on conceptualizations of gender, power, discourse, and subjectivity, this book also addresses the ways in which reader responses may reinscribe, transgress, or reinvent existing gendered scripts.

Krasny, K. (2007). Seeking the affective and the imaginative in the act of reading: Embodied consciousness and the evolution of the moral self. In D. Vokey (Ed.), *Philosophy of education 2006* (pp. 429–37). Normal, IL: Philosophy of Education Society.

Issues related to empathetic identification and moral imagination are discussed in relation to readers' literary encounters. Krasny suggests that reader responses to literature may provide a critical point of self-reflection that can lead to one's more robust understanding of self and others.

Pace, B. G., & Townsend, J. S. (1999). Gender roles: Listening to classroom talk about literacy characters. *English Journal* 88, no. 3, 43–49.

Pace and Townsend examine the ways in which instructional context determines how students may engage with literature as a means towards deconstructing societal frameworks. The authors analyze instructors' instructional techniques, questions of voice and interpretation in the classroom, as well as the relationship between gender and literary engagement.

Zimet, S. (1966). Children's interests and story preferences. *The Elementary School Journal* 67, 122–30.

In this early review of the literature on children's reading interests, Zimet suggests that there is a close relationship between children's reading interests and their social, cultural, and political circumstances. As reading interests are sociohistorically situated and fluid, Zimet also acknowledges the ways in which reading interests are shaped by the historical time period and the reader's age, gender, and socioeconomic background.

Suggested Reading for Chapter 6: Reading Gender in Children's and Adolescent Literature

Harper, H. (2007). Studying masculinity(ies) in books about girls. *Canadian Journal of Education* 30, no. 2, 508–30.

Harper explores the nature and performance of masculinity portrayed in five popular young adult novels with female protagonists. Her study demonstrates the importance of employing masculinity as a lens for textual analysis. The researcher argues that these works can offer readers more complex renderings of gendered identity to temporarily disrupt the connection between sex and gender.

Lehr, S. (2001). *Beauty, brains, and brawn: The construction of gender in children's literature*. Portsmouth, NH: Heinemann, 2001.

This collection of essays written from diverse perspectives explores how femininities and masculinities are constructed in children's literature. Renowned children's literature scholar Charlotte Huck writes the introduction in which she suggests that reading practices and literacy are related to broader social ideas regarding feminine and masculine gender norms. Questions about hegemony, resistance, compliance, and equity are discussed.

Nodelman, P., & Reimer, M. (2003). *The pleasures of children's literature*. Boston, MA: Allyn and Bacon.

Nodelman and Reimer examine children's literature as a site where readers may grapple with conventional subject positions and ask after the unequal division of power in society. Through their engagement with issues related to literary response, the authors open a space for readers to think across questions stemming from literary theory, cultural studies, psychology, and educational theory. Educators will find the practical suggestions for literary exploration helpful in engaging students in critical readings of classic and contemporary texts.

Rothbauer, P. M. (2002). Reading mainstream possibilities: Canadian young adult fiction with lesbian and gay characters. *Canadian Children's Literature* 108, 10–26.

Rothbauer's analysis of 15 Canadian fictional works that contain lesbian or gay characters considers the representation of these characters and the possibilities they offer for gay teens. Issues related to underrepresentation, coming-out narratives, and the mainstream portrayal of homosexual characters are addressed.

Trites, R. S. (1997). *Waking sleeping beauty: Feminist voices in children's novels*. Iowa City: University of Iowa Press.

In her critical feminist analysis of young adult and children's literature, Trites initiates discussion around questions of feminine voice, subjectivity, and cultural narratives. Working with themes derived from her analysis of this literature, Trites offers interpretations of the ideological stakes related to the construction of feminist novels and female protagonists generally.

Zipes, J. (2001). *Sticks and stones: The troublesome success of children's literature from Slovenly Peter to Harry Potter*. New York: Routledge.

Renowned children's literature scholar Jack Zipes presents a series of essays in which he demonstrates the danger associated with adults' overinvestment in children. He argues that children are succumbing to cultural homogenization that limits their imagination and creativity.

Suggested Reading for Chapter 7: Policy, Practice, and Research: How Schools and Communities Take Action

Coulter, R. (1996). Gender equity and schooling: Linking research and policy. *Canadian Journal of Education* 21, no. 4, 433–52.

In this historical review of educational research and policy making in gender equity and schooling, Coulter demonstrates how the two have been linked through the work of teachers and their organizations. In addition to sex-role stereotyping theory that has been influential in shaping government policy and pedagogical practice, teachers have accessed a wider body of research to inform their work in schools.

Ellsworth, E. (1989). Why doesn't this feel empowering? Working through the repressive myths of critical pedagogy. *Harvard Educational Review* 59, no. 3, 297–325.

Ellsworth turns a critical lens to critical pedagogy to open up a conversation about the assumptions and power dynamics that have not been theorized by critical pedagogues. A provocative and critical assessment of key concepts such as empowerment, dialogue, and voice is put forth.

Jackson, P. W. (1968). *Life in classrooms*. New York: Holt, Rinehart and Winston.
This classic text convincingly argues that classrooms are sites of social reproduction but may also be conceptualized as venues for social change. Jackson recognizes educational institutions as key agents of socialization that are implicated in existing power relations and social inequalities.

Khayatt, D. (2006). What's to fear: Calling homophobia into question. *McGill Journal of Education* 41, no. 2, 133–44.
Khayatt examines the interplay between gender and sexuality through a cross-cultural analysis of hegemonic masculinities to account for several reasons why mainstream society cannot bear homosexuality or any expression of resistance to heteronormative behavior.

Martino, W., & Pallotta-Chiarolli, M. (2003). *So what's a boy? Addressing issues of masculinity and schooling*. Maidenhead, UK: Open University Press.
Martino and Pallotta-Chiarolli offer insight into the construction of masculinity and the ways in which boys negotiate their gendered identity within educational institutions. Focusing on the forms of power, hegemonic discourses, and boundary policing of "normal" masculinity, the authors offer both analyses and recommendations.

Tannen, D. (1995). The power of talk: Who gets heard and why. *Harvard Business Review* 73, no. 5 (September–October): 138–48.
The linguistic styles of men and women are analyzed as social constructions that reinforce existing gender inequalities. Language is conceptualized as a site governed by unequal power relations, and thus conversational rituals and expectations are understood to be indicative of social and political issues.

Suggested Reading for Chapter 8: Taking Action in the Classroom

American Association for University Women. (2004). *Harassment-free hallways: How to stop sexual harassment in school: A guide for students, parents, and schools*. Washington, DC: American Association of University Women Education Foundation.
This AAUW guide responds to the results of 2001 and 2003 surveys showing that 8 in 10 students experience some form of sexual harassment at some point during their school lives. This practical guide is intended to help parents, students, schools, and school districts in assessing present strengths and weaknesses with regard to existing policy, in developing user-friendly policies, and in helping them understand their respective rights and responsibilities for dealing with reports of sexual harassment. The Avondale Middle School model in which students drafted school sexual harassment policy is presented in this document.

Wallowitz, L. (2004). Reading as resistance: Gendered messages in literature and media. *The English Journal* 93, no. 3 (January): 26–31.

By introducing feminism as a critical perspective to senior high students, Wallowitz argues that individuals may be better able to understand how social ideas about gender impact their experiences as men and women. Teaching feminist analyses of language, literature, or popular culture permitted students to think deeply about what it means to be male or female in one's society.

Literature and Media Cited

LITERATURE

Alcott, L. M. (1868). *Little women*. New York: Bantam Dell.

Anderson, L. (1999). *Speak*. New York: Penguin.

Atwood, M. (1986). *The handmaid's tale*. Toronto: Seal Books

Bauer, M. D. (1994). *Am I blue? Coming out from silence*. Toronto: Harper Collins.

Baum, F. (2000). *The wonderful wizard of Oz: 100th anniversary edition*. New York: Harper Collins.

Bell, W. (1992). *No signature*. Toronto: Doubleday.

Block, F. L. (2004). *Weetzie Bat*. Harper Collins Publishers.

Bouchard, D. (2001). *Buddha in the garden*. Vancouver, BC: Raincoast Books.

Boyd, D. (1996). *Bottom drawer*. Oakville, ON: Rubicon.

Brett, C. (1989). *S. P. likes A. D*. Toronto: Women's Press.

Bronte, C. (1847/1969). *Jane Eyre*. New York: Oxford University Press.

Brooks, M. (1994). *Traveling on into the light and other stories*. Orchard Books.

Brown, C. (2003). *Louis Riel: A comic-strip biography*. Montreal: Drawn and Quarterly.

Buck, P. S. (1931). *The good earth*. New York: Washington Square Press.

Burnett, F. H. (1905/2000). *A little princess*. Mineola, NY: Dover Publications.

Capote, T. (1958). *Breakfast at Tiffany's*. New York: Random House.

Cleary, B. (1983). *Dear Mr. Henshaw*. New York: Harper Trophy.

Colodi, C. (1946). *Pinocchio: The adventure of a little wooden boy*. New York: World Publishing.

Dahl, R. (1988). *Matilda*. London: Puffin Books.

Dickens, C. (1850/1996). *David Copperfield*. Toronto: Penguin.

Dickens, C. (1861/1996). *Great expectations*. New York: Penguin.

Donovan, J., & Urie, M. (1969). *I'll get there, it better be worth the trip*. Toronto: HarperCollins.

Ellis, D. (2000). *The breadwinner*. Toronto: Groundwood Books.

Fielding, H. (1996). *Bridget Jones's diary*. New York: Penguin.
Fielding, H. (1749/2005). *The history of Tom Jones, a foundling*. New York: Penguin.
Fitzhugh, L. (1964). *Harriet the spy*. New York: Yearling.
Flack, M. (1933/1977). *The story about Ping*.
Flyers Novice Team. (2009). *I love my hockey mom*. Toronto: Key Porter Books.
Flyers Novice Team. (2009). *Thanks to my hockey dad*. Toronto: Key Porter Books.
Friesen, B. (1995). *The seasons are horses*. Saskatoon, SK: Thistledown Press.
Goethe, J. (1795/1917). *The apprenticeship of Wilhelm Meister*. New York: P. F. Collier & Son.
Golding, W. (1971). *Lord of the flies*. London: Faber and Faber.
Greenwald, S. (1980). *It all began with Jane Eyre: Or, the secret life of Franny Dilman*.
Hamilton, V. (1987). *A white romance*. New York: Philomel Books.
Hansberry, L. (1958). *A raisin in the sun*. New York: Signet/Penguin.
Hawthorne. N. (1978). The birthmark. In N. Hawthorne and B. Perry (Ed.), *Dr. Heidegger's experiment; The birthmark; Ethan Brand; Wakefield; Drowne's wooden image; The ambitious guest*. Whitefish, MT: Kessinger.Herman, H. (1996). *In your face*. New York: Bantam Skylark.
Ho, M. (1986). *Rice without rain*. New York: Harper Collins.
Holeman, L. (1995). *Saying goodbye*. Markham, ON: Fitzhenry and Whiteside.
Hosseini, K. (2003). *The kite runner*. Toronto: Random House.
Hrdlitschka, S. (2002). *Dancing naked*. Victoria, BC: Orca Book Publishing.
Hunter, M. (1972). *A sound of chariots*. Toronto: Harper Collins.
Huser, G. (1999). *Touch of the clown*. Toronto: Groundwood.
Jackson, Shelley. (1995). *Patchwork Girl: A modern monster*. CD-ROM.
Konigsburg, E. L. (1972). *From the mixed-up files of Mrs. Basil E. Frankweiler*. New York: Aladdin.
Konigsburg, E. L. (1993). *T-backs, T-shirts, COATS, and suit*. New York: Macmillan.
Lee, H. (1960). *To kill a mockingbird*. New York: Grand Central.
Le Guin, U. *(1990). Tehanu*. New York: Simon & Schuster.
Le Guin, U. (1969). *The left hand of darkness*. London: Macdonald Science Fiction.
Levinson, R. (1988). *Our home is the sea*. New York: Puffin.
Lewis, C. S. (1959). *The lion, the witch and the wardrobe*. London: Penguin Books.
Lewis, W. (2000). *Graveyard girl*. Markham, ON: Red Deer Press.
Lingren, A. (1950). *Pippi Longstocking*. Toronto: Puffin Books.
Little, J. (1970). *Look through my window*. Toronto: Harper Collins.
Lobel, A. (1970). *Frog and toad are friends*. New York: Scholastic.
Lowry, L. (1979) *Anastasia Krupnik*. New York: Houghton Mifflin.
Lowry, L. (1989). *Number the stars*. New York: Yearling.
Maguire, G. (1995). *Wicked: The life and times of the Wicked Witch of the West*. Harper Collins Publishers.
Martin, A. M. (1999). *Karen's big sister*. Topeka, KS: Econo-Clad Books.
Matas, C. (1994). *The burning time*. Toronto: Harper Collins.
Matas, C. (1998). *Telling; What girls really talk about*. Toronto: Key Porter Books.

Mayer, M. (1995). *Turandot*. Toronto: Harper Collins.

McCully, E. A. (1998). *Beautiful warrior*. New York: Arthur A. Levine.

McCulley, J. (1924). *The mask of Zorro*. New York: Grosset & Dunlop.

McDonald, M. (1998). *Carving my name*. Saskatoon, SK: Thistledown Press.

McKenna, C. (1994). *Roger Friday: Live from the fifth grade*. New York: Scholastic.

Mitchell, D. (2007). *Black swan green*. Toronto: Vintage.

Montgomery, L. M. (1908/1989). *Anne of Green Gables*. New York: Scholastic.

Mosel, A. (1968). *Tikki Tikki Tembo*. New York: Macmillan.

Munsch, R. (1994). *Where is Gah-Ning?* Toronto: Annick Press.

Paterson, K. (1995). *Lyddie*. New York: Puffin.

Peters, J. A. (2004). *Luna, a novel*. New York: Little, Brown, and Co.

Porter, C. (1993). *Addy learns a lesson*. Middleton, WI: American Girl Publishing.

Puzo, M. (1969). *The godfather*. New York: Penguin.

Rawlings, M. K. (1938). *The yearling*. New York: Aladdin.

Rousseau, J. J. (1761). *Emile*. London: J. M. Dent.

Rowling, J. K. (1997). *Harry Potter and the sorcerer's stone*. New York: Scholastic.

Rowling, J. K. (2000). *Harry Potter and the goblet of fire*. New York: Scholastic.

Salinger, J. D. (1951). *The catcher in the rye*. Boston: Little, Brown and Company.

Sander, S. (2010). *Lego city adventures: Ready for takeoff!* New York: Scholastic.

Selvadurai, S. (1994). *Funny boy*. Toronto: McCelland and Stewart.

Sendak, M. (1963). *Where the wild things are*. New York: Scholastic.

Singer, I. B. (1983). "Yentl the yeshiva boy." New York: Farrar, Straus and Giroux.

Soto, G. (2006). *Accidental love*. Orlando, FL: Harcourt.

Spiegelman. A. (1973). *MAUS: A survivor's tale*. New York: Pantheon Books.

Spinelli, J. (2000). *Stargirl*. New York: Alfred A. Knopf.

Steig, W. (1990). *Shrek*. New York: Farra, Strauss and Giroux.

Taylor, M. B. (1981). *Let the circle be unbroken*. New York: Puffin.

Taylor, M. B. (1990). *The road to Memphis*. New York: Puffin.

Toews, M. (2004). *A complicated kindness*. Toronto: Knopf.

Toten, T. (2001). *The game: Haunting teen fiction*. Markham, ON: Red Deer Press.

Travers, P. L. (1934). *Mary Poppins*. New York: Odyssey/Harcourt Brace.

Twain, M. (1876). *The adventures of Tom Sawyer*. New York: Oxford University Press.

Twain, M. (1884). *The adventures of Huckleberry Finn*. London: Harrap.

Voigt, C. (1985). *Jackaroo*. New York: Simon Pulse.

Voigt, C. (1990). *On fortune's wheel*. New York: Simon Pulse.

Voigt, C. (1993). *The wings of a falcon*. New York: Scholastic.

Waber, B. (1973). *Lyle, Lyle, crocodile*. Boston: Houghton Mifflin.

White, E. B. (1945). *Stuart Little*. New York: Harper Collins.

Wieler, D. (1989). *Bad boy*. Toronto: Groundwood.

Wiese, K., and Flack, M. (1933). *The Story about Ping*. Scholastic Book Services.

Winton, T. (2006). *Lockie Leonard, human torpedo*. London: Penguin Books.

Withrow, S. (2001). *Box girl*. Toronto: Groundwood.

Yep, L. (1977). *Child of the owl*. New York: Harper Collins.

Yolen, Jane. (2004). *The devil's arithmetic*. New York: Puffin Books.

FILMS

Ardolino, E. (Director), & Bergstein, E. (Writer). (1987). *Dirty dancing.* Great American Films/Vestron.

Cameron, J. (Director and writer). (1997). *Titanic.* Twentieth Century-Fox/ Paramount Pictures.

Campion, J. (Director and writer). (1993). *The piano.* The Australian Film Commission.

Capra, F. (Director and writer), Goodrich, F., Hackett, A., Swerling, J., Van Doren Stern, P., & Wilson, M. (Writers). (1946). *It's a wonderful life.* Liberty Films/RKO Radio Pictures.

Coppola, F. F. (Director and writer), & Puzo, M. (Writer). (1972). *The godfather.* Paramount Pictures.

Coraci, F. (Director), & Herlihy, T. (Writer). (1998). *The wedding singer.* Juno Pix/ New Line Cinema.

Donen, S. (Director), & Krasna, N. (Writer). (1958). *Indiscreet.* Warner Bros.

Edwards, B. (Director), Capote, T., & Axelrod, G. (Writers). (1961). *Breakfast at Tiffany's.* Jurow-Sheperd/Paramount Pictures.

Ephron, N. (Director and writer), Arch, J., & Ward, D. S. (Writers). (1993). *Sleepless in Seattle.* Tri-Star Pictures.

Ephron, N. (Director and writer), László, M., & Ephron, D. (Writers). (1998). *You've got mail.* Warner Bros.

Fickman, Andy (Director). (2006). *She's the man.* Lakeshore Entertainment Studio.

Flemming, V., Cukor, G., Wood, S. (Directors), Mitchell, M. (Writer), & Howard, S. (Writer). (1939). *Gone with the wind.* Metro-Goldwyn-Mayer.

Fletcher, A. (Director), & Chiarelli, P. (Writer). (2009). *The proposal.* Touchstone Pictures.

Howard, R. (Director), Goldsman, A., & Nasar S. (Writers). (2001). *A beautiful mind.* Universal.

Katselas, M. (Director), & Gershe, L. (Writer). (1972). *Butterflies are free.* Frankovich Productions/Columbia Pictures.

Lucas, G. (Director and writer). (1977). *Star wars. Episode IV: A new hope.* Lucasfilm/Twentieth-Century Fox.

Maguire, S. (Director), Fielding, H., Davies, A., & Curtis, R. (Writers). (2001). *Bridget Jones's diary.* Miramax/Universal/Studion Canal.

Parker, A. (Director and writer), Rice, T. (Writer), & Stone, O. (Writer). (1996). *Evita.* Hollywood Pictures.

Ray, N. (Director and writer), Stern, S., & Shulman, I. (Writers). (1955). *Rebel without a cause.* Warner Bros.

Scott, R. (Director), O'Bannon, D., & Shusett, R. (Writers). (1979). *Alien.* Brandywine Productions/Twentieth Century-Fox.

Shyer, C. (Director and writer), Goodrich, F., Hackett, A., & Meyers, N. (Writers). (1991). *Father of the bride.* Sandollar Productions/Touchstone Pictures.

Soderbergh, S. (Director), & Grant, S. (Writer). (2000). *Erin Brockovich.* Jersey Films/Universal Pictures.

Speilberg, S. (Director), Kasdan, L., Lucas, G., & Kaufman, P. (Writers). (1981). *Raiders of the Lost Ark.* Paramount Pictures/Lucasfilms.

Stevenson, R. (Director), Walsh, B., DaGradi, D., & Travers, P. J. (1964). *Mary Poppins*. Walt Disney Productions.

Streisand, B. (Director and writer), Rosenthal, J., & Singer, I. B. (Writers). (1983). *Yentl*. MGM/ United Artists.

Van Sant, G. (Director), Damon, M., & Affleck (Writers). (1997). *Good Will Hunting*. Be Gentlemen Limited/Lawrence Bender/Miramax.

Verbinski, G. (Director), Elliott, T., Rossio, T., Beattie, S., & Wolpert, J. (Writers). (2003). *Pirates of the Caribbean: The curse of the black pearl*. Walt Disney Pictures/ Jerry Bruckheimer Films.

Zucker, J. (Director), & Rubin, B. J. (Writer). (1990). *Ghost*. Paramount Pictures.

TELEVISION SERIES CITED

Berman, R., Roddenberry, G., Piller, M., & Wagner, M. (Executive producers). (1987). *Star trek: The next generation*. Paramount Television.

Bloomfield, G., King, J., Slevin, K., Siracusa, F., Bray, P., Carney, R., Gross, P., Haggis, P., Wertheimer, R., Denver, N., & Cole, D. (Producers). (1994). *Due south*. Alliance Atlantis Communications.

Brooks, J. L., Burns, A., Weinberger, E., Ephraim, L., Daniels, S., Cherry, B., Davis, D., & Zinberg M. (Producers). (1970). *Mary Tyler Moore*. MTM Enterprises/Columbia Broadcasting System.

Burrows, J., Charles, G., Charles, L., & Berry, T., Steinkellner, B., Steinkellner, C., Sutton, P. (Executive producers). (1982). *Cheers*. Charles/Burrows/Charles Productions/Paramount Television.

Daniels, G., Gervais, R., Merchant, S., Novak, B. J., Silverman, B., Klein, H., Lieberstein, P., Kaling, M., Weinberg, T., Shure, A., Chun, D., Schur, M., Zbornak, K., Eisenberg, L., Stupnitsky, G., Feig, P., & Ocko, P. (Executive producers). (2005). *The office*. Reveille Productions/NBC Universal Television.

King, M. P., Melfi, J., Parker, S. J., Bicks, J., Chupack, C., & Jossen, B. (Executive producers). (1998). *Sex in the city*. Darren Starr Productions/Home Box Office.

Kuzui, F. R., Kuzui, K., Whedon, J., Berman, G., Gallin, S., & Noxon, M. (Executive producers). (1997). *Buffy the vampire slayer*. Mutant Entertainment/Kuzui Enterprises/Sandollar Television.

Lorre, C., Medavoy, B., More, E., & Prady, B., (Executive producers). (1997). *Dharma and Greg*. American Broadcasting Corporation.

Lorre, C., Prady, B., Goetsch, D., Molaro, S., Kaplan, E., Aronsohn, L., Reynolds, J., Cohen, R., & Litt, D. (Executive producers). (2007). *The Big Bang Theory*. Chuck Lorre Productions/Warner Bros. Television.

Roddenberry, G. (Executive producer). (1966) *Star Trek*. Desilu Productions.

Anticipation Guide

An anticipation guide is an instructional strategy used to activate prior knowledge about a particular topic and incite curiosity. As a comprehension strategy, anticipation guides are intended to help establish a purpose for reading and generate postreading reflection and discussion.

Students are asked to respond to a series of statements related to the content of the material.

STEPS

1. Preview the text to identify themes or important content.

2. Create a one-page anticipation guide with 8 to 10 general statements about the theme (e.g., "Humankind should always strive for technological progress.") or content (e.g., "The arctic ice is home to living organisms."), each requiring students to agree or disagree and provide a brief justification for their response.

3. Distribute anticipation guides to students before reading the text under study and ask them to complete the exercise, explaining that the purpose is to provide them with an opportunity to explore their thoughts and ideas.

4. Students complete the guide individually and may be invited to compare and discuss their responses with a partner.

5. Conduct a whole-class discussion by asking students to share their thinking on each of the statements.

6. Students read to confirm or change their opinions.

7. After reading, students record evidence from the text confirming or revising their original response.

SAMPLE THEME STATEMENTS FOR MARY SHELLEY'S *FRANKENSTEIN*

Before Reading	Statement	After Reading
Agree/Disagree Reason: _____ _____	1. Humankind should always strive for technological progress.	Agree/Disagree Reason: _____ _____
Agree/Disagree Reason: _____ _____	2. Human pride will be our undoing.	Agree/Disagree Reason: _____ _____

Directed Reading Thinking Activity (DRTA) and Directed Listening Thinking Activity (DLTA)

The DRTA and DLTA strategies (Stauffer, 1970) engage students in the activation of prior knowledge and in making inferences while they listen and read. In these activities, built on an understanding that reading should be taught as a thinking process (Stauffer, 1969), the teacher guides students through a shared reading selection, encouraging them to take risks and set purposes for reading by asking them to formulate questions, make predictions, and read further to confirm or reject their predictions.

DRTA adapts to a wide range of instructional contexts and is helpful in motivating reluctant readers and engaging students in new texts. Guided experience with strategies like the DRTA leads to more independent habits of action that can contribute to readers' skill and confidence in the comprehension of a variety of genres. The same principles can be applied in a Directed Viewing Thinking Activity (DVTA) as students work together to make meaning from film and other media resources.

STEPS

1. The teacher asks students to examine the title, pictures, and any other textual features of the selected text and to share what they already know about the subject.

2. The teacher invites students to make predictions about the text and to support their predictions.

3. Students read silently or listen attentively to a section of the text and formulate predictions.

4. At a certain point in the selection, students are directed to record their predictions and cite evidence from the text or knowledge that relates to the particular events and characters.

5. Students turn and talk to share and revise their predictions with a partner.

6. Students read on or listen further to confirm, reject, or modify their predictions, giving evidence from the text.

7. The steps are repeated with the next section of reading or listening.

REFERENCES

Stauffer, R. G. (1969). *Teaching reading as a thinking process.* New York: Harper & Row.

Stauffer, R. G. (1970). *The language experience approach to the teaching of reading.* New York: Harper & Row.

Female and Male Archetypes

Literary archetypes have come to stand for familiar and predictable character types. Through repetition across time and cultures, the conventional patterns of behavior provoke expectations and emotional responses in the minds of readers and lend coherence to plot structure. The following is a list of archetypes frequently found in literature and popular culture. Readers are asked to consider how these character prototypes have socially reified attitudes and assumptions about gender.

HERO ARCHETYPES (FEMALE)

The Boss: Goal-oriented and tough, she fights her way to the top and demands respect. Like Sandra Bullock in *The Proposal*, she takes charge and isn't scared to ruffle a few feathers along the steep climb up the ladder of success.

The Seductress or Enchantress: Manipulating and often mysterious, like Vivien Leigh in *Gone with the Wind* or Madonna in *Evita*, she possesses a strong will to survive and will do anything to come out ahead.

The Kid: A young woman, loyal and likeable and at times a bit vulnerable, she is the kind you always want to root for. Popular film and television yield numerous examples. She's the girl with spunk, like Mary Richards in the classic sitcom *The Mary Tyler Moore Show*. More recent examples include the Bridget Jones character in Helen Fielding's 1996 novel *Bridget Jones's Diary*, a role later played by Renee Zellweger in the 2001 film and Meg Ryan in both *Sleepless in Seattle* and *You've Got Mail*.

The Free Spirit: Eternally optimistic and committed to following her heart, this is a role made famous by Audrey Hepburn as Holly Golightly in the film *Breakfast at Tiffany's* based on the 1958 novella by Truman Capote. Goldie Hawn's role in the 1972 film *Butterflies Are Free* embodied the free spirit of the hippie subculture, a movement that inspired Jenna Elfmann's character a generation later in the 1990s sitcom *Dharma and Greg*.

The Waif: A damsel in distress who possesses the strength to endure, she can compel an urge to protect in even the toughest or least likely of heroes, but her victory ultimately owes a greater debt to her sheer will to survive. Examples include Dorothy in Frank L. Baum's *The Wizard of Oz* and the Demi Moore character in the film *Ghost*.

The Librarian: Poised and proper, the Librarian appears competent and in complete control, but beneath that stern exterior lies the beating heart of a passionate woman. Readers will recognize her as Hermione Granger in J. K. Rowling's *Harry Potter* series, and television viewers know her as Diane, played by Shelley Long in the long-running sitcom, *Cheers*.

The Crusader: The Joan of Arc figure is the female character with dedication and commitment, and she is on a mission. Think of real-life Norma Rae played by Oscar-winning Sally Field and Sigourney Weaver in *Alien*.

The Nurturer: The nurturing caregiver is serene and capable. Anticipating your every need, she can see you through the most difficult of situations. She listens well, is patient, and is a good manager. In literature, she is Mary Poppins in P. J. Travers's children's novel, ably played by Julie Andrews in the 1964 Disney film, and the sensitive Lena Younger ("Mama") in Lorraine Hansberry's 1959 play *A Raisin in the Sun*.

HERO ARCHETYPES (MALE)

The Chief or Leader: Tough and decisive, the leader works incessantly whether he was born to lead or fought his way to the top. At times he is overbearing and rather inflexible. Science fiction buffs will recognize these traits in William Shatner and Patrick Stewart's roles as captains of the Starship *Enterprise* on *Star Trek*. These characteristics are equally identifiable in Marlon Brando's role as Vito Corleone in Francis Ford Coppola's *The Godfather*, a film based on Mario Puzo's bestselling novel.

The Bad Boy: He's the boy from the wrong side of the tracks and is carrying a chip on his shoulder. He's the rebel in town willing to take a walk on the wild side. The Bad Boy may be bitter and damaged, but he has charisma. Without a doubt, the role has been epitomized by James Dean as Jim Stark in the 1955 film *Rebel without a Cause*. More recent examples include Patrick Swayze as Johnny Castle in the 1987 film *Dirty Dancing* and Matt Damon as Will Hunting in the 1997 film *Good Will Hunting*.

The Best Friend: Always there for you, he is a regular Mr. Nice Guy. He doesn't want to hurt anyone's feelings, so he works hard at appeasing everyone. Perhaps no actor best portrays the nice-guy image better than Jimmy Stewart as George Bailey in Frank Capra's 1946 film *It's a Wonderful Life*. Young viewers will recognize the Best Friend as Adam Sandler in the role of Robbie Hart in the 1998 film *The Wedding Singer*.

The Charmer: He may be smooth, suave, and sophisticated or a little rough around the edges. The Charmer is fun and totally irresistible but doesn't necessarily want to be tied down. He's the Cary Grant of yesteryear in the 1958 film *Indiscreet*, Harrison Ford as Hans Solo in the *Stars Wars* films, Leonardo DiCaprio in James Cameron's (1997) *Titanic*, and Johnny Depp as Captain Jack Sparrow from the *Pirates of the Caribbean* films.

The Lost Soul: Often the outcast, the Lost Soul is brooding and secretive. He may be a creative artist but is most assuredly a loner and vulnerable. Vampires are perfectly suited to the type as we see in the character Angel in *Buffy, the Vampire Slayer*. Steve Carell cuts a more comic figure of the Lost Soul as Michael Scott of *The Office*.

The Professor: He is analytical, introverted, and, like the Leader, inflexible. He may like to deal with the cold hard facts, but he has feelings, too. Kelsey Grammer as television's Frasier Crane and Russell Crowe's portrayal of real-life mathematician John Nash in the 2001 film *A Beautiful Mind* fill the bill.

The Swashbuckler: Dashing and daring, the Swashbuckler is fearless. He lives a life of excitement and adventure with charm to boot. Familiar Swashbuckler characters include Robin Hood, the heroic outlaw of English folklore; Zorro, the masked avenger featured in books, films, and television; and Indiana Jones, played by Harrison Ford in *Raiders of the Lost Ark* and other films.

References

Abel, E., Hirsch, M., & Langland, E. (Eds.). (1983). *The voyage in: Fictions of female development*. Hanover, NH: Dartmouth.

Abi-Mershed, O. (2010). *Trajectories of education in the Arab world: Legacies and challenges*. New York: Routledge.

Allan, J. (1993). Male elementary teachers: Experiences and perspectives. In C. Williams (Ed.), *Doing "woman's work": Men in non-traditional occupations* (pp. 113–27). Newbury Park: Sage.

Allison, R. (2003). Rowling books "for people with stunted imaginations." *The Guardian*, July 11. http://www.guardian.co.uk/uk/2003/jul/11/books.harrypotter.

Alloway, N. (2007). Swimming against the tide: Boys, literacies, and schooling—an Australian story. *Canadian Journal of Education* 30, no. 2, 582–605.

Alvermann, D. E. (1993). Student voice in class discussion: A feminist poststructuralist perspective. In D. E. Alvermann (Chair), *Expanding the possibilities: How feminist theories inform traditions and positions in reader response, classroom discussion, and critical thinking*. Symposium at the Annual Meeting of the National Reading Conference, Charleston, SC.

Alvermann, D. E. (1995). Peer-led discussions: Whose interests are served? *Journal of Adolescent and Adult Literacy* 39, 282–89.

Alvermann, D. E., Commeyras, M., Young, J. P., Randall, S., & Hinson, D. (1997). Interrupting gendered discursive practices in classroom talk about texts: Easy to think about, difficult to do. *Journal of Literacy Research* 29, 73–104.

Alvermann, D. E., Young, J. P., & Green, C. (1997). *Adolescents' negotiations of out-of-school reading discussion*. Reading Research Report No. 77. Athens, GA: University of Georgia, National Reading Research Center.

American Association of University Women. (1991). *Shortchanging girls, shortchanging America*. Washington, DC: American Association of University Women Education Foundation. http://aauw.org/learn/research/upload/SGSA-2.pdf.

American Association of University Women. (1992). *How schools shortchange girls: The AAUW report: A study of major findings on girls and education*.

Washington, DC: American Association of University Women Education Foundation.

American Association of University Women. (2001). *Beyond the "Gender Wars": A conversation about girls, boys, and education.* Washington, DC: American Association of University Women Education Foundation. http://aauw.org/learn/research/upload/BeyondGenderWar.pdf.

American Association of University Women. (2004). *Harassment-free hallways: How to stop sexual harassment in school.* Washington, DC: American Association of University Women Education Foundation.

American Association of University Women. (2008). *Where the Girls (and Boys) Are —and Where the Real Crisis Is.* Washington, DC: American Association of University Women Education Foundation.

Appleman, D. (2000). *Critical encounters in high school English: Teaching literary theory to adolescents.* New York: Teachers College Press.

Archer, J. (1997). The influence of testosterone on human aggression. *British Journal of Psychology* 82, 1–28.

Arendt, H. (1961). *Between past and future.* New York: Viking.

Arnot, M., David, M. E., & Weiner, G. (1999). *Closing the gender gap: Postwar education and social change.* Malden, MA: Blackwell Publishers.

Baer, J. D., Kutner, M. A., Sabatini, J., & White, S. (2009). *Basic reading skills and the literacy of America's least literate adults: Results from the 2003 National Assessment of Literacy (NAAL) supplemental studies.* Washington, DC: National Center for Education Statistics.

Baker, B. M. (2011). *New times: Globalization, curriculum studies, and strategies of subjectification.* Paper presented at the American Educational Research Association Annual Meeting, April, New Orleans, LA.

Bakhtin, M. (1981). Discouse in the novel. In M. Holquist & C. Emerson (Eds.), *The dialogic imagination* (pp. 259–422). Austin: University of Texas Press.

Bakhtin, M. M. (1986). *Speech genres and other late essays.* Austin: University of Texas Press.

Bangert-Drowns, R. L., Kulik, J. A., & Kulik, C.-L. C. (1985). Effectiveness of computer-based education in secondary schools. *Journal of Computer-Based Instruction* 12, 59–68.

Banks, J. A. (2002). *An introduction to multicultural education* (3rd ed.). Boston, MA: Allyn and Bacon.

Baraks, N., Hoffman, A., & Bauer, D. (1997). Children's book preferences: Patterns, particulars, and possible implications. *Reading Psychology* 18, 309–41.

Bardsley, D. (1999). *Boys and reading: What reading fiction means to sixth grade boys.* Unpublished doctoral dissertation, Arizona State University, Phoenix, AZ.

Barrs, M., Pidgeon, S., & Centre for Language in Primary Education. (1998). *Boys and reading.* London: Centre for Language in Primary Education.

Barton, D., & Hamilton, M. (1998). *Local Literacies: reading and writing in one community.* New York: Routledge.

Batcher, E., Brackstone, D., Winter, A., & Wright, V. (1975). *And then there were none.* Toronto: Federation of Women Teachers' Associations of Ontario.

Baumann, J., Hoffman, J., Moon, J., & Duffy-Hexter, A. M. (1998). Where are teachers' voices in the phonics/whole language debate? Results from a survey of U.S. elementary teachers. *Reading Teacher* 51, 636–52.

Bean, T., & Harper, H. (2007). Reading men differently: Alternative portrayals of masculinity in contemporary young adult fiction. *Reading Psychology* 28, 11–30.

Beck, L. G., & Murphy, J. (1996). *The four imperatives of a successful school*. Thousand Oaks, CA: Corwin Press.

Bell, C. (2009). *Ritual: Perspectives and dimensions*. Oxford, UK: Oxford University Press.

Best, R. (1983). *We've all got scars: What boys and girls learn in elementary school*. Bloomington: Indiana University Press.

Biddulph, S. (1998). *Raising boys: Why boys are different-and how to help them become happy and well-balanced men*. Berkeley, CA: Celestial Arts.

Bils, M., & Klenow, P. (2000). Does schooling cause growth? *American Economic Review* 90, 5, 1160–83.

Birru, M., & Steinman, R. (2004). Online health information and low-literacy African Americans. *Journal of Medical Internet Research* 6, no. 3, e26. doi:10.2196/jmir.6.3.e26.

Bitz, M. (2004). The Comic Book Project: The Lives of Urban Youth. *Art Education*, 57, no. 2, 33–39.

Blackburn, M., & Clark, C. (2011). Analyzing talk in a long-term literature discussion group: Ways of operating within LGBT-inclusive and queer discourses. *Reading Research Quarterly* 46, no. 3, 222–48.

Blair, H., & Sanford, K. (1999). TV and zines: Media and the construction of gender for early adolescents. *Alberta Journal of Educational Research* 45, no. 1, 103–5.

Bloom, H. (2003). Dumbing down American readers. *The Boston Globe*, September 24. http://www.boston.com/news/globe/editorial_opinion/oped/articles/2003/09/24/dumbing_down_american_readers/.

Booth, D. (2002). *Even hockey players read: Boys and reading*. Markham, ON: Pembroke Publishers.

Braaksma, M., Rijlaarsdam, G., Couzijn, M., & van den Bergh, H. (2002). Learning to compose hypertext and linear text: Transfer or inhibition? In R. Bromme & E. Stahl (Eds.), *Writing hypertext and learning: Conceptual and empirical approaches. Advances in Learning and Instruction Series* (pp. 15–37). London: Pergamon.

Britzman, D. (1995). Is there a queer pedagogy? Or, stop reading straight. *Education Theory* 45, no. 2, 151–165.

Browman, M. T., & Templin, M. C. (1959). Stories for younger children in 1927–29 and in 1952–55. *The Elementary School Journal* 59, no. 6, 324–27.

Brown, L. M., & Gilligan, C. (1992). *Meeting at the crossroads: Women's psychology and girls' development*. Cambridge, MA: Harvard University Press.

Brown, S., & Patterson, A. (2010). Selling stories: Harry Potter and the marketing plot. *Psychology & Marketing* 27, no. 6, 541–56.

Brozo, W. G. (2010). *To be a boy, to be a reader: Engaging teen and preteen boys in active literacy* (2nd ed.). Newark, DE: International Reading Association.

Bundy, B. A. (1983). *The development of a survey to ascertain the reading preferences of fourth, fifth and sixth graders.* Doctoral dissertation. Retrieved from *Dissertation Abstracts International* 44, 68A.

Burman, E. (2005). Childhood, neo-liberalism and the feminization of education. *Gender and Education* 17, 351–67.

Bus, A. G., van Ijzendorn, M. H., & Pellegrini, A. D. (1995). Joint book reading makes for success in learning to read: A meta-analysis on intergenerational transmission of literacy. *Review of Educational Research,* 65, no. 1, 1–21.

Butler, D., & Christianson, R. (2003). Mixing and matching: The effect on student performance of teaching assistants of the same gender. *Political Science and Politics* 36, 781–86.

Butler, J. (1990). *Gender trouble: Feminism and the subversion of identity.* London: Routledge.

Cameron, D. (1998). *The feminist critique of language: A reader.* London: Routledge.

Campbell, Joseph. (1998/2008). *The Hero with a thousand faces.* Novato, California: New World Library.

Carlsen, G. R. (1967). *Books and the teen-age reader.* New York: Harper and Row.

Carrington, B., & Skelton, C. (2003). Re-thinking role models: Equal opportunities in teacher recruitment in England and Wales. *Journal of Educational Policy* 12, no. 3, 353–65.

Carrington, B., Tymms, P., & Merrell, C. (2005). *Role models, school improvement and the "gender gap"—Do men bring out the best in boys and women the best in girls?* Paper presented at the EARLI conference, August, University of Nicosia, Cyprus.

Carter, B., & Harris, K. (1982). What junior high student like in books. *Journal of Reading* 26, 42–46.

Chang, M. (2001). "Are authors rewriting folklore in today's image?" In S. Lehr (Ed.), *Beauty, Brawn and Brains: The construction of gender in children's literature.* Portsmouth, NH: Heinemann.

Cherland, M. R. (1992). Gendered readings: Cultured restraints upon response to literature. *The New Advocate* 5, 187–97.

Cherland, M. R. (1994). *Private practices: Girls reading fiction and constructing identity.* London: Taylor and Francis.

Chiu, S. S. (1997). Reorienting the English classroom: Asian American writers in the canon. *The English Journal* 86, no. 8, 30–33.

Clark, C., & Blackburn, M. (2009). Reading LGBT-themed literature with young people: What's possible? *English Journal* 98, no. 4, 25–32.

Clark, R. (1985). Confounding in educational computing research. *Journal of Educational Computing Research* 1, 137–48.

Comaroff, J., & Comaroff, J. L. (2000). Millennial capitalism: First thoughts on a second coming. *Public Culture* 12, no. 2, 291–343.

Connell, R. W. (1995). *Masculinities.* Berkeley: University of California Press.

Constantino, J., Grosz, D., Saenger, P., Chandler, D., Nandi, R., & Earls, F. (1993). Testosterone and aggression in children. *Journal of the American Academy of Child and Adolescent Psychiatry* 32, 1217–22.

Correll, S. J. (2001). Gender and the career choice process: The role of biased self-assessments. *American Journal of Sociology* 106, no. 6, 1691–730.

Coulter, R. (1996). Gender equity and schooling: Linking research and policy. *Canadian Journal of Education* 21, no. 4, 433–52.

Coulter, R., & McNay, M. (1993). Exploring men's experiences as elementary school teachers. *Canadian Journal of Education* 18, 398–413.

Culler, Jonathan. (1982). "Reading as a woman," in *On Deconstruction: Theory and criticism after structuralism*. New York: Cornell University Press, 43–63.

Cummins, H. J. (2000). The phenomenon that is Harry Potter. *Minneapolis Star Tribune*, July 6. http://www.startribune.com/templates/Print_This_Story ?sid=11475271.

Cummins, J., & Schecter, S. (2003). *Multilingual education in practice: Using diversity as a resource*. Portsmouth, NH: Heinemann.

Damasio, A. (2003). *Looking for Spinoza: Joy, sorrow, and the feeling brain*. New York: Harcourt.

Daniels, H. (1994). *Literature circles: Voice and choice in the student-centered classroom*. York, ME: Stenhouse.

Darling-Hammond, L. (2004). The color line in American education: Race, resources, and student achievement. *Du Bois Review* 1, 213–46.

Davies, B. (1993). *Shards of glass: Children reading and writing beyond gendered identities*. Cresskill, NJ: Hampton Press.

Davies, J. (2002). Expressions of gender: An analysis of gendered discourse styles in small classroom discussions. *Discourse & Society* 14, 115–32.

De Beauvoir, S. (1949/1952). *The second sex*. New York: Vintage Books.

de Castell, S. (2000). Literacies, technologies, and the future of the library in the "information age." *Journal of Curriculum Studies* 32, no. 3, 359–76.

de Certeau, M. (1984). *The practice of everyday life*. Berkeley: University of California Press.

Dee, T. S. (2007). Teachers and the gender gaps in student achievement. *Journal of Human Resources* 42, no. 3, 528–54.

Delpit, L. D. (1988). The silenced dialogue: Power and pedagogy in educating other people's children. *Harvard Educational Review* 58, no. 3 (August): 280–98.

Dewey, J. (1915). *Democracy and education*. In J. Boydston, (Ed.), *The Middle Works of John Dewey, 1899–1924*, Vol. 9 (pp. 1–3). Carbondale: Southern Illinois University Press.

Dewey, J. (1922/1983). Human nature and conduct: An introduction to social psychology. In J. Boydston (Ed.), *The Middle Works of John Dewey, 1899–1924*, Vol. 14 (pp. 1–12). Carbondale: Southern Illinois University Press.

Doty, D., Popplewell, S., & Byers, G. (2001). Interactive CD-ROM storybooks and young readers' reading comprehension. *Journal of Research on Computing and Education* 33(4), 374–384.

Dudley-Marling, C. (2007). Return of the deficit. *Journal of Educational Controversy* 2, no. 1. http://www.wce.wwu.edu/Resources/CEP/eJournal/v002n001/a004 .shtml. Dutro, E. (2000). *Reading gender/gendered readers: Girls, boys and popular fiction*. University of Michigan.

Dutro, E. (2001). "But that's a girls' book!" Exploring gender boundaries in children's reading practices. *The Reading Teacher* 55, no. 4, 376–84.

Edelman, G. (1992). *Bright air, brilliant fire: On the matter of the mind*. New York: Basic Books.

Egale Canada. (March 2009). Egale Canada first national climate survey on homophobia in Canadian schools: Phase 1 Report. Toronto: Egale.

Ehrenberg, R., Goldhaber, D., & Brewer, D. (1995). Do teachers' race, gender and ethnicity matter? Evidence from the national education longitudinal study of 1988. *Industrial and Labour Relations Review* 48, 547–61.

Eisenhart, M. A., & Finkel, E. (1998). *Women's science: Learning and succeeding from the margins*. Chicago: University of Chicago Press.

Ellsworth, E. (1989). Why doesn't this feel empowering? Working through the repressive myths of critical pedagogy. *Harvard Educational Review* 59, no. 3, 297–325.

Emerson, R., Fretz, R., & Shaw, L. (1995). *Writing Ethnographic Fieldnotes*. Chicago: University of Chicago Press.

Evans, K., Alvermann, D., & Anders, P. (1998). Literature discussion groups: An examination of gender roles. *Reading Research and Instruction* 37, 107–22.

Faludi, S. (1999). *Stiffed: The betrayal of the American man*. New York: W. Morrow and Co.

Fausto-Sterling, A. (2000). *Sexing the body: Gender politics and the construction of sexuality*. New York: Basic Books.

Fennema, E., Carpenter, T. P., Jacobs, V. R., Franke, M. L., & Levi, L. (1998). A longitudinal study of gender differences in young children's mathematical thinking. *Educational Researcher* 27, no. 5, 6–11.

Fetterley, J. (1978). *The resisting reader: A feminist approach to american fiction*. Bloomington: Indiana University Press.

Fish, S. (1980). Interpreting the "Variorum." In S. Fish, *Is there a text in this class?: The authority of interpretive communities* (pp. 147–73). Cambridge, MA: Harvard University Press.

Fish, S. (1997). Boutique multiculturalism, or why liberals are incapable of thinking about hate speech. *Critical Inquiry*, 23, no. 2 (Winter): 378–96.

Flowerday, T., & Schraw, G. (2000). Teacher beliefs about instructional choice: A phenomenological study. *Journal of Educational Psychology* 92, no. 4, 634–45.

Fokias, F. (1998). Changing practice through reflection. In M. Barrs & S. Pidgeon (Eds.), *Boys and reading*. London: Centre for Language in Primary Education.

Foucault, M. (1972). *The archeology of knowledge*. London: Routledge.

Foucault, M. (1978). *The history of sexuality* (1st American ed.). New York: Pantheon Books.

Fox, M. (1993). Men who weep, boys who dance: The gender agenda between the lines in children's literature. *Language Arts* 70, 84–88.

Frank, E. (2006). Interactive booktalking at the high school. *The School Librarian's Workshop* 26, no. 4, 14.

Freire, P. (1970). *Pedagogy of the oppressed* (30th Anniversary Ed.). Trans. M. Bergman Ramos. New York: Continuum.

Freire, P., & Macedo, D. (1987). *Literacy: Reading the word and reading the world*. South Hadley, MA: Bergin and Garvey.

Froude, L. (2002). Study defies the "boys need men" credo. *Times Educational Supplement* 4471, 3–9.

Frow, J. (2005). *Genre*. New York: Routledge.

Gallo, D. R. (1983). Students' reading interests: A report of a Connecticut survey. *Resources in Education* 18, no. 12, 36.

Garbarino, J. (2000). *Lost boys: Why our sons turn violent and how we can save them*. New York: Anchor.

Gee, J. P. (2005). *Why video games are good for your soul: Pleasure and learning*. Common Ground Publishing.

Gee, J. P., Hull, G., & Lankshear, C. (1996). *The new work order*. Boulder, CO: Westview Press.

Gilbert, R., & Gilbert, P. (1998). *Masculinity goes to school*. New York: Routledge.

Gilbert, S., & Gubar, S. (1979). *The madwoman in the attic: The woman writer and the nineteenth-century literary imagination*. New Haven, CT: Yale University Press.

Gillborn, D., & Youdell, D. (2000). *Rationing education: Policy, practice, reform, and equity*. Philadelphia: Open University Press.

Gilligan, C. (1993). *In a different voice: Psychological theory and women's development*. Cambridge, MA: Harvard University Press.

Gilligan, C. (2003). *The birth of pleasure*. (Reprint). New York: Vintage.

Gilligan, C., Brown, L. M., & Rogers, A. G. (1990). Psyche embedded: A place for body, relationships, and culture in personality theory. In Albert Rabin et al. (Eds.), *Studying persons and lives*. (pp. 86–147), New York: Springer.

Gilligan, J. (1997). *Violence: Reflections on a national epidemic*. New York: Vintage.

Ginsberg, A., Shapiro, J. P., & Brown, S. P. (2000). Opening GATE (gender awareness through education): A doorway to gender equity. *Women's Studies Quarterly* 28, nos. 3–4 (Fall–Winter): 164–76.

Graham, S. A. (1986). Assessing reading preferences: A new approach. *New England Reading Association Journal* 21, 8–11.

Grant, L. (1984). Black females' "place" in desegregated classrooms. *Sociology of Education* 57 (April): 98–111.

Gritsavage, M. (1997). *Examining dominance in discourse in the graduate course, gender, culture and literacy*. Unpublished doctoral dissertation, Arizona State University, Tempe.

Grove, N. (1984). Challenge '76: Sexism in education. *The B.C. Teacher*, 64, no. 1, 13.

Gurian, M. (1996). *The wonder of boys: What parents, mentors and educators can do to shape boys into exceptional men*. New York: J. P. Tarcher.

Gurian, M., Henley, P., & Trueman, T. (2001). *Boys and girls learn differently: A guide for teachers and parents*. San Francisco, CA: Jossey-Bass.

Guzzetti, B. (1998). Texts and talk: The role of gender in learning physics. Research Report, ERIC Document ED 422 164. http://www.eric.ed.gov/ERICWeb Portal/search/detailmini.jsp?_nfpb=true&_&ERICExtSearch_SearchValue_0= ED422164&ERICExtSearch_SearchType_0=no&accno=ED422164.

Guzzetti, B., & Bean, T. (2012). *Adolescent literacies and the gendered self: (Re)constructing identities through multimodal literacy practices*. New York: Routledge.

Guzzetti, B., Young, J., Gritsavage, M., Fyfe, L., & Hardenbrook, M. (2002). *Reading, writing, and talking gender in literacy learning*. Newark, DE: International Reading Association.

Halberstam, J. (1998). *Female masculinity*. Durham, NC: Duke University Press.

Hall, C., & Coles, M. (1999). *Children's reading choices*. New York: Routledge.

Harper, H. (2007). Studying masculinity(ities) in books about girls. *Canadian Journal of Education* 30, no. 2, 508–30.

Harste, J. (2002). *Debriefing the work of the task force on critical literacy*. Paper presented at the Annual Convention of the International Reading Association, San Francisco, CA, May.

Hawkins, S. (1983). Reading interests of gifted children. *Reading Horizons* 24, 18–22.

Heath, S. B., & McLaughlin, M. W. (1993). *Identity and inner-city youth: Beyond ethnicity and gender*. New York: Teachers College Press.

Heit, M., & Blair, H. (1993). Language needs and characteristics of Saskatchewan Indian and Métis students: Implications for educators. In M. Danesi, K. A. McLeod, & S. Morris (Eds.), *Aboriginal languages and education: The Canadian experience* (pp. 103–28). Oakville, ON: Mosaic.

Hey, V. (1997). *The company she keeps: An ethnography of girls' friendships*. Philadelphia, PA: Open University Press.

Hill, C., Corbett, C., & St. Rose, A. (2010). *Why so few? Women in science, technology, engineering and mathematics*. American Association of University Women. http://www.aauw.org/learn/research/whysofew.cfm.

Hirsch, M. (1979). From Great Expectations to Lost Illusions: The novel of formation as genre. *Genre* 12, no. 3, 293–311.

Holmes, J. (1986). Function of you know in women's and men's speech. *Language in Society* 15, 1–21.

hooks, b. (2000). *Feminist theory: From margin to center*. Cambridge, MA: South End Press.

Huck, C. (2001). Introduction. In E. Lehr (Ed.), *Beauty, brains, and brawn: The construction of gender in children's literature* (p. vii). Portsmouth, NH: Heinemann.

Hunter, L. (1984). *Rhetorical stance in modern literature: Allegories of love and death*. London: Macmillan.

Irvine, J. J. (1986). Teacher-student interactions: Effects of student race, sex, and grade level. *Journal of Educational Psychology* 78, 14–21.

Jackson, P. W. (1968). *Life in classrooms*. New York: Holt, Rinehart and Winston.

Jacobs, Dale. (January 2007). More than Words: Comics as a Means of Teaching Multiple Literacies. *English Journal*, 96, no. 3, 19–25.

Jenkins, C. (1994). Review of *Am I blue? Coming out from the Silence* by M. D. Bauer and B. Underwood. *School Library Journal*, (June): 144.

Jenkins, C. (1998). From queer to gay and back again: Young adult novels with gay/lesbian/queer content, 1969–1997. *Library Quarterly*, 68 (July): 298–334.

Julien, L. (1987). *Women's issues in education in Canada: A survey of policies and practices at the elementary and secondary levels*. Toronto: Council of Ministers of Education.

Keddie, A., & Mills, M. (2008). *Teaching boys*. Crows Nest, NSW: Allen and Unwin.

Kenway, J. Willis, Sr. (1998). *Answering back: Girls, boys and feminism in schools*. London: Routledge.

Kerr, B. (1997). *Smart girls: A new psychology of girls, women, and giftedness*. Scottsdale, AZ: Gifted Psychology Press.

Khayatt, D. (2006). What's to fear: Calling homophobia into question. *McGill Journal of Education* 41, no. 2, 133–44.

Kilbourne, J. (1999). *Can't buy my love: How advertising changes the way we think and feel.* New York: Touchstone.

Kim, K. (1998). The Disney peril. *Salon,* July 7, 1998.

Kindlon, D., & Thompson, M. (1999). *Raising Cain: Protecting the emotional life of boys.* New York: Ballantine.

Kimmel, M. S. (2002, February 8). Gender, class and terrorism. *Chronicle of Higher Education,* 48, B11–12.

Kohlberg, L. (1976). Moral stages and moralization: The cognitive-developmental approach. In T. Lickona (Ed.), *Moral development and behavior: Theory, research and social issues,* (pp. 31–53). Holt, NY: Rinehart and Winston.

Kosciw, J. G. (2004). *The 2003 National Climate Survey: The school-relate experience of our nation's lesbian, gay, bisexual and transgendered youth.* New York: GLSEN.

Kozol, J. (1992). *Savage inequalities: Children in America's schools.* New York: Harper Perennial.

Kozol, J. (2005). *The shame of the nation: The restoration of apartheid schooling in America.* New York: Crown Publishers.

Krasny, K. (2006). Into a new light: Re-envisioning educational possibilities for biography. *Language and Literacy: A Canadian Educational E-Journal* 8, no. 2, 1–28.

Krasny, K. (2007). Seeking the affective and the imaginative in the act of reading: Embodied consciousness and the evolution of the moral self. In D. Vokey (Ed.), *Philosophy of Education 2006* (pp. 429–37). Normal, IL: Philosophy of Education Society.

Krasny, K. (2010). *Shifting ground: Reading subjectivities in a virtual world. Panel: Ethics and the new literacies.* Paper presented at the annual conference of the Canadian Society for the Study of Education, Montreal, QC, May.

Krasny, K. (2011). The book—kindle'ing for the mind. *Journal of the Canadian Association for Curriculum Studies* 8, no. 2, 6–18.

Krasny, K. (2012). Taking patriarchy to task: Youth, YouTube, and young adult literature. In B. Guzzetti & T. Bean (eds.), *Adolescent literacies and the gendered self: (Re)constructing identities through multimodal literacy practices.* New York: Routledge.

Kristeva, J. (1974). *La revolution du langage poétique.* Paris: Seuil.

Landsburg, M. (1986). *Michelle Landsberg's guide to children's books.* Toronto, ON: Penguin.

Landy, S. (1977). Why Johnny can read, but doesn't. *Canadian Library Journal* 34, 379–87.

Lanier, C., & Schau, H. J. (2007). Culture and co-creation: Exploring the motivation behind Harry Potter on-line fan fiction. In R. Belk and J. Sherry (Eds.), *Consumer culture theory: Research in* consumer behaviour (pp. 321–42). New York: Elsevier.

Leathwood, C. (2005). "Treat me as a human being—don't look at me as a woman": Femininities and professional identities in further education. *Gender and Education* 17, no. 4, 387–409.

Lefever-Davis, S., & Pearman, C. (2005). Early readers and electronic texts: CD-ROM storybook features that influence reading behaviors. *The Reading Teacher* 58, no. 5, 446–54.

Leu, D. J., Jr. (2000). Literacy and technology: Deictic consequences for literacy education in an information age. In M. L. Kamil, P. Mosenthal, P. D. Pearson, and R. Barr (Eds.), *Handbook of reading research*, Vol. III (pp. 743–70). Mahwah, NJ: Erlbaum.

Leu, D., & Kinzer, C. (1999). *Effective literacy instruction* (4th ed.). Upper Saddle River, NJ: Prentice Hall.

Lewin, C. (1996). *Improving talking book software design: Emulating the supportive tutor*. Bradford, UK: Open University, Centre for Information Technology in Education.

Lingard, B., & Douglas, P. (1999). *Men engaging feminisms: Pro-feminism, backlashes and schooling*. Philadelphia: Open University Press.

Lingard, B., Martino, W., & Mills, M. (2009). *Boys and schooling: Beyond structural reform*. New York: Palgrave.

Lingard, B., Martino, W., Mills, M., & Bahr, M. (2002). *Addressing the educational needs of boys; Report to Department of Education, Science and Training (DEST)*. Canberra, Australia: DEST.

Linville, D. (2009). Queer theory and teen sexuality: Unclear lines. In J. Anyon (Ed.), *Theory and Educational Research. Toward critical social explanation* 153–177. New York: Routledge.

Liu, M. (1998). The effect of hypermedia authoring on elementary students' creative thinking. *Journal of Educational Computing Research* 19, 27–51.

Lopez, A. J. (2008). "Everybody else just living their lives": 9/11, race and the new postglobal literature. *Patterns of Prejudice* 42, nos. 4–5, 509–29.

Lorde, A. (2007). The master's tools will never dismantle the master's house. In A. Lorde, *Sister outsider: Essays and speeches* (pp. 110–13). Berkeley, CA: The Crossing Press.

Luce-Kapler, R. (2004). *Writing with, through and beyond the text: An ecology of language*. Mahwah, NJ: Lawrence Erlbaum.

Luce-Kapler, R. (2006). Creative fragments: The subjunctive spaces of e-literature. *English Teaching: Practice and Critique 5*, 6–16.

Luke, A., Freebody, P., & Land, R. (2000). *Literate futures: Review of literacy education*. Brisbane, Queensland, Australia: Education Queensland.

Luke, C. (1996). Reading gender and culture in media discourses and texts. In G. Bull & M. Anstey (Eds.), *The Literacy lexicon.* (pp. 177–192) New York: Prentice-Hall.

Lynch, J. (2009). Print literacy engagement of parents from low-income backgrounds: Implications for adult and family literacy programs. *Journal of Adolescent and Adult Literacy* 52, no. 6, 509–21.

Lynch-Brown, C. (1997). Procedures for determining children's book choices: Comparison and criticism. *Reading Horizons* 17, 243–50.

MacLeod, A. S. (1998). Writing backward: Modern models of historical fiction. *The Horn Book Magazine* 74 (January/February): 26.

Mahiri, J. (1998). *Shooting for excellence: African American and youth culture in new century schools*. Urbana, IL: Teachers College Press.

Mahony, P. (1985). *Schools for boys: Co-education reassessed*. London: Hutchinson, in association with the Explorations in Feminism Collective.

Mariage, T.V. (1995). Why students learn: The nature of teacher talk during reading. *Learning Disability Quarterly*, 18, no. 3, 214–234.

Marks, T. (1995). Gender differences in third graders' oral discourse during peer-led literature discussion. Doctoral dissertation, University of Maryland, 1995. *Dissertation Abstracts International* 56, 2997.

Martin, A. (2003). Primary school boys' identity formation and the male role model: An exploration of sexual identity and gender identity in the UK through attachment theory. *Sex Education* 3, no. 3, 257–71.

Martino, W. (1995a). Boys and literacy: Exploring the construction of hegemonic masculinities and the formation of literate capacities for boys in the English classroom. *English in Australia* 112, 11–24.

Martino, W. (1995b). Deconstructing masculinity in the English classroom: A site for reconstituting gender subjectivity. *Gender and Education* 7, 205–20.

Martino, W. (1998). "Dickheads", "poofs", "try-hards" and "losers": Critical literacy for boys in the English classroom. *Aotearoa* 25, 31–57.

Martino, W. (2001). Boys and reading: Investigating the impact of masculinities on boys' reading preferences and involvement in literacy. *Australian Journal of Language and Literacy* (February). http://findarticles.com/p/articles/mi_hb3336/is_1_24/ai_n28862169/.

Martino, W., & Kehler, M. (2007). Gender-based literacy reform: A question of challenging or recuperating gender binaries. *Canadian Journal of Education* 30, no. 2, 406–30.

Martino, W., Kehler, M., & Weaver-Hightower, M. (Eds.). (2009). *The problem with boys' education: Beyond the backlash*. New York: Routledge.

Martino, W., & Mellor, B. (2000). *Gendered fictions*. Urbana, IL: National Council of Teachers of English.

Martino, W., & Pallotta-Chiarolli, M. (2003). *So what's a boy? Addressing issues of masculinity and schooling*. Maidenhead, UK: Open University Press.

Mastoon, A. (1997). *The shared heart: Portraits and stories celebrating lesbian, gay, and bisexual young people*. New York: HarperCollins.

Mathews, K. (1996). The impact of CD-ROM storybooks on children's reading comprehension and attitudes. *Journal of Educational Multimedia and Hypermedia* 5, 379-394.

Matthews, G.H. (1987). Gender, home range, and environmental cognition. *Transactions of the British Geographers* 12, 43–56.

Mayes-Elma, R. (2006). *Females and Harry Potter: Not all that empowering*. Lanham, MD: Rowman and Littlefield.

Maynard, T. (2002). *Boys and literacy: Exploring the issues*. New York: Routledge Falmer.

McBroom, G. (1981). Research: Our defense begins here. *English Journal* 70, 75–77.

McCarthy, S.J. (1998). Constructing multiple subjectivities in classroom literacy contexts. *Research in the Teaching of English* 32, no. 2, 126–59.

McVeigh, B. J. (2000). How Hello Kitty commodifies the cute, cool and camp: "Consumutopia" versus "control" in Japan. *Journal of Material Culture 5* (July): 225–45.

Mendelson, M. (2009). *Why we need a First Nations Education Act*. Ottawa, ON: Caledon Institute of Social Policy.

Millard, E. (1994). *Developing Readers in the Middle* Years. Buckingham: Open University Press.

Millard, E. (1997) *Differently literate: Boys, girls and the schooling of literacy*. London: Falmer Press.

Moffatt, L. (2006). Boys and girls in the reading club: Conversations about gender and reading in an urban elementary school. *English Quarterly 3*, nos. 2–3), 42–48.

Moje, E. (2000). "To be part of the story": The literacy practices of gangsta adolescents. *Teachers College Record 102*, 651–90.

Money, J., & Ernhardt, A. (1972). *Man and woman, boy and girl: The differentiation and dimorphism of gender identity from conception to maturity*. Baltimore, MD: John Hopkins University Press.

Moss, G. (2007). *Literacy and gender: Researching texts, contexts and readers*. New York: Routledge.

Mullis, I. V. S., Martin, M. O., Kennedy, A. M., & Flaherty, C. L. (Eds.). (2002). *PIRLS 2001 encyclopedia: A reference guide to reading education in the countries participating in IEA's progress in international reading literacy study*. Chestnut Hill, MA: Boston College.

The New London Group. (1996). A pedagogy of multiliteracies: Designing social futures. *Harvard Educational Review 66*, no. 1, 60–92.

Niemiec, R., & Walberg, H. (1985). Computers and achievement in elementary schools. *Journal of Educational Computing Research 1*, 435–40.

Noble, J. (2004). *Masculinities without men?: Female masculinity in twentieth-century fictions*. Vancouver: University of British Columbia.

Nodelman, P. (2002). Making boys appear: The masculinity of children's fiction. In J. Stephens (Ed.), *Ways of being male: Representing masculinities in children's literature and film* (pp. 1–14). New York: Routledge.

Nodelman, P., & Reimer, M. (2003). *The pleasures of children's literature*. Boston, MA: Allyn and Bacon.

North York Board of Education. (1975). *Interim report no. 2, Ad Hoc Committee Respecting the Status of Women in the North York System*. North York, Ontario: The Committee.

Novogrodsky, M., Kaufman, M., Holland, D., & Wells, M. (1992). Retreat for the future: An anti-sexist workshop for high schoolers. *Our Schools/Our Selves*, 3, no. 4, 67–87.

Ogbu, J. U. (2003). *Black American students in an affluent suburb: A study of academic disengagement*. Mahwah, NJ: L. Erlbaum Associates.

Ogbu, J. U., & Fordham, S. (1986). Black students' school success: Coping with the burden of "acting white." *The Urban Review 18*, no. 3, 176–206.

Olweus, D., Limber, S. P., & Mihalic, S. (1999). *The Bullying Prevention Program: Blueprints for violence prevention*, Vol. 10. Boulder, CO: Center for the Study and Prevention of Violence.

Ontario Ministry of Education. (2004). *Me read? No way: A practical guide to improving boys' literacy skills.* Toronto: Ontario Ministry of Education.

Ontario Ministry of Education. (2007). *The Ontario Curriculum,* grades 1-8: Language. Ottawa: Queen's Printer.

Orellana, M., & Gutiérrez, K. (2006). What's the problem? Constructing different genres for the study of English learners. Research in the Teaching of English 41, no. 1, 118–23.

Orenstein, P. (1994). *School girls: Young women, self-esteem, and the confidence gap.* New York: Doubleday.

Organisation for Economic Co-operation and Development (2000). *Knowledge and skills for life: First results from the OECD Programme for International Student Assessment (PISA) 2000.* http://www.oecd.org/document/4/0,3746, en_32252351_32236159_33668932_1_1_1_1,00.html.

Organisation for Economic Cooperation and Development. (2003). *Learning for tomorrow's world: First results from the OECD Programme for International Student Assessment (PISA) 2003.* http://www.oecd.org/document/55/0,3746, en_32252351_32236173_33917303_1_1_1_1,00.html.

Organisation for Economic Co-operation and Development. (2009). *PISA 2009 Results: What student know and can do: Student performance in reading, mathematics and science (Volume 1).* http://www.oecd.org/document/53/ 0,3746,en_32252351_46584327_46584821_1_1_1_1,00.html.

Organisation for Economic Co-operation and Development. (2010). *The high cost of low educational performance.* http://www.oecd.org/document/58/0,3746,en _32252351_32236191_44417722_1_1_1_1,00.html.

Pace, B. G., & Townsend, J. S. (1999). Gender roles: Listening to classroom talk about literacy characters. *English Journal* 88, no. 3, 43–49.

Paechter, C. (1998). *Educating the other: Gender, power and schooling.* London: Falmer Press.

Paley, V. G. (1997). *The girl with the brown crayon.* Cambridge, MA: Harvard University Press.

Parker, L., & Lepper, M. (1992). The effects of fantasy contexts on children's learning and motivation: Making learning more fun. *Journal of Personality and Social Psychology* 2, 625–33.

Patterson, A., & Brown, S. (2009). Harry Potter and the service-dominant logic of marketing: A cautionary tale. *Journal of Marketing Management* 25, nos. 5–6, 519–33.

Pearman, C. (2003). *Effects of CR-ROM story books on the independent reading comprehension of second grade students.* Doctoral dissertation, University of Arkansas, 2003. *Dissertation Abstracts International* 64(07a), 2427.

Pearson, D., & Gallagher, M. C. (1983). The instruction of reading comprehension. *Contemporary Educational Psychology* 8, 317–44.

Pipher, M. B. (1994). *Reviving Ophelia: Saving the selves of adolescent girls.* New York: Ballantine Books.

Pollack, W. S. (1998). *Real boys: Rescuing our sons from the myths of boyhood.* New York: Random House.

Price, L. H., van Kleek, A., & Huberty, C. J. (2009). Talk during book sharing between parents and preschool children: A comparison between storybook and expository book conditions. *Reading Research Quarterly* 44, no. 2, 171–194.

Propp, V. (1928/1968). *Morphology of the folk tale.* University of Texas Press.

Purves, A. C., & Beach, R. (1972). *Literature and the reader: Research in response to literature, reading interests, and the teaching of literature.* Urbana, IL: National Council of Teachers of English.

Radway, Janice. (1984). *Reading the romance: Women, patriarchy, and popular literature.* Chapel Hill: University of North Carolina Press.

Ranker, J. (2008). Composing across multiple media: A case study of digital video production in a fifth grade classroom. *Written Communication* 25, 196–234.

Reinking, D., Labbo, L., & McKenna, M. (2000). From assimilation to accommodation: A developmental framework for integrating digital technologies into literacy research and instruction. *Journal of Research in Reading* 23, 110–22.

Riesterer, L. (2002). (Book) talk them into reading. *Book Report* 21, no. 3, 8. http:// connection.ebscohost.com/c/articles/7693760/book-talk-them-reading. Retrieved November 30, 2011.

Rogers, A. (1993). Voice, play and a practice of ordinary courage in girls' and women's lives. *Harvard Educational Review* 63, no. 3, 265–95.

Rose, J. (1984). *The case of Peter Pan: Or the impossibility of children's fiction.* New York: Palgrave Macmillan.

Rothbauer, P. M. (2002). Reading mainstream possibilities: Canadian young adult fiction with lesbian and gay characters. *Canadian Children's Literature* 108, 10–26.

Rothbauer, P. M., & McKechnie, L. (1999). Gay and lesbian fiction for young adults: A survey of the holdings in Canadian public libraries. *Collection Building* 18, no. 1, 32–39.

Rowan, L., Knobel, M., Bigum, C., & Lankshear, C. (2002). *Boys, literacies and schooling: The dangerous territories of gender-based literacy reform.* Philadelphia, PA: Open University Press.

Sadker, M., & Sadker, D. M. (1994) *Failing at fairness: How America's schools cheat girls.* New York: Charles Scribners Sons.

Said, E. (1978). *Orientalism.* New York: Random House.

Salisbury, J., & Jackson, D. (1996). *Challenging macho values: Practical ways of working with adolescent boys.* London: Falmer Press.

Sanders, M. G. (Ed.) (2000). *Schooling students placed at risk: Research, policy, and practice in the education of poor and minority adolescents.* Mahwah, NJ: L. Erlbaum Associates.

Sanders, M. G. (2003). Community involvement in schools: From concept to practice. *Education and Urban Society* 35, no. 2, 161–81.

Sax, L. (2002). How common is intersex?: A response to Anne Fausto-Sterling. *Journal of Sex Research* 39, no. 3, 174–78.

Sax, L. (2005). *Why gender matters: What parents and teachers need to know about the emerging science of sex differences.* New York: Doubleday.

Schoefer, C. (2000). *Harry Potter's girl trouble: The world of everyone's favorite kid wizard is a placed where boys come first.* Salon.com, January 13. http://www .salon.com/books/feature/2000/01/13/potter.

Schraw, G., Flowerday, T., & Lehman, S. (2001). Increasing situational interest in the classroom. *Educational Psychology Review* 13, no. 3, 211–24.

Schraw, G., Flowerday, T., & Reisetter, M. (1998). The role of choice in reader engagement. *Journal of Educational Psychology* 90, no. 4, 705–14.

Schwartz, A., & Rubenstein-Avila, E. (2006). Understanding the manga hype: Uncovering the multimodality of comic-book literacies. *Journal of Adolescent and Adult Literacy*, 50, no. 1, 40–49.

Schweickart, P. (1989). Reading ourselves: Toward a feminist theory of reading. In E. Showalter (Ed.), *Speaking of gender* (pp. 17–44). New York: Routledge.

Sears, J. (1997). Centering culture: Teaching for critical sexual literacy using the sexual diversity wheel. *Journal of Moral Education* 26, 273–83.

Sebesta, S. L., & Monson, D. L. (1991). Reading preferences. In K. Flood, J. Jensen, D. Lapp, & J. Squire (Eds.), *Handbook of research on teaching the English language arts* (pp. 664–73). New York: MacMillan.

Sebesta, S. L., & Monson, D. L. (2003). Reading preferences. In J. Flood, D. Lapp, J. R. Squire, & J. M. Jensen (Eds.), *Handbook of research on teaching the English Language arts* 2nd ed., 835–847. Mahwah, NJ: Lawrence Erlbaum.

Shea, J. A., Beers, B. B., McDonald, V. J., Quistberg, D. A., Ravenell, K. L., & Asch, D. A. (2004). Assessing health literacy in African American and Caucasian adults: Disparities in Rapid Estimate of Adult Literacy in Medicine (REALM) scores. *Family Medicine* 36, no. 8, 575–81.

Showalter, E. (1977). *A literature of their own: British women novelists from Bronte to Lessing.* Princeton, NJ: Princeton University Press.

Showalter, E. (1981). Feminist criticism in the wilderness. *Critical Inquiry* 8, no. (Winter): 179–205.

Shuto, L. (1974). *Background paper on the BCTF Status of Women Program.* Cited in Coulter, R. P. (1996) Gender equity and schooling: linking research and policy. *Canadian Journal of Education* 21, no. 4, 444.

Singh, M. (2007). Official discourse and challenges of building a learning society in India. In M. Kuhn (Ed.), *New society models for a new millennium: The learning society in Europe and beyond,* (pp. 531–554). New York: Peter Lang Publishing, Inc.

Sizer, T. R. (2004). *The red pencil: Convictions from experience in education.* New Haven, CT: Yale University Press.

Slattery, P., Krasny, K. A., & O'Malley, M. P. (2007). Hermeneutics, aesthetics, and the quest for answerability: A dialogic possibility for reconceptualizing the interpretive process in curriculum studies. *Journal of Curriculum Studies* 39, no. 5, 537–58.

Smith, C., & Lloyd, B. (1978). Maternal behavior and perceived sex of infant: Revisited. *Child Development* 49, 1263–65.

Smith, M. L., & Eno, L. V. (1961). What do they really want to read? *English Journal* 50, 343–45.

Smith, M. W., & Wilhelm, J. D. (2002). *Reading don't fix no Chevys: Literacy in the lives of young men.* Portsmouth, NH: Heinemann.

Snow, C. E., Burns, M. S., & Griffin, P. (eds.) (1998). *Preventing reading difficulties in young children.* Washington, DC: National Academy Press.

184 *References*

Sokal, L. (2010). Long term effect of male reading tutors, choice of text and computer-based text on boys reading achievement. *Language and Literacy: A Canadian E-Journal* 12, no. 1, 97–115.

Sokal, L., Katz, H., Adkins, M., Grills, T., Stewart, C., Priddle, G., et al. (2005). Factors affecting inner-city boys' reading: Are male teachers the answer? *Canadian Journal of Urban Research* 14, no. 1, 107–30.

Sommers, C. H. (2000). *The war against boys: How misguided feminism is harming our young men.* New York: Simon & Schuster.

SparkNotes. http://www.sparknotes.com/.

Spender, D., & Sarah, E. (1980). *Learning to lose: Sexism and education.* London: Women's Press.

Stack, M., & Kelly, D. M. (2006). Popular media, education, and resistance. *Canadian Journal of Education* 29, no. 1, 5–26.

Stanworth, M. (1981). *Gender and schooling: A study of sexual divisions in the classroom.* London: Hutchinson.

Stauffer, R. G. (1969). *Teaching reading as a thinking process.* New York: Harper & Row.

Stauffer, R. G. (1970). *The language experience approach to the teaching of reading.* New York: Harper & Row.

Stephens, J. (2002). *Ways of being male: Representing masculinities in children's literature and film.* New York: Routledge.

Stipek, D. (1984). Sex differences in children's attributions for success and failure on mathematics and spelling tests. *Sex Roles* 11, 969–981.

Strang, R. E. (1946). Reading interests. *English Journal* 35, 477–82.

Sullivan, M. (2009). *Serving boys through readers advisory.* Chicago, IL: American Library Association.

Sumara, D. (2002). *Why reading literature in school still matters: Imagination, interpretation, insight.* Mahwah, NJ: Lawrence Erlbaum Associates.

Sussman, N. M., & Tyson, D. H. (2000). Sex and power: gender differences in computer-mediated interaction. *Computers in Human Behavior* 16, 381–94.

Sutton, R. (1999). Potter's field. *Horn Book Magazine* 75, no. 5 (September–October): 500–501.

Tannen, D. (1984). *Conversational style: Analyzing talk among friends.* New York: Oxford University Press.

Tannen, D. (1995). The power of talk: Who gets heard and why. *Harvard Business Review* 73, no. 5 (September–October): 138–48.

Telford, L. (1999). A study of boys' reading. *Early Childhood Development and Care* 149, 87–124.

Thompson, E. (2007). *Mind in life: Biology, phenomenology and the sciences of mind.* Cambridge, MA: Harvard University Press.

Thompson, E., & Varela, F. J. (2001). *Between ourselves: Second-person issues in the study of consciousness.* Charlottesville, VA: Imprint Academic.

Thorne, B. (1993). *Gender play: Girls and boys in school.* New Brunswick, NJ: Rutgers University Press.

Topping, K., Valtin, R., Roller, C., Brozo, W., & Dionisio, M. L. (2003). *Policy and practice implications of the Program for International Student Assessment*

(PISA) 2000: Report of the International Reading Association PISA Task Force. Newark, DE: International Reading Association.

Tracy, K., & Eisenberg, E. (1990/1991). Giving criticism: A multiple-goal case study. *Research on Language and Social Interaction* 24, 37–70.

Trites, R. S. (1997). *Walking sleeping beauty: Feminist voices in children's novels.* Iowa City: University of Iowa Press.

Turner-Bowker, D. (1996). Gender stereotyped descriptors in children's picture books: Does "Curious Jane" exist in the literature? *Sex Roles: A Journal of Research* 35, nos. 7–8, 461–88.

U.S. Department of Education. (Various years). National Assessment of Educational Progress (NAEP). http://nces.ed.gov/nationsreportcard/.

Valentine, G. (1999). "Oh please, Mum, oh please, Dad": Negotiating children's spatial boundaries. In L. McKie, S. Browlby, & S. Gregory (Eds.), *Gender, power and the household* (pp. 137–57). New York: Macmillan.

Vickers, Jill., Rankin, Paulline, & Appelle, Christine. (1993). Politics as if women mattered: A political analysis of the national action committee on the status of women. Toronto: University of Toronto Press.

Vygotsky, L. (1962). *Thought and language.* Cambridge, MA: MIT Press.

Vygotsky, L. (1978). *Mind in society: The development of higher psychological processes.* President and Fellows of Harvard College.

Wagner-Martin, L. (1994). *Telling women's lives: The new biography.* New Brunswick, NJ: Rutgers University Press.

Walkerdine, V. (1981). Sex, power, and pedagogy. *Screen Education* 38, 14–24.

Walkerdine, V. (1988). *The mastery of reason.* London: Routledge.

Walkerdine, V. (1990). *Schoolgirl fictions.* London: Verso.

Walkerdine, V. (1998). *Counting girls out: Girls and mathematics.* London: Falmer Press.

Walkerdine, V., Lucey, H., & Melody, J. (2001). *Growing up girl: psychosocial explorations of gender and class.* London: Macmillan.

Wallowitz, L. (2004). Reading as resistance: Gendered messages in literature and media. *The English Journal* 93, no. 3 (January): 26–31.

Weaver-Hightower, M. (2003). The "boy turn" in research on gender and education. *Review of Educational Research* 73, no. 4, 471–98.

Weedon, C. (1987). *Feminist practice and post-structural theory.* Oxford, UK: Blackwell.

Weiner, G. (1994). *Feminisms in education: An introduction.* Philadelphia, PA: Open University Press.

Weiss, L., & Fine, M. (1993). *Beyond silenced voices: Class, race, and gender in United States schools.* Albany: State University of New York Press.

White, B. (2007). Are girls better readers than boys? Which boys? Which girls? *Canadian Journal of Education* 30, no. 2, 554–81.

Whitley, B. (1997). Gender differences in computer-related attitudes and behaviors: A meta-analysis. *Computers and Human Behaviour* 13, 1–22.

Willinsky, J. (1990). *The triumph of literature/the fate of literacy: English in the secondary school curriculum.* New York: Teachers College Press.

Willinsky, J. (2005). *The access principle: The case for open access to research and scholarship.* Cambridge: Massachusetts Institute of Technology.

Wilson, B. (2005). More lessons from the superheroes of J. C. Holtz: The visual culture of childhood and the third pedagogical site. *Art Education* 58, no. 6, 18–24.

Wolfson, B. J., Manning, G., & Manning, M. (1984). Revisiting what children say their reading interests are. *Reading World* 24, 4–10.

Women in Teaching. (1975). *Text book study*. Vancouver: British Columbia Teachers' Federation.

Yasin, F., & Krasny, K. (2010). Comics as a multimodal means of exploring adolescent identity. Paper presented at the 2010 National Council of Teachers of English Annual Convention (Research Strand), Orlando, FL, November.

Yates, L. (2000). The 'Facts of the Case': gender equity for boys as a public policy issue. In Lesko, Nancy. *Masculinities at School: research on men and masculinities*, 305. Thousand Oaks, California: SAGE.

Younger, M., Warrington, M., & McLellan, R. (2005). *Raising boys' achievement*. Maidenhead, UK: Open University Press.

Zimet, S. F. (1966). Children's interest and story preferences: A critical review of the literature. *The Elementary School Journal*, 67, no. 3, 122–130.

Zipes, J. (2001). *Sticks and stones: The troublesome success of children's literature from Slovenly Peter to Harry Potter*. New York: Routledge.

Zipes, J. (2002). *Breaking the magic spell: Radical theories of folk and fairy tales*. Lexington: University Press of Kentucky.

Index

About the Author

KAREN A. KRASNY, PHD, is Director of the Graduate Program in Education and Associate Professor of Language and Literacy at York University, Toronto, Canada, where she teaches graduate seminars in language, culture and teaching, and adolescent and children's literature. She received her doctorate in 2004 from Texas A&M University, College Station, TX. Dr. Krasny is Past President of the Canadian Association for Curriculum Studies and Co-Editor-in-Chief of the association's journal. A longtime educator, Dr. Krasny previously worked as a teacher and curriculum coordinator in the fields of English and French language arts. Her early contributions were recognized with a nomination for the Lieutenant Governor's Medal for Literacy in the province of Manitoba and a secondment as Manitoba's English Language Arts Provincial Specialist. Dr. Krasny continues to maintain a keen interest in K–12 literacy and has worked with university faculty, teachers, and students in Canada, the United States, Ukraine, China, and Saudi Arabia. She collaborated on a coedited collection of students' responses to representations of the Holocaust titled *We Are Their Voice: Young People Respond to the Holocaust*, published with Second Story Press. Her recent scholarly work appears in *Oral History Forum*, *Review of Educational Research*, *Journal of Curriculum Studies*, *Canadian Modern Language Review*, and *Language and Literacy: A Canadian Educational E-Journal*.